Charros

AMERICAN CROSSROADS

Edited by Earl Lewis, George Lipsitz, George Sánchez, Dana Takagi, Laura Briggs, and Nikhil Pal Singh

Charros

HOW MEXICAN COWBOYS ARE REMAPPING
RACE AND AMERICAN IDENTITY

Laura R. Barraclough

UNIVERSITY OF CALIFORNIA PRESS

University of California Press, one of the most distinguished university presses in the United States, enriches lives around the world by advancing scholarship in the humanities, social sciences, and natural sciences. Its activities are supported by the UC Press Foundation and by philanthropic contributions from individuals and institutions. For more information, visit www.ucpress.edu.

University of California Press
Oakland, California

Library of Congress Cataloging-in-Publication Data

Names: Barraclough, Laura R., author.
Title: Charros : how Mexican cowboys are remapping race and American identity / Laura R. Barraclough.
Description: Oakland, California : University of California Press, [2019] | Includes bibliographical references and index. |
Identifiers: LCCN 2018050981 (print) | LCCN 2018055040 (ebook) | ISBN 9780520963832 (ebook and ePDF) | ISBN 9780520289116 (cloth : alk. paper) | ISBN 9780520289123 (pbk. : alk. paper)
Subjects: LCSH: Charros—West (U.S.)—History. | Mexican Americans—West (U.S.)—Race relations.
Classification: LCC F596.3.M5 (ebook) | LCC F596.3.M5 B37 2019 (print) | DDC 978.00468/72—dc23
LC record available at https://lccn.loc.gov/2018050981

Manufactured in the United States of America

26 25 24 23 22 21 20 19
10 9 8 7 6 5 4 3 2 1

For Alessandro

CONTENTS

ILLUSTRATIONS

PHOTOS

MAPS

ACKNOWLEDGMENTS

Writing a book is a tremendous journey. I relish the opportunity to thank the many people who traveled with me and made my scholarship better.

This book is rooted in the intellectual foundation I received as an undergraduate student of ethnic studies and urban planning at the University of California, San Diego, and as a graduate student in American Studies and Ethnicity at the University of Southern California. Years later, the lessons and ways of thinking that I first developed in those fine programs continue to guide me. I am indebted to the faculty who mentored me, especially Laura Pulido, George Sánchez, Bill Deverell, Roberto Lint Sagarena, Leland Saito, Ruthie Gilmore, Jennifer Wolch, Carolyn Cartier, George Lipsitz, Ross Frank, and Ruby Tapia.

One of the biggest challenges—and greatest pleasures—of writing this book was visiting archives and special collections across the U.S. Southwest. Many thanks to the archivists and staff at the following institutions, who guided my research in ways big and small: the Chicano Studies Research Center, Special Collections, and Film and Television Archive at UCLA; the City of Los Angeles Records and Archives Division; the Institute for Texas Cultures in San Antonio; the Denver Public Library's Western Heritage Center; the Pueblo City-County Public Library; the Stephen H. Hart Library and Research Center at the History Colorado Center; the National Archives and Records Administration regional office in Broomfield, Colorado; the legislative research libraries in Arizona, Nevada, and Texas; and the special collections departments at California State University, Northridge; Colorado State University, Pueblo; the University of Southern California; and the University of Texas, San Antonio. My ability to visit these archives and special collections was made possible by the following funders: the American Philosophical Society, the Whitney Humanities Center at Yale, and the provost's office at Kalamazoo College. Thanks also to the following research assistants, who tracked down additional materials and conducted new research: David Duffield, Amy Jimenez, and Oscar Morales. I am also deeply indebted to Julian Nava and Toby de la Torre for speaking with me at length about their personal experiences with charrería.

I had the good fortune of sharing sections of the draft manuscript with many seminars, working groups, and conferences. My sincere thanks to participants in the University of Michigan's American History Workshop, the Departments of Chicana/o Studies and Urban Planning at UCLA, the Radcliffe Institute at Harvard University, Brown University's Center for the Study of Race and Ethnicity in America, the Borderlands History Workshop and Multidisciplinary Urban Research Seminar at New York University, the Borderlands and Latinx Studies Seminar at the Newberry Library, the Symposium on Gender and Intimacy in the U.S.-Mexico Borderlands at the University of California, Santa Barbara, the Immigration and Urban History seminar at the Massachusetts Historical Society, the American Studies program at Yale, and conference sessions at the American Studies Association, Urban History Association, and Western History Association. Much gratitude to the conveners of those sessions for inviting me to share my work and providing generative feedback at crucial stages: Eric Ávila, Xochitl Bada, Geraldo Cadava, Verónica Castillo-Muñoz, Miroslava Chávez-García, Ryan Enos, Desirée García, Adam Goodman, Yalidy Matos, Maria Montoya, Andrew Needham, Tricia Rose, and Rachel St. John.

So often, the "aha" moments of writing a book come through informal conversations with good friends and trusted mentors, for whom I am deeply grateful. Extra big thanks to Arlene Dávila, Sally Deutsch, George Lipsitz, Mary Lui, Natalia Molina, Steve Pitti, Brandon Proia, Alicia Schmidt Camacho, and an anonymous reviewer for reading the entire draft manuscript and sharing their deep knowledge of Mexican American cultural politics and the U.S. Southwest with me. Genevieve Carpio, Michael Denning, Kate Dudley, Dolores Hayden, Maria Montoya, Jacqueline Moore, and Laura Pulido read draft chapters, asked tough questions, and offered important insights that moved the project forward. Numerous other people served as generative thinking partners or took the time to dig up leads and share archival finds: José Alamillo, John Bezís-Selfa, Jerry González, Laura Hernández-Ehrisman, Fawn-Amber Montoya, Marci McMahon, and Alex Tarr, among others. I am fortunate to have many brilliant and gracious colleagues at Yale who have helped me become a better scholar and writer, but I'll single out Rene Almeling, Dan HoSang, Isaac Nakhimovsky, Albert Laguna, Greta LaFleur, Chitra Ramalingam, and Dixa Ramírez for being not just colleagues, but also dear friends (and awesome lunch dates).

The editorial staff at UC Press ably shepherded this project to completion. Special thanks to Niels Hooper, who saw its potential at a very early stage, challenging me and supporting me at just the right moments. Bradley Depew, Sabrina Robleh, and Kate Hoffman provided unparalleled support at every stage of the publication process, and Sue Carter copyedited the book thoughtfully. Many thanks to the editors of the American Crossroads series for their leadership and vision over the years. Outside of UC Press, I am grateful to the American Studies program and the dean's office at Yale for funding a manuscript colloquium, to Jennifer Tran and Alexander Tarr for preparing the maps, and to Al Rendon for the great honor of reproducing his beautiful photographs on the cover and throughout the book.

I completed most of this book while raising my extraordinary son, Alessandro, as a single parent. Alessandro accompanied me, in utero, on my first research trip to San Antonio. Since then, throughout a cross-country move, starting a new job at Yale, and figuring out how to live and thrive in New England, Alessandro has served as my constant and best companion. But it would have been impossible to do any of it alone, and I am immensely grateful to the family, friends, and babysitters who provided us with support of all kinds. My mother, Bette Barraclough, deserves a special shout-out for accompanying me to conferences and research trips where she traipsed with Alessandro to aquariums, zoos, and the occasional Wild West Town, often in 100+ degree weather, while I worked. I am deeply grateful, as well, to the Anne Coffin Hanson Fund at Yale, an extraordinary resource that provides funding for childcare so that faculty can travel for conferences or research; every institution should have something like it. The Single Parents in Academia Facebook group, aka the best thing on the Internet, provided daily emotional support even though I have yet to meet any of its members in person. At the end of the day, though, I consider myself luckiest of all that I get to share life with my sweet, smart, sensitive, and kind son. Alessandro, I am so proud of who you are and who you are becoming. In all respects, this book is for you.

Introduction

ON JUNE 11, 2013, ELEVEN-YEAR-OLD MARIACHI STAR Sebastien de la Cruz—best known for his performance on *America's Got Talent*—sang the U.S. national anthem at San Antonio's AT&T Center, setting the Internet on fire. Introduced by his moniker "El Charro de Oro," de la Cruz opened Game Three of the NBA Finals by belting out a moving rendition of "The Star-Spangled Banner."[1] The *Daily Dot* applauded his superb performance and impressive vocal range: "The kid was dynamic. He was [as] theatrical as it gets. He hit all the high notes. He stayed long on the low notes."[2] But others took to Twitter to express outrage at a Mexican American boy singing the U.S. national anthem, calling him a "wetback," "beaner," and "illegal" with the hashtags #yournotamerican and #gohome.[3]

The tweeters were especially incensed by de la Cruz's outfit: a perfectly pressed, light blue *traje de charro*. Most recognizable as the suit worn by mariachi musicians, the traje de charro references a broad set of cultural forms associated with lo ranchero—Mexican ranch life and ranch culture.[4] Among these are the *charro,* a term sometimes translated as "Mexican cowboy," though the charro is better understood as a gentleman horseman associated with Mexico's elite. He is also a deeply nationalist figure. Ranchero cultural forms, including the charro, have signified lo mexicano (Mexicanness) since the aftermath of the Mexican Revolution (1910–20); *charrería* (the art and sport of charros) is now Mexico's national sport, and the *charreada* (Mexican rodeo) is as popular with some Mexican audiences as soccer.[5] Yet the charro also has evidentiary claims to be the "original cowboy"—the skilled horseman who introduced ranching and rodeo to the region that became the U.S. Southwest. The nativist tweeters intuited the Mexican nationalist history in de la Cruz's charro suit, even if they didn't know the specifics, and rejected the implication that U.S. ranching and rodeo might owe a great deal to Mexicans. One person tweeted: "Is this the American National Anthem or the Mexican Hat Dance? Get this lil kid out of here," while another wrote: "Why was the kid singing the national anthem wearing a mariachi band outfit? We ain't Mexican."[6]

The tweeters may not have considered the collective "we" they invoked to be Mexican, but neither did de la Cruz, who told a reporter, "I'm not from Mexico, I'm from San Antonio born and raised, a true San Antonio Spurs fan."[7] Like countless ethnic Mexicans in the United States since at least the 1930s, de la Cruz viewed the charro and lo ranchero as powerful means to express his pride in being Mexican *and* his rights to occupy central spaces in American life; for him, there was no contradiction between these goals. Many reporters, politicians, and entertainers shared de la Cruz's view of the charro and its symbolic potential for Mexican Americans. San Antonio mayor Julian Castro, U.S. president Barack Obama, and actor Eva Longoria all rallied to de la Cruz's defense, appealing for a multicultural America where a brown-skinned boy wearing a charro suit could sing the U.S. national anthem with pride.[8]

Clearly, the public debate over de la Cruz's traje de charro was about far more than sports or patriotism. Rather, it invoked an ongoing struggle over the relationships between race, masculinity, and national identity in the United States, particularly in the U.S. Southwest and U.S.-Mexico border region. This struggle has taken shape through contests over the meanings of the American cowboy and the Mexican charro—two iconic forms of masculinity derived from the multicultural ranching societies of the Americas but now firmly associated with the nationalist projects of their respective states. For nearly a century, ethnic Mexicans in the United States have navigated between these two racial and nationalist formations in flexible but strategic ways. Drawing on the figure of the charro—symbol of Mexican identity *and* a distinguished horseman with claims to be the "original cowboy"—they have expressed their attachment to Mexican culture while claiming rights and opportunity in the United States.

This book documents their visions, hopes, and struggles. I focus on the many ways in which ethnic Mexicans in the United States have mobilized the charro in the service of civil rights, cultural citizenship, and place-making since the 1930s. Traversing a range of cities with distinctive histories, geographies, cultures, and social structures, I show how ethnic Mexicans have used the figure of the charro to nurture their cultural heritage, to resist subjugation and challenge inequality, and to transform the landscapes and institutions of the places in which they live. The charros' work across these domains has inevitably required them to engage—and sometimes challenge—the presumed whiteness and U.S. nationalism of the American cowboy. Thus, the book considers how U.S. charros have transformed core narratives of American history and identity centered on the cowboy, rodeo, and ranching in order to create more inclusive and equitable conditions.

Although the history of charrería within Mexico is well documented (indeed, romanticized), few have studied its meaning or practice in the United States. This book seeks to fill that silence, by offering the first history of charros in the United States. Those studies of U.S.-based charros that do exist were conducted in the 1990s and early 2000s by anthropologists Kathleen Mullen Sands and Olga Nájera-Ramírez; their ethnographic accounts explain the contemporary expression of charrería, its internal dynamics, and its importance to participants.[9] Building on this important work, *Charros* contributes a historical and cultural geography of charros and charrería in the U.S. Southwest. Taking the long view, I show that charros have been ubiquitous in Mexican American communities since at least the 1930s, and that they have consistently galvanized ethnic Mexicans' pursuit of equity, inclusion, and belonging. Indeed, the charro has been as important to Mexican American history, culture, and politics as his better-known counterparts, the bracero, the pachuco, and the Chicano activist. At the same time, U.S. charros have played key roles in transforming the Mexican nationalist formation of charrería from abroad. They have sustained vibrant transnational cultural linkages amid the waxing and waning of U.S.-Mexico geopolitics, and they have infused migrant sensibilities into Mexican nationalist culture. Working at multiple scales, then, charros have been crucial agents in the simultaneous coproduction of U.S., Mexican, southwestern, and border cultures.

The main protagonists in this story are members of the U.S.-based charro associations. These are formal organizations of ten to twenty men, often from the same extended family or place of origin, who ride, practice, and compete together in the regional, national, and transnational circuits of Mexican rodeo. The first U.S. charro associations formed in Texas and California in the 1940s, just after World War II, and facilitated ethnic Mexicans' engagement with institutions that had proved key to their racial subjugation since U.S. conquest, namely law enforcement and the capitalist economy. Many other charro associations formed in the 1970s, at the height of the Chicano movement and Mexican Americans' struggles for land and dignity, when the charro guided ethnic Mexicans' work to create more responsive and multicultural public institutions. Still more charro associations were established in the 1990s, in the aftermath of the North American Free Trade Agreement and the tremendous migration it unleashed. In the face of discursive constructions of "illegality" and corresponding racial violence, charrería since the 1990s has cohered Mexican migrants with Mexican Americans in affirming their cultural heritage and galvanizing political action. Yet the charro associations have never had a monopoly on the meaning or political utility of the charro, who circulates in popular culture and politics as much as in the *lienzo* (the distinctive keyhole-shaped arena used for charreadas). Thus, while centering the leadership of the charro associations in remapping race and national identity, this book also traces the efforts of public figures such as elected officials, school principals, county sheriffs, business owners, and artists, all of whom have used the charro for a wide range of political, economic, and cultural purposes.

The charro associations and their supporters represent a particular perspective on ethnic Mexican empowerment in the United States—one that is middle class, masculine, and aligned with Spanish-Mexican histories of colonialism and aspirations to whiteness. The charros' initiatives reflect their position at the intersection of these social identities. Much of their work, as we shall see, has focused on securing ethnic Mexican men's access to institutions from which they were historically excluded, such as law enforcement and business, and to public space and the agencies governing its use. Charros have lobbied for inclusion in these spheres by invoking their patriarchal control of family, community, and ethnic identity and by forging masculine networks that transcend ethnicity, race, and citizenship in order to access the privileges of middle-class status and whiteness. Still, even those groups that are relatively subjugated within charro culture—women, workers, and indigenous peoples—have sometimes used the charro and other ranchero practices to claim greater power. Women, in particular, have mobilized the charro to create more inclusive public institutions, especially in areas related to social reproduction, such as education. Women have also found in charro culture the expansion of personal opportunities for marriage, family formation, competition, and travel. While ethnic Mexicans' relationship to nation and colonialism in the U.S. Southwest is complex, charrería has been attractive to many ethnic Mexican women because, as Elleke Boehmer explains, the concept of the nation "remains a place from which to resist the multiple ways in which colonialism distorts and disfigures a people's history."[10]

Incorporating these diverse figures and their work into the fold of Mexican American history requires a capacious sense of politics—one that exceeds a focus on electoral politics, grassroots organizing, or direct action and that transcends neat divisions between liberal and conservative agendas. Until very recently, most members of the charro associations have not been involved in formal politics. However, they *have* nurtured meaningful partnerships with well-known politicians, business owners, and cultural producers, both ethnically Mexican and not, and from across the political spectrum. Using strategies of collaboration and persuasion rather than protest or direct action, they have mostly labored to transform U.S. institutions and spaces from within. As a result, charros often lurk in the background—both literally and symbolically—of the most important struggles for inclusion, equality, and justice that ethnic Mexicans have waged for nearly a century. Many of their goals and accomplishments have corresponded with those of better-known and more explicitly political Mexican American and Chicano organizations, from the League of United Latin American Citizens (LULAC) in the 1940s and '50s to the immigrant rights movement of today. Though quieter and less obviously politicized, their work has been equally important in enabling ethnic Mexicans to claim citizenship, belonging, and rights.

The charro has proven an enduring and transcendent figure for a simple but compelling reason: as a representation of skilled masculinity, economic autonomy, and landownership, he allows ethnic Mexicans to resist the core processes through which they have been racially subjugated in the United States. The U.S. military conquest of Mexican land, people, and culture that began in the 1830s unleashed processes of displacement, migration, proletarianization, and barrioization that are still very much in motion, sustained in the present through neoliberal trade arrangements, processes of "illegalization," and racial violence. In the face of these contentious histories and contested geographies, the charro promises power: power over land, over the conditions and fruits of one's labor, over the ability to bind family and community, over the meaning of ethnic and cultural identity. As we shall see in the chapters to come, that power has not always been actualized, nor has it come without struggle even when the outcomes are successful. Nonetheless, for many ethnic Mexicans, identification with and organizing around the charro galvanizes hope for a more autonomous, dignified, and equitable future. It is that sense of hope—and the collective action it guides—that I trace in this book.

The remainder of this introduction proceeds in three parts. First, it documents the social history of ranching in colonial Mexico and its spread north into the region that would become, after 1848, the U.S. Southwest. Generated through the interactions among wealthy hacendados and working-class, often indigenous vaqueros (ranch workers), the ranching culture of the Americas became even more complex when it migrated north, where Anglo-Americans, African Americans, and indigenous peoples of the North joined the mix. The introduction then explains how, in the early twentieth century, amid industrialization, urbanization, and the rise of the modern nation-state, elite men and the mass culture industries in both the U.S. and Mexico abstracted the working horseman from his hybrid, multicultural origins and constructed the cowboy and the charro as racially and nationally distinct cultural icons. Finally, it gives an overview of how ethnic Mexicans in the United States have strategically mobilized charros and charrería since the 1930s, detailing the scope of the chapters to come and the methods and sources used for the analysis. Following this introduction is a photographic interlude that describes the spaces, rituals, and competitive events of the charreada, which adapts the historical conditions of ranching to the urban sporting context.

A SOCIAL HISTORY OF RANCHING IN MEXICO
AND THE UNITED STATES

The charro's origin story begins in the sixteenth century with the Spanish import of horses, as well as riding equipment and techniques adapted from the Moors, to the Americas as a deliberate strategy of colonization. The high costs of equine transport as well as frequent illness and death en route meant that the breeding of horses and cattle within the colonies became a top priority. Colonists established vast and profitable cattle ranches on the Caribbean islands and Mexico's central plateau. In 1549, Viceroy Luís de Velasco ordered that cattle ranching be moved north, to spread Spain's economic and "civilizing" missions to what were then the far-flung colonial frontiers of Jalisco, Aguascalientes, Querétaro, and Guanajuato—a region known as the Bajío. The ranchers who took up this charge, typically creoles born in New Spain, fashioned a group identity and political consciousness as resourceful, rugged, and rebellious subjects; they tended to oppose and resent the Spanish colonial elite's concentration of wealth and power in Mexico City. Despite their sense of marginalization, they benefited substantially from the domestic labor of women who ran the vast households of the hacienda, as well as the

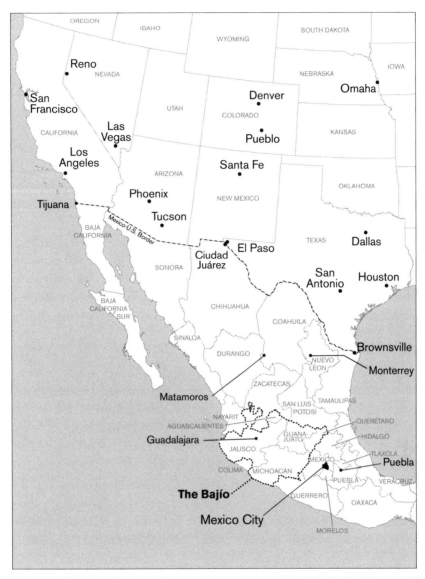

The United States and Mexico, featuring important locations for the development of charrería. By Jennifer Tran and Alexander Tarr.

coerced labor of indigenous and mestizo (mixed-race) vaqueros.[11] Indeed, it was the vaqueros who developed most of the materials and techniques that made large-scale cattle ranching possible. Denied the luxury goods that the hacendados enjoyed, they invented or adapted what they needed for their craft. These included magüey rope, which was woven of local fibers; intricate roping techniques, now called fancy or trick roping; and the use of leather chaps to protect the workers' legs.[12]

These materials and techniques were shared and ritualized among hacendados, workers, and visitors during the annual rodeos (round-ups) in which cattle were gathered and branded. At the rodeos, hacendados and vaqueros engaged in practices such as the *cola,* or grabbing the tail of a bull or steer and twisting it under the rider's boot or around the saddle horn to flip the animal to the ground; *piales,* which involves roping a running horse around the back legs to slow it down and bring it to a standstill without injury; and *ternas,* or team roping techniques used to down cattle for branding. The rodeos also included other events that had little to do with the work of the ranch but showcased riders' skill and bravery, such as bull and bronc riding, sliding stops, bullfighting, and roping displays. These were social occasions, too, featuring food, entertainment, and music as well as opportunities for courtship that were rare in the sparsely settled, isolated ranching society of colonial Mexico. Collectively, these techniques, materials, and social rituals constitute the prehistories of charrería—the art, sport, and culture of charros.[13]

Although the early rodeos served pragmatic and social purposes, they were also essential opportunities for the performance of masculinity and for the negotiation (and sometimes transgression) of the class and ethnic fissures that characterized Spanish colonial society. Nájera-Ramírez explains that for the wealthy sons of the hacendado, the charreada was an important occasion to prove they were worthy inheritors of their father's land and business, while for the laboring vaqueros, the events were a chance to show they were just as skillful as their social superiors. For these reasons, "charreadas were a means by which men of any social class might prove themselves to be worthy charros and thus greatly enhance their status as real men."[14] This sense of masculine unity across class differences rested on men's shared patriarchal status over women. According to Spanish law, a father made most decisions for his daughters until his death or until they married, at which point their husbands assumed control. The hacendado was expected and assumed to rule and protect his wife and children, just as men of lower social status ruled over women and children within and below their rank.[15]

The world of the rodeos/charreadas did not exist on the far northern frontier of New Spain—the area that would become the U.S. Southwest—in any meaningful way until the early nineteenth century, on the eve of Mexican independence.[16] Although Spanish settlers brought horses, cattle, and other livestock on their colonial expeditions to the North, the region's sparse population, near-constant warfare with powerful American Indian nations, the monopoly on land held by the Franciscan missions, and extremely limited access to material goods stalled the development of an elite hacienda society.[17] During the 1820s and especially the 1830s, however, the newly independent Mexican government made extensive land grants to both Mexicans and foreigners on the condition they attract settlers and make capital improvements. The Mexican government also liberalized trade and immigration policies, which enriched access to material goods among settlers of the far northern frontier, and permitted mestizos to hold political office for the first time. The net impact of these changes was the creation of a newly propertied, politically empowered class of Mexican landowners in the North who formed the core of an emergent but tenuous hacienda society by the 1830s.[18]

Hacendados and vaqueros, later grouped uneasily under the name "charros," created a culture in the Mexican North that was similar, though not identical, to that which existed in central-western Mexico. Like their counterparts farther south, the newly empowered hacendados of el Norte depended almost totally on the labor of women, indigenous, and mestizo workers, insisting on their superiority as gente de razón (people of reason). Also like their southern counterparts, they created a world marked by leisure and lavishness—not as extensive as their counterparts in the Bajío, to be sure, but definitively so relative to the vaqueros with whom they were co-creating a distinctly norteña version of Mexican ranching and charro culture. The hacendados or charros of the North consumed and flaunted luxury goods such as clothing, imported furniture, and ornately tooled saddles. They constructed and maintained elaborate ranch homes with the red tile roofs, archways, and ornate woodwork that would later be associated with the Mission Revival and Spanish Colonial Revival architectural styles. They also hosted elaborate fandangos and festivals, including rodeos, that sustained a sense of community and kinship among the region's emerging elite class.[19] Through their cultural rituals and efforts to shape the physical landscape, they mimicked what they perceived as the more "authentic" ranching and charro cultures of central Mexico, even as they adapted to the distinct political, economic, and geographic conditions of the North. This core tension, between the perceived authenticity of charrería in central Mexico and the heterogeneous ranchero practices of el Norte/the U.S. Southwest, has been an enduring feature of charrería ever since.

One key difference in the Mexican North was its intercultural nature, especially the presence and influence of well-capitalized Anglo-American men. Concerned more with local issues and private gain than with nationalist attachments, elite landowning men in the North formed families, engaged in business partnerships, and shared political power across ethnic and racial lines. Although the degree of collaboration differed from place to place, elite Mexican men and elite Anglo men were partners, if unevenly so, in shaping the region's social structure and ranching culture both before and after U.S. military conquest in 1848. They mingled together in the homes, ranchos, and plazas of the region's pueblos; they established business partnerships; they campaigned for elected office in roughly equal numbers; and they participated together in violent mobs that criminalized the region's indigenous and working-class inhabitants.[20] Laborers, too, joined together in crafting a transnational, working-class ranch culture of significant hybridity. When white and Black American cowboys sought work on the long cattle drives from Texas after the end of the U.S. Civil War, they adopted the style, equipment, language, and ranching practices that mestizo and indigenous vaqueros had been using in Texas and Mexico for decades. It was also common for ethnic Mexicans to compete in events organized by white promoters, and for Anglo-American and African American cowboys to cross the newly delineated border line to participate in bullfights and rodeo-style contests in Mexico.[21]

The interculturalism of the nineteenth-century U.S. Southwest generally, and of ranching culture specifically, shifted dramatically with U.S. military conquest and the maturation of American capitalism. The Treaty of Guadalupe Hidalgo, signed in 1848 to end the U.S. war with Mexico, ceded approximately half of Mexico's territory to the United States—the future states of California, New Mexico, Arizona, Texas, Utah, Nevada, and Colorado. The treaty gave the hundred thousand Mexicans living in the region the choice of relocating within Mexico's newly established borders or converting to U.S. citizenship; over 90 percent chose the latter. Though the treaty was supposed to protect the religious, linguistic, civil, and property rights of those who opted to stay in the new U.S. territories, it usually failed to do so. Much of the land previously held by the hacendado elite was systematically transferred to Anglo corporate ranchers and agriculturalists, who fenced their lands and restricted access to public waterways, ending the era of the open range. Anglo ranchers also adopted scientific breeding methods and modern management techniques, deskilling ranch work and alienating the large pool of working-class, multi-ethnic cowboys and vaqueros.[22]

While U.S. conquest and the introduction of American corporate methods affected all cowboys and vaqueros to some degree, they did so in ways sharply delineated by race and citizenship. Native laborers, who had worked extensively in ranching and agriculture at the missions and the ranchos, were routinely subjugated by laws and vigilantes that criminalized their cultural and spatial practices in order to secure a cheap, captive labor force.[23] African American and ethnic Mexican laborers, who made up between one-quarter and one-third of the cowboy workforce, were also structurally subordinated within the industry. They held the lowest-status positions, were frequently paid less than their Anglo-American counterparts, had little chance for upward mobility, and faced significant interpersonal hostility and institutional discrimination.[24] Ethnic Mexicans experienced these processes in direct relationship to the military conquest and territorial dispossession that increasingly structured their racialization in the United States. As the nineteenth century wore on, Mexicans of all class backgrounds, including many members of the elite class, were displaced from the land, concentrated in the region's rapidly expanding wage labor forces (especially in agriculture, construction, and manufacturing), and confined to urban barrios and agricultural colonias. These racialized spaces expanded still further when hundreds of thousands of Mexican nationals fled the violence and economic instability of the Mexican Revolution in the early twentieth century, seeking political peace as well as work in the Southwest's burgeoning economy.[25]

All of these changes signaled the modernization and economic maturation of the region, now rapidly urbanizing and industrializing, as well as the institutionalization of white American settler power and the growing rigidity of national borders. But they also created significant and widespread anxiety about the shifting relationships between race, masculinity, and national identity in the early twentieth century. During the Spanish and Mexican eras, elite Mexican men *and* elite American men in the U.S. Southwest had enjoyed shared social status through their paternalistic control of land, animals, workers, women, and children. After U.S. conquest, this form of patriarchy was replaced by a new conception of manhood defined by control of mobile capital and industry, ownership of private property, command of republican democracy and the instruments of republican citizenship, and adherence to Victorian gender and sexual ideals. Similar processes were under way in Mexico as dictator Porfirio Díaz opened the Mexican economy, land base, and natural resources to foreign investment in the name of modernizing the country, a process that some postrevolutionary Mexican leaders tried to redirect, with only partial success. Elite and middle-class men in both the U.S. and Mexico struggled to perform the emerging masculine ideals of their respective states in these rapidly changing political-economic contexts. Their collective reaction, remarkably similar in both societies, was to seek a unifying masculine symbol of nationhood: the cowboy in the United States, the charro in Mexico. Along the way, each figure would become racialized and nationalized—the cowboy became "whitewashed" and the charro became "brownwashed"—in ways that elided the significantly more complex, pluralistic, and hybrid social history of ranching in both central-west Mexico and the U.S.-Mexico borderlands.

MAKING RACE AND NATION THROUGH RURAL HORSEMEN

Throughout the late nineteenth and early twentieth centuries, elites in both the U.S. and Mexico responded to profound social change with cultural and political initiatives that sanctified the premodern rural horseman as the foundation of emerging national narratives. The point was not to return to the agrarian world of the cowboy or the charro, but rather to celebrate him as part of the nation-state's origin story, thus freeing the modern nation to chart a progressive course forward under the leadership of a conservative elite.[26] In both the U.S. and Mexico, these nationalist cultural projects corresponded with, and mollified resistance to, the hardening of economic and political inequalities along the lines of race and citizenship.

In the United States, the most prominent example of this phenomenon is Teddy Roosevelt's self-fashioning as a "rough rider." Criticized for being genteel and effeminate in his early career, Roosevelt remade himself as a cowboy to restore public perceptions of his manhood. This strategy carried him to election to the U.S. presidency and helped him win support for his foreign policy initiatives, especially those that brought new imperial possessions into the American fold.[27] Other elite American and European (especially British) men dressed in "Indian" clothing, coordinated "Indian" spiritual gatherings, and established exclusive hunting clubs throughout the American West as well as Australia, Canada, East Kenya, and other British colonies.[28] They also sent their sons to ranch schools in the U.S. West that were, as Melissa Bingmann explains, meant to "inculcate individualism, bravery, strength, democracy, hard work, and fortitude ... at the same time as they preserved boys' status as the next generation of American leaders."[29]

By the 1930s, the U.S. mass culture industries spread similar practices of "playing cowboys and Indians" to the working classes, among whom they were meant to inculcate modern notions of masculinity and citizenship through reference to—and implicit distancing from—a shared premodern past. Corporate organizations such as the Professional Rodeo Cowboys Association (PRCA), which formed in 1936, promoted the idea that rodeo was an outgrowth of informal contests among Anglo—and *only* Anglo— cowboys on the Texas open range. In this way, the PRCA's shows and institutional histories of rodeo differed markedly not only from the social history of ranching in Mexico and the U.S. Southwest, but also the Wild West Shows of the 1890s, which had featured charros, vaqueros, and other diverse characters in their casts.[30] The country western music industry likewise transformed the radical, ethnically inflected working-class politics of individual musicians into a collective celebration of conservative, and increasingly suburban, whiteness.[31] The Western film industry, which reached its height from the 1930s through the 1950s, also depicted the cowboy as a white American figure while relegating Mexicans, African Americans, and indigenous characters to limited and stereotypical roles.[32] Collectively, these cultural products and practices mass-produced the idea that the cowboy was a working-class, white, and American male hero, obscuring the historic and ongoing participation of ethnic Mexicans, other Latinos, African Americans, and indigenous people in rodeo and ranching.[33]

At the same time, their Mexican counterparts were engaged in a remarkably similar process via their efforts to "brownwash" the charro. Mexican presidents and political elites from across the ideological spectrum had long called upon the charro's symbolism to bolster their authority and forge national unity, but this agenda accelerated after the Mexican Revolution (1910–20) amid land reforms, the commercialization of agriculture, industrialization, and the mass migration that these structural changes unleashed.[34] In order to consolidate their power and legitimacy while subduing social tensions, the emergent Mexican state and the Mexican cultural elite created elaborate mythologies of the country's haciendas and ranchos. Popular culture, such as música ranchera (ranch/country music) and comedia ranchera (ranch comedy, a cinematic genre similar to the American Western) constructed Mexico's ranch life as a much simpler time and place, where traditional gender roles and family structures held sway and where diverse social classes lived peacefully together under the benevolent leadership of the patriarchal hacendado/charro. These cultural forms elevated the charro to a heroic and quintessentially Mexican national icon, while sweeping the tensions and inequalities of Mexican ranch life—past and present—under the rug.[35]

Meanwhile, elite men in Mexico's rapidly growing urban centers institutionalized the sporting culture of charrería in ways that commemorated the historic ranching activities of the creole hacendado elite while eliding the roles of vaqueros, women, and people of indigenous and African descent. In 1921, they established the first formal charro association in Guadalajara, Jalisco; others soon followed in Mexico City and elsewhere. In 1932, a coalition of these charro associations successfully lobbied for September 14 to be declared Mexico's "Day of the Charro," and in 1933, they established the Federación Mexicana de Charrería (FMCH) in Mexico City to regulate the sport's practice. Under its elite, urban leadership, the FMCH assumed an authoritative role in defining the structure and culture of charrería. It established measurements for the size and shape of the lienzo and formalized the nine official *suertes* (events) of the charreada, which can be seen in the photographic interlude following this introduction. The FMCH also developed guidelines for the number and use of the various trajes de charro, and passed a code of conduct mandating sobriety, personal dignity, commitment to brotherhood, religiosity, and loyalty to Mexico.[36]

Equally important, the FMCH's officers wrote and published "official" histories of charrería, many of which remain highly influential today. These texts emphasized charrería's evolution as a distinctly Mexican, not Spanish, cultural form and centered on the role of landowning Mexican men, rather than workers and women, in its making.[37] These same histories located the origins of the charro most decisively in Mexico City and the west-central states of Mexico, especially the Bajío—the states of Jalisco, Aguascalientes, Querétaro, and Guanajuato—and Michoacán; according to Ricardo Pérez Montfort, they "reduced the tremendous regional diversity of lo mexicano and emptied charro culture of any indigenous signs or traces of class conflict."[38] Reductionist narratives of Mexico's ranching history were linked to policy. Wealthy landowners opposed agrarian reform on the grounds that it threatened a treasured way of life that they claimed to protect, via their practice of charrería and other ranchero cultural forms. Collectively, the FMCH's codes, rules, and histories framed postrevolutionary Mexican manhood around whiteness, social class privilege, and the geographies of central-western Mexico in ways that reproduced historic inequities of race, class, gender, and citizenship into the mid-twentieth century—much like the cowboy narratives and institutions then being created in the United States.

In both the United States and Mexico, then, the elevation of the cowboy and the charro to masculine nationalist icons proceeded in strikingly similar ways and toward similar ends. In both nations, the rural horseman channeled nostalgia for a premodern, patriarchal, and colonial past at a time of widening inequality and growing dissent, helping to unify diverse national populations through invocation of a supposedly shared cultural heritage. Though constructed as distinct figures, however, the cowboy and the charro were produced in relationship to each other. Indeed, the parallel construction of each figure reflected and helped to define the prevailing cultural norms and values of each nation-state, as well as their unequal positions within the global political economy. Constructed as an individualized symbol of working-class, white, rugged manhood who guided the nation's divinely ordained western expansion, the cowboy was an emblem of the United States' position as a settler nation and American elites' growing control of territorial possessions and colonies—as well as Mexico's economy—in the late nineteenth and early twentieth centuries. The charro, on the other hand, helped cultivate attachment to Mexico after decades of war, conquest, and revolution, as its leaders struggled to define a modern economic and political system amid debt and corruption, as well as territorial loss and ongoing migration to the United States.

To this day, these historical, cultural, and geopolitical differences are fully apparent in the stylistic differences between the cowboy and the charro. Spectators and journalists who encounter the two cultural forms inevitably comment on their differences. Cowboys embrace a rugged, informal, and utilitarian aesthetic that communicates the cowboy's working-class symbolism and American emphasis on economic efficiency: they wear Wrangler jeans, plaid button-up shirts, and cowboy boots, with only a prized silver belt buckle for ornamentation. Charros, by contrast, wear formal and elegant trajes de charro, handcrafted sombreros, intricately tooled leather belts, and boots of the highest-quality calfskin, all of which are meant to signal their dignity, skill, and cultural pride. Individualism versus collectivism are powerful differences as well: U.S. rodeo cowboys mostly compete as individuals, whereas charros specialize in particular events but ride, practice, travel, and compete as members of teams. In addition, while U.S. rodeo cowboys tend to be professionals who travel a competitive circuit in search of prize money, charros are amateurs who compete primarily for tradition, status, and pride. Aside from prizes such as saddles, belt buckles, or horse trailers (increasingly, with growing corporate sponsorship of events), winners of charro competitions do not receive money. The stylistic differences between the cowboy and the charro circulate in the spaces and events of the American-style rodeo and the Mexican charreada, as well, where the national, racial, and gender identities associated with both practices are performed and negotiated. As Kathleen Sands notes, "In rodeo, speed and strength are dominant values, reflecting the value Americans place on efficiency, practicality, endurance, and power. In charreada, style and precision dominate, reflecting the emphasis Mexican culture places on elegance, colorful embellishment, baroque richness, and mastery."[39]

The cultural and stylistic differences between charrería and American-style rodeo matter greatly to charros in the United States, as they navigate their complex relationships to both nationalist formations and their associated logics of race, class, gender, and citizenship. For many ethnic Mexicans in the United States, the charro's noble, dignified, communal, and prideful character facilitates subtle resistance to the histories of U.S. imperial expansion, economic dominance, and racial violence through which ethnic Mexicans have been persistently subjugated. This is a key reason why the charro has been such a popular figure among ethnic Mexicans in the United States for over a century. For them, the charro is at once the "original cowboy," an elite form of patriarchal manhood, and a revered symbol of Mexican identity. As a composite of these multiple meanings, values, and potentials, the charro has cohered ethnic Mexicans in the United States in their collective resistance to conquest, displacement, and institutionalized racism.

CHARROS AND CHARRERÍA IN THE UNITED STATES

Like diasporic subjects around the world, both past and present, ethnic Mexicans in the United States have drawn on the figure of the charro to address their distinct needs and experiences in the U.S. while simultaneously shaping the Mexican nationalist project of charrería from abroad.[40] Beginning in the 1880s but especially after the 1930s, ethnic Mexicans turned to the charro to demonstrate their loyalty to Mexico and their authenticity as Mexican cultural subjects in diaspora while also laboring to transform their living conditions in the United States. In doing so, they challenged all-too-recent histories of dispossession, alienation, and subjugation and began the work of remapping race and national identity.

This project was, at first, concentrated among elite Mexicans and their descendants living in the U.S. Southwest, especially through late nineteenth-century literature that remembered and honored the world of the hacienda.[41] But such commemorations gained steam in the 1920s and '30s amid the tremendous transnational migration unleashed by the Mexican Revolution and subsequent efforts to rebuild postrevolutionary Mexico. During this period, Mexican elected officials, diplomats, businessmen, and filmmakers traveled extensively throughout the U.S. Southwest and sometimes beyond, to New York City and other influential urban centers on the eastern seaboard. As they traveled through the United States, these elite figures tried to cultivate both political and economic opportunities for themselves and loyalty to the nation among Mexicans living in diaspora.[42] Among them were officers of the newly organized Federación Mexicana de Charrería, who were not only charros but also businessmen and politicians.[43] Entertainers and performers such as Tito Guízar, Pedro Infante, Jorge Negrete, and Antonio Águilar, to name just a few of the more famous, also traveled extensively throughout the United States during the early and mid-twentieth century, infusing ranchero cultural ideas and practices into American popular culture.[44]

The ranchero nationalism that these Mexican figures promoted during their travels provided a framework within which working-class Mexicans in the U.S. Southwest negotiated the complexities of their daily lives. Across the U.S. Southwest during the 1920s and '30s, working-class Mexican migrants and Mexican Americans immersed themselves in charro- and ranch-themed mass culture. They sang along to the ranchera songs that played on Spanish radio stations and watched comedias rancheras at Spanish-language theaters in San Antonio, El Paso, Tucson, Los Angeles, and other cities and towns. They dressed as charros and chinas poblanas (a traditional style of women's dress) for Cinco de Mayo and Mexican Independence Day parades, often sponsored by the Mexican consulates, that wound through the streets of the U.S. Southwest's growing Mexican barrios. The expanding class of ethnic organizations and mutual aid societies that served Mexican migrants and their communities also drew on ranchero cultural forms. For example, they sponsored events at "Spanish"-themed locations like Olvera Street in Los Angeles or La Villita in San Antonio—many of which had been conceived, designed, and financed by the Anglo elite—where they encouraged Mexican migrants to dress up as charros and dance the jarabe tapatío (often referred to as the "Mexican hat dance").[45]

Ethnic Mexicans' embrace of charros, charrería, and other ranchero cultural forms during this period complicates current scholarly understanding of the so-called Spanish fantasy past. The term was first coined by critic and journalist Carey McWilliams, who used it to describe the constellation of Anglo-American cultural projects that glorified the Spanish colonial era and justified indigenous genocide and Mexican dispossession in the U.S. Southwest.[46] The Spanish fantasy past took many forms, among them a relentless parade of "Spanish"-themed costume parties and pageants; preservation of the Spanish missions as well as Spanish Revival and Mission Revival architecture; and mission-themed school curricula. The Spanish fantasy past reached its heyday in the 1920s and '30s, when it worked to boost local identity and attract tourists and settlers. Institutionalized in civic organizations and concretized in the physical landscape, it persists in the public culture of southwestern cities to this day.[47] Yet ethnic Mexicans' attachment to the charro and other ranchero cultural forms from the 1930s onward should give us pause in dismissing the Spanish fantasy past as *only* an expression of white Americans' imperialist nostalgia or modernist anxieties. Their use of the charro and associated ranchero forms, whether through moviegoing, fashion, parades, performances, or parties, allowed them to exercise cultural citizenship through the claiming of public space in ways that were otherwise often denied.[48] At a time when the U.S.-Mexico border was selectively but violently patrolled, and when pressures for Americanization were especially intense, ethnic Mexicans could work within the "Spanish" fantasy past to express their longings for Mexico and the pains of dislocation, migration, and racial subjugation. And they could do so in ways that were both supported by powerful Mexican institutions and palatable to Anglo-Americans, who may not have even recognized the Mexican nationalist impulses at work within the "Spanish" culture they valorized.

Amid widespread economic affluence, the ascendance of postwar liberalism, and the burgeoning Mexican American civil rights movement after World War II, the charro became a much more focused and intentional conduit for organized political and cultural activity. In this period, middle-class and upwardly mobile ethnic Mexican men—many of them now veterans, parents, homeowners, and business owners—went from watching charros on stage or screen to competing and performing as charros themselves. As they formed charro associations and rode and competed together, ethnic Mexican men used the symbolic power of the charro and the organizational structure of the charro associations to pursue opportunity and inclusion in U.S. institutions. The chapters that follow consider a range of these initiatives, organized by time period, geography, and the kinds of institutions that U.S. charros targeted for change. The first four chapters explore charros' work at the local level as they labored to transform the institutions that had been key to their racial subjugation in those places, from state violence in Los Angeles to economic disenfranchisement in San Antonio to school segregation in Denver and suburban public space in Southern California. The final chapter then considers how U.S. charros have "scaled up" to the national level in recent years, becoming formal actors in the American political system as they respond to animal welfare concerns in the Mexican rodeo.

As will become apparent, the scope of the U.S. charros' work has been wide-ranging and diverse. The charro's flexibility as a symbol of dignity, autonomy, skill, and cultural pride has made him useful for a wide spectrum of social struggles, and the opportunities pursued by charros in one city have not necessarily made sense for their counterparts in another. Instead, their initiatives have generally responded to the local geographies of racial subjugation, as well as the unique opportunities born by the particularities of place. In exploring this geographic variability, this book aims to nurture the burgeoning field of Chicanx and Latinx geographies, which explores how the social production of space and place shapes Latinx identity, the location of Latinx people within structures of inequality, and the form and content of their resistance to the spatial conditions of their lives. With regard to this study, it is not only that the social world of the charro has been historically more complex than is often remembered, but that the spatial form of the hacienda and its chief protagonist, the charro, developed across the Spanish empire and postindependence Mexico, including the region that became the U.S. Southwest, in highly uneven ways. These differentiated geographies have affected not only *how* ethnic Mexicans since the 1930s have understood and mobilized the charro, but also whether the charro "sticks" at all as a meaningful way of knowing the land, forming collective consciousness, and advocating for change. The diversity and unevenness of these initiatives illustrates sociologist Wendy Wolford's contention that any social movement "is shaped by—and shapes—the way people internalize and engage with their specific material and symbolic spatial environments."[49] Put differently, the historic and ongoing production of space matters in terms of whether and how ethnic Mexicans find the charro to be meaningful, useful, or effective as an instrument of social change.

The charro emerged first as a unifying force for social change in California and Texas—places where elite hacienda culture developed most fully under Spanish and Mexican rule, where ethnic Mexicans retained significant power for a brief period after U.S. conquest, and where the largest numbers of Mexican migrants moved during and after the Mexican Revolution. For these reasons, ethnic Mexicans who mobilized the charro in these border states were able to achieve some significant political, economic, and spatial gains. The first two chapters document their efforts, looking at the establishment and early work of the first U.S. charro associations, founded in San Antonio and Los Angeles just after World War II. In Los Angeles, as chapter 1 shows, working-class charros from the East Los Angeles barrio negotiated an alliance with Eugene Biscailuz, the elite descendant of Spanish-Mexican Californios who headed the Los Angeles Sheriff's Department (LASD) from 1932 to 1958. This relationship allowed the East L.A. charros to join the LASD's mounted posse program and to serve as extras in *The Young Land* (1959), an important film about racial justice in California during the transition to U.S. settler rule. These activities enabled working-class and middle-class ethnic Mexican men to claim a limited form of state power at a time when the city's law enforcement agencies were otherwise targeting Mexicans for harassment and persecution. Meanwhile, in San Antonio, as chapter 2 explains, the city's tiny class of Mexican American businessmen formed a charro association that worked with a wide range of civic groups, in both South Texas and northern Mexico, to build the city's postwar tourist economy. Their focus on entrepreneurship and business networking gave them power over the shaping of San Antonio's culture and landscape in ways denied most other ethnic Mexican groups in South Texas at the time, though their initiatives primarily benefited middle-class men with a pro-capitalist outlook.

Beginning in the late 1960s and well through the 1980s, a period marked by the rise and demise of the Chicano movement, struggles for land, and pride in Mexican cultural heritage, charros and their associations operated in the service of ethnic Mexicans' efforts to integrate public institutions and public spaces. Buoyed by an increasingly influential cadre of Mexican American politicians, businessmen, and cultural producers, charros began making more direct claims upon American institutions and social spaces, frequently deploying the language of "original cowboys" to do so. In Colorado, as chapter 3 explains, ethnic Mexicans used the charro as a resource for bilingual education in Denver Public Schools, the integration of the Colorado State Fair in Pueblo, the expansion of Hispanic participation in celebrations of the American Bicentennial in 1976, and the diversification of public art at the state capitol in Denver. Back in Los Angeles, as chapter 4 shows, ethnic Mexican men used charrería to make claims upon public space in their new suburban neighborhoods, even while they assumed increasing financial risk as Latino-majority suburbs weathered the worst of Southern California's economic restructuring.

In the 1990s, hemispheric free-trade agreements and neocolonial interventions by the U.S. and other nations in Mexico's economy propelled unprecedented displacement and migration to the United States, with many migrants settling in new areas in the interior and Midwest. The expansion of migrant communities and their ranchero cultural practices, especially in new locations, made U.S. charros subject to a new force of racialization from an unlikely (and progressive) source: the animal welfare movement. Since the 1990s, animal welfare activists have objected to several events in the charreadas, which are now banned and criminally prosecuted in more than a dozen U.S. states. Adopted alongside other high-profile laws directed at ethnic Mexicans, such as California's Proposition 187 and Arizona's SB 1070, these laws have contributed to the production of Mexican immigrant "illegality" by constructing ethnic Mexicans and other Latinos—regardless of citizenship status—as illegitimate, criminal subjects and by curtailing their access to public space. Yet, as chapter 5 also shows, these same laws have galvanized U.S. charros to organize as formal political subjects for the first time, scaling up to impact the U.S. legislative system while propelling important conversations about the ethics of charrería in both the United States and Mexico.

Considered collectively, the initiatives documented here illuminate key historical and spatial processes in the racialization of ethnic Mexicans, as well as transformative moments in their politicization and ongoing resistance via the charro and lo ranchero. They also offer a number of new perspectives and theoretical insights for American history, southwestern history, and ethnic studies, especially Chicanx and Latinx studies. Among these are the significance of the ethnic Mexican middle class in Mexican American history and in the shaping of the Southwest's racial geographies; the tension between ethnic Mexicans' interlocking histories as both colonizers and colonized in the U.S. Southwest; the complex relationships to whiteness and modernity that this tension has produced; and the negotiation of masculinity as it intersects with race, class, citizenship, and place.

One important thread relates to class formation among middle-class ethnic Mexicans in the United States. Most participants in charrería are middle class, upwardly mobile, even elite. To be sure, "middle class" is a vast category that includes people with a range of incomes, education levels, and social statuses, and ethnic Mexicans' experience of middle-class status in the United States has been sharply influenced by their racial position—all of which will soon become apparent in this book. Even so, participation in Mexican rodeo, like other equestrian sports, requires significant disposable income. Charros must pay for their own well-trained horses, saddles, bridles, trajes, horse trailers, travel expenses, and leasing fees for rough stock (steers, horses, and other animals they use in practice and competition). Though charrería is still more accessible in the U.S. than in Mexico, where it remains the province of the elite, in the U.S. the sport is limited to those with some degree of economic security and capital. However, it is this same class status, as well as the charro's symbolism as a respectable and culturally conservative figure, that has given charros and their associations significant institutional power, especially in areas that have been unavailable to their working-class counterparts. It also means that the charros have focused on aspects of social life that are particularly relevant to the middle class: small business entrepreneurship, home ownership, and suburban space, for example. In documenting these initiatives with attention to their class politics, this book contributes to a burgeoning scholarship on the Mexican American middle class, whose experiences, perspectives, and social change strategies have sometimes differed markedly from their working-class co-ethnics.[50]

Charros' relatively privileged class standing has made them especially effective in transforming racial geographies—the racial organization and meanings of space. Charrería resembles sports like soccer, which, as Juan Javier Pescador has argued, provide an opportunity for players, food vendors, musicians, and spectators to "mexicanize the urban landscape and manifest their right to public facilities."[51] Charrería accomplishes this same goal to an even greater extent because the charreada requires distinctive facilities: a large keyhole-shaped arena known as a lienzo, as well as corrals and stables to keep horses and other livestock, grandstands, and other structures. These physical landscapes are both more permanent and more expensive than those required by soccer, baseball, boxing, and other sports in which Latinos participate in large numbers. As such, they require significant private and public investment. As middle-class figures with connections to Anglo-American, Mexican, and Mexican American power structures, charros have played a crucial role in brokering these investments and the relationships on which they rest. In doing so, charros have mexicanized the southwestern landscape via their production of urban lienzos—the modern spatial counterparts of the historic ranchos and haciendas—and are reclaiming the territorial power of ethnic Mexicans in the region.

In this respect, the practice of charrería in the United States invokes simultaneously a colonial imaginary and a nationalist one. As Chicanx studies scholars Nicole Giudotti-Hernández, Laura Pulido, Rosaura Sánchez, Beatrice Pita, and others have argued, Mexicans in what became the U.S. Southwest were historically both active agents of Spanish and Mexican colonialism before 1848 *and* victims of U.S. empire and racialized class structures thereafter.[52] When mobilized as sports culture or strategy of civil rights and place-making, charrería celebrates the first process in order to challenge the second. It commemorates historic Spanish and Mexican colonial ranching societies in order to resist the conquest, displacement, and exploitation of Mexicans by U.S. institutions, but it largely ignores the ways in which haciendas and ranchos did the same for indigenous inhabitants. The practice of charrería among Mexicans in the United States has thus involved a process of whitening: claims to power rest on invocations of a violent colonial past. These fissures reverberate with the tensions around social class, race, and region that have long simmered within articulations of Mexican nationalism. Given the charro's roots in the west-central states of Mexico—a region associated with whiteness, haciendas, and the nationalist elite—for example, he has had little appeal to migrants who hail from states such as Veracruz, with its Afro-Caribbean heritage and connections, or the southern, largely indigenous states of Oaxaca and Chiapas.

The tensions related to class privilege, whiteness, and colonialism are also intimately bound up with gender identity and performance, because the charro is an indisputably masculine form of power. The operation of masculinity among U.S. charros is complex and multifaceted, echoing the findings of recent scholarship on Latino masculinities, especially in contexts of migration, in which no one model of masculine identity performance necessarily dominates.[53] Although the world of charrería is certainly built on men's violence and control, especially of animals, the men who perform as charros typically aspire to caballerismo—a form of masculinity that values nurturance, protection of the family, dignity, wisdom, hard work, and emotional connectedness. To be a caballero, in their view, is to protect, care for, and speak on behalf of the family and community—all of which they view as positive qualities.[54] The charro also represents masculine skill and dignity in a way that stands in explicit contrast to the image of stoop labor—the bent-over, faceless, laboring brown body—that otherwise frames so much of the Mexican experience in the United States.[55] Finally, participation in charrería, like other sports popular among Latino men, allows male participants to develop leadership skills, build social networks that transcend geography and generation, and travel extensively throughout the United States, Mexico, and beyond.[56] Small wonder that ethnic Mexican men have admired and emulated this figure so consistently across time and place.

Still, the very qualities that make charro masculinity appealing to many ethnic Mexican men also facilitate its reproduction as a patriarchal, aggressive, and violent form of masculinity. As historian José Alamillo and sociologist Michael Messner have both demonstrated, building on the work of Chicana feminists, competitive sports like charrería tend to cultivate masculine cultures of violence, risk, and aggression that are damaging not only to women, non-normative men, and animals, but also the male charros themselves.[57] Despite the codes of conduct developed by the FMCH and individual men's aspirations to caballerismo, drinking, fighting, sexual harassment, and animal abuse sometimes do occur, especially at nonsanctioned charreadas or *jaripeos* and *coleadores* (bull-riding and steer-tailing events, respectively).[58] Sexism is also woven into the very structure of the sport. Women participate in charrería, but only in highly gendered, stereotypical roles—as queens, *escaramuzas* (female riders), and wives and mothers laboring behind the scenes—through which they reproduce what Rosa Linda Fregoso has called the "masculine family drama" of Mexican cultural nationalism.[59] Nonhuman animals, especially cattle and horses but also dogs, sheep, and chickens, play a similar role: they are expected to labor on behalf of the reproduction of Mexican nationalist culture, even when doing so means risking significant violence and harm.[60]

These tensions will figure prominently in this book, as will the challenges levied against charros and charrería on the basis of class and gender. Yet they have also spurred the ongoing evolution of charrería as both nationalist and transnational Mexican cultural practice. The women who participate in charrería as escaramuzas and queens, for example, have found creative ways to exercise agency within the sport, while also pushing for subtle changes to gender roles and structures—changes that at least some male charros also support.[61] Outside the lienzo, in the cultural spheres of literature, reality television, and mariachi music, Mexican and Mexican American artists and writers have used the figure of the charro to imagine productive new relationships between gender, sexuality, and nation.[62] For all its pretenses to nostalgically represent the premodern agrarian past of modern Mexico, charrería is a living and changing cultural form. It has consistently responded to the shifting realities and perspectives of diverse subjects, both in Mexico and in diaspora, enabling those subjects to constantly remap the intersections of race, class, gender, and national identity.

METHODS, SOURCES, AND COMMITMENTS

Before moving on, I want to situate myself more explicitly in relationship to this study. I came to this project through my experiences growing up in a horse-keeping neighborhood in suburban Los Angeles during the late 1980s and early '90s. My family and I lived in Shadow Hills, one of four neighborhoods in the City of Los Angeles where the right to keep and ride horses is protected by municipal zoning. After school and on weekends, my friends and I rode our horses in Hansen Dam, a flood control channel that the U.S. Army Corps of Engineers constructed in the 1950s. Because of regulations attached to flood control projects in the mid-twentieth century, Hansen Dam also functions as a regional recreation center. It is full of trails and shallow streams where my friends and I rode our horses, splashing in the cool water and enjoying the shade during Los Angeles's blistering hot summer days. But Hansen Dam was also the site of immense racial tensions between the majority-white residents of my neighborhood, which abutted Hansen Dam to the south, and the Latino residents who lived in residential communities on the northern and western sides of the dam. I documented some of these conflicts in my book, *Making the San Fernando Valley: Rural Landscapes, Urban Development, and White Privilege,* which explored the relationships between intentional rural landscapes and the reproduction of white privilege in Los Angeles, especially as the city became majority Latino in the late twentieth century. Tensions between white and Latino users of public space in that corner of the San Fernando Valley spiked during my young adulthood in the 1990s, amid the anti-immigrant sentiment that gripped California at the time. They continue to simmer today, albeit at a lower boil.

For me, one of the most puzzling tensions at that time centered on the figure of the Mexican horseman—the same figure I now recognize as the charro. Occasionally, while out riding in Hansen Dam, my friends and I encountered Mexican men riders who wore trajes de charro, complete with silky bowties and wide sombreros. They rode prancing, well-groomed horses outfitted in intricately carved saddles and bridles, decorated with flashes of silver. My friends and I, riding bareback and barefoot in our cutoff denim shorts, had no idea what to make of these men; we simply said "hello" as we passed, as we did to everyone we met out riding. Afterward, though, I can recall my friends saying things like, "Those Mexicans—always trying to show off on their horses. Always trying to be macho." White adults in the neighborhood made similar remarks. These casual comments imprinted in my young mind the idea that cultural conflict was bound up with competing histories of horsemanship, and that those competing histories were connected to contemporary struggles over physical space.

Years later, while doing research for *Making the San Fernando Valley,* I stumbled upon evidence of a group of charros, the Charros Emiliano Zapata, who had subleased part of Hansen Dam from the City of Los Angeles during the mid-1970s in order to host charreadas for the San Fernando Valley's growing Latino population. Due to protests from animal welfare and environmental activists, that group lost their lease in 1980—the same moment when homeowner activists in my own majority-white neighborhood were successfully lobbying municipal officials to create zoning codes that protected horse-keeping and the "rural" lifestyle. I explore the story of the Charros Emiliano Zapata more fully in chapter 4. But my initial encounter with the archival materials of this group confirmed my childhood impressions: horses, horsemen, and the claims on private property and public space they enable were important axes of struggle and inequality in Los Angeles. Later, I would discover that such struggles were not limited to my corner of Southern California, nor were they a unique feature of suburban life in the late twentieth century. Quite the contrary: they dated at least to the 1930s and were rooted in even deeper histories of conquest, racial subjugation, and labor exploitation—all of which still structure life and landscape in the region.

My formative encounters with the charro, as a young white woman riding horses in a city that was rapidly becoming majority Latino in the late twentieth century, shape the way I relate to and narrate the stories in this book. This book is not an ethnographic account, and while I am attentive to internal conversations within ethnic Mexican communities about the evolving meanings of the charro and charrería, especially in relationship to gender and animal welfare, my primary goal is to analyze the charro's public-facing work. My focus is on how ethnic Mexicans have mobilized the charro to nurture cultural and social connections with Mexico while transforming the economies, institutions, public cultures, and spatial arrangements of the U.S. cities where they live, work, and play. Given my own background in a majority-white community that was devoted to myths of the "Wild West," where I observed the racialized construction of nationalist renditions of American history in physical space, I am especially interested in how the charro challenges whitewashed histories of the frontier and the cowboy—how their claims to be the "original cowboys," whether explicit or implicit, enable Mexican Americans' pursuit of equity, access, and inclusion.

To understand these processes, then, let us begin with Los Angeles, which is both the city where I first encountered the charro in the late 1990s *and* the place where he had first emerged as a guiding force for ethnic Mexicans' collective action, more than a half-century before.

The charreada is held in and around the *lienzo charro*—a keyhole-shaped arena that includes two distinct but connected spaces. A long rectangular lane measuring 39 feet wide by 200 feet long leads into a circular area, the *ruedo,* which is 130 feet in diameter. The lienzo is usually surrounded by metal bleachers and a judges' platform where officials can safely observe and score the events; a dance floor for entertainment may be nearby. Attached to the lienzo are holding pens for the horses, bulls, and steers, which are released into the lienzo as needed. Outside of the lienzo are stables, practice areas, outbuildings, parking lots, concession stands, and other landscape features. Pictured here is the Lienzo Charro de la Viga in Mexico City, 2014. Photo by Comisión Mexicana de Filmaciones, licensed under Creative Commons Attribution-Share Alike 2.0 Generic license.

The first of nine charreada events is the *cala,* a series of reining maneuvers in which the rider races the horse down the long, narrow part of the lienzo to arrive in the ruedo, then brings the horse to a sliding stop, or *raya*. The rider then urges the horse to spin rapidly on one back foot, first in one direction and then the other. Finally, the rider backs the horse all the way out of the arena. The purpose of the cala is to show the horse's dexterity and nimbleness, as well as the rider's mastery of subtle cues conveyed through leg pressure, shifts in body weight, and nearly imperceptible applications of the reins. In this photo, the charro performs the sliding stop while the judge and the announcer look on. Photo by Al Rendon, used with permission.

The second charreada event is the *piales en lienzo,* in which members of competing teams attempt to rope a running mare who is racing down the long narrow section of the lienzo. The riders throw a loop in front of the mare, then allow her to race through it and be caught by the hind legs. Once the horse's hind legs have been captured—a difficult task—the charro brings her to a slow, gradual stop. He has three chances to do so. The purpose of this event, historically, was to catch a loose horse for branding, feeding, or medical care on the open range. Nowadays, the piales serve to demonstrate the charro's capacity to use exceptionally long ropes in a confined space. It has become one of the more controversial charreada events, and in some U.S. states it is no longer performed. Photo by Louis DeLuca for the *Dallas Morning News,* 2016, used with permission.

The third charreada event is the *cola,* which translates literally as "tail," and in the context of charreada refers to the practice of "tailing a bull" (or, much more commonly, a steer—a castrated bull). The rider runs alongside a fleeing steer, tries to grab the animal's tail, and, if successful, wraps the tail around his leg or boot, using both his arm strength and the leverage of his body weight to flip the animal to the ground. Like the piales and the manganas, this activity originated on the Mexican range before the use of ropes, when vaqueros needed to bring loose animals to the ground. Also like these other events, the cola has drawn the attention of animal welfare activists concerned about damage to the steer's spine. However, charros are quick to note that the event is equally risky for human riders: the cola is a physically demanding event that frequently burns the rider's hand as the rope sizzles through his palm, and sometimes breaks fingers. Despite the risk of injury, it remains an important and valued event, in both full-fledged charreadas and in separate events called *coleaderos,* because it allows charros to demonstrate their strength and dexterity. Photo by Smiley Pool for the *Dallas Morning News,* 2015, used with permission.

The fourth charreada event is the *jinete de toro*—bull riding. U.S.-style rodeo has an almost identical event, but requires the rider to stay on the bull for only eight seconds. In the Mexican version, the rider not only tries to stay on until the bull is subdued, but also earns extra points by spurring the animal when it begins to slow down, thus prolonging the ride. The jinete may also use two hands to hold onto the grab rope, whereas in the U.S. style of bull riding the cowboy may use only one hand. Unlike the other charreada events derived from practical skills required for working with cattle, bull riding developed as a form of skillful play during the recreational parts of the historic roundup. Photo by Al Rendon, used with permission.

The fifth charreada event, which begins as soon as the bull rider has dismounted in jinete de toro and involves the same bull or steer, is the *terna en el ruedo,* or team roping. Much like U.S.-style team roping, this event features teams of riders trying to rope the head and hind legs of the steer, then stretch it on the ground in a subdued position. In American rodeo, team roping is the only event where men and women compete alongside each other in professionally sanctioned competition. In the charreada, it remains an exclusively male event. Unlike U.S.-style team roping, in which a time limit of thirty seconds is imposed, charros have eight minutes to complete the task. With the extended time, charros demonstrate fancy and trick roping; the style and execution of the rope flourishes are as important as accuracy in the event's scoring. Judges also award points depending on the distance from which the lasso is thrown to catch the bull. Photo by Al Rendon, used with permission.

The sixth charreada event is the *jinete de yegua,* or bronc riding. As in the bull-riding event, the charro rides a wild mare until she stops bucking, becomes calm, and can be dismounted quietly. Photo by Al Rendon, used with permission.

The seventh and eighth charreada events are the *manganas a pie* and *manganas a caballo,* in which competitors on foot or on horseback, respectively, rope a running mare's front legs in order to bring her to the ground in a shoulder roll. Mounted team members chase the mare around the ruedo to ensure she keeps running. Often called "horse-tripping" by critics, the manganas have become the most controversial of the charreada events in the United States; as of this writing, they have been banned by a dozen U.S. states, and U.S. charros have agreed they will no longer perform the event in its traditional form anywhere in the United States. This photograph, by Al Rendon and used with permission, was taken prior to that change. Charros in Mexico continue to perform the manganas in their traditional, unaltered form.

The final competitive event of the charreada is the *paso de la muerte,* which translates as "pass of death" or death leap. In this event, the contestant races his own well-trained horse alongside an untamed horse around the outside of the ruedo as his teammates try to keep the wild horse against the curving wall. When the two horses are directly alongside each other, the contestant leaps from his own horse to the bare back of the galloping wild mare, with only her mane to grab onto, then rides her to a stop before dismounting. This is considered the most dangerous of all the charreada events, as the rider is in serious jeopardy of being trampled by the mare or his own teammates. It tends to be practiced and performed by the youngest, fittest, and most daring men on a team. Photo by Al Rendon, used with permission.

Many charreadas also include one event for women: the *escaramuza,* which translates literally as "skirmish," but in the context of the charreada, it refers to a women's mounted drill team. Six to twelve young women—usually the daughters, granddaughters, or nieces of male charros—execute complicated maneuvers while riding their horses sidesaddle at breakneck speed. They typically perform their routines halfway through a charreada, as a sort of intermission or exhibit, and their performance is not scored or judged (though escaramuzas may compete against each other in separate women-only events). Escaramuzas wear clothing that honors the women who participated in the Mexican Revolution as officers, combatants, and camp followers, known as "Adelitas," after Adela Velarde Pérez. Photo by Al Rendon, used with permission.

ONE

Claiming State Power in Mid-Twentieth-Century Los Angeles

IN HIS SPANISH-LANGUAGE BOOK *El Charro en U.S.A.*, Miguel Flores—resident of Los Angeles, charro, and amateur historian—observed that L.A.'s ethnic Mexicans began donning the traje de charro for parades and celebrations of Mexico's patriotic holidays in the 1920s. The suit became especially popular in the 1930s and '40s, when comedias rancheras and canciones rancheras circulated across the U.S.-Mexico borderlands.[1] By the mid-1940s, a group of ethnic Mexicans in Los Angeles had gone beyond merely wearing the outfit on foot, and instead began riding and performing as charros on horseback. They did so not as an autonomous charro association, but rather as members of the Los Angeles Sheriff's Department (LASD). Performing as charros in one of the nation's most powerful—and most violent—law enforcement agencies enabled middle-class ethnic Mexicans to demonstrate their capacity for citizenship at this important historical juncture. Membership in the LASD, via the symbolism of the charro, also opened avenues to the city's culture industries and some of its public spaces and elite institutions. In all of these venues, ethnic Mexicans in Los Angeles used the charro to claim new forms of state power and to resist the city's long history of anti-Mexican violence at the hands of the state. Their work in these intersecting domains is the subject of this chapter.

Contemporary L.A. is renowned for its police brutality and the bouts of corruption that have plagued its law enforcement agencies. However, state violence in Los Angeles is as old as the city itself, fully imbricated in the region's histories of colonialism and directed initially at its indigenous peoples. At the Spanish missions in what would become Los Angeles County—Mission San Gabriel (est. 1771) and Mission San Fernando (est. 1797)—friars and soldiers forced indigenous people to convert to Catholicism, participate in Christian weddings, and labor on behalf of the Spanish Crown. Spanish authorities also banned indigenous subsistence practices, prohibited Native people from riding horses, and criminalized vagrancy, disorderly conduct, and public drunkenness almost exclusively among indigenous and mixed-race people. Punishment took the form of incarceration, corporal punishment, and convict labor, through which Native people built much of the city's infrastructure. Rape and sexual assault of indigenous women, especially by Spanish soldiers, was also a persistent fact of Spanish colonial life.[2]

After Mexican independence from Spain was won in 1821, the new political elite embraced liberal philosophies and policies. Ultimately, however, and in conjunction with incoming white settlers, they created a class structure nearly as hierarchical as their Spanish predecessors, and a police and juridical state just as violent.[3] From the 1830s through the 1870s, in what David Torres-Rouff refers to as Los Angeles's "transitional period," the city's intercultural elite used the pueblo's legal and carceral systems to enforce order, discipline poor and indigenous people, and maintain their social status. They passed civic ordinances that penalized adultery, gambling, interracial sex, vagrancy, and horse thievery, and then selectively enforced these among the city's poor, indigenous, Asian, and Black populations. As punishment, they meted out gruesome beatings, lynchings, and other acts of mob violence that endured well into the 1870s, after U.S. conquest, in what historian William Deverell has called the "unending Mexican War."[4] The Los Angeles County Sheriff's Department, established in 1850 as the city's first law enforcement agency, proved unable or unwilling to manage the conflicts. In recognition of this fact, in 1853 the LASD created volunteer posses, which often carried out the more spectacular acts of violence while members of the sheriff's department looked on with tacit approval. Indeed, the line between law enforcement and posse/lynch mob sometimes proved hard to decipher.[5]

With the swelling of the city's white American population in the 1870s and '80s and the demographic decline of the Mexican elite, the state's policies and practices became racialized in new ways by now targeting ethnic Mexicans of all class backgrounds, as well as indigenous peoples, for violent persecution.[6] The state's racial violence played out, on the one hand, through the repeated displacement of ethnic Mexicans from the land. The adjudication of land ownership in the conquered territories after 1848 resulted in Mexicans' overwhelming land loss, downward class mobility, and movement to the urban barrios around the plaza and nearby Sonoratown.[7] Then, in the early twentieth century, ethnic Mexicans were removed from those same central barrios, this time in the name of urban renewal, and relocated to neighborhoods east of the Los Angeles River: Boyle Heights, Lincoln Heights, Hollenbeck Park, Belvedere, and Maravilla. Collectively referred to as East Los Angeles, these neighborhoods would, by World War II, constitute one of the most politically and culturally significant Mexican barrios in the United States.[8]

At the same time, as the rising Anglo-American elite aggressively pursued agricultural and industrial development, it relied on local law enforcement to squash labor disputes and maintain the conditions for profitability. With support and urging from the Merchants and Manufacturers' Association (a coalition of businessmen and their supporters), the LAPD's "Red Squad" arrested picketers, broke up public demonstrations, infiltrated leftist organizations and labor unions, and arrested radicals on trumped-up charges.[9] Although many groups were targeted, Mexican migrants and Mexican Americans, whose population in Los Angeles swelled during and after the Mexican Revolution (1910–20), bore the brunt of this violence.[10] Not only were ethnic Mexicans the city's largest racial minority group, but they also showed a persistent inclination to organize in support of leftist politics.[11] Police and sheriffs routinely broke up strikes among Mexican workers, arrested Spanish-language speakers at the plaza, and spied on labor movements and revolutionary organizations led by Mexican nationals. Throughout the 1920s and '30s, instances of police misconduct and brutality against Mexican nationals in L.A. grew so rapidly that even the Mexican consulate, which had formerly supported the LAPD's open shop and anti-radical initiatives, protested.[12]

Not surprisingly, then, given this history, resistance to state violence was an enduring preoccupation for ethnic Mexicans as well as other communities of color in Los Angeles. This was especially true in the mid-twentieth century, as ethnic Mexicans experienced upward mobility through their participation in the military and unionized defense industries and began to integrate some of the city's institutions. As they pushed for civil rights at this key historical moment, the state and its capacity for violence was a foremost concern. Indeed, historian Edward Escobar has argued that "while other issues may have forced people to think of themselves as Mexican Americans, no other issue made people act politically *as* Mexican Americans."[13]

Much of the scholarship on ethnic Mexicans and state violence in mid-twentieth-century Los Angeles has focused on working-class experiences of and resistance to police brutality. For example, scholars have extensively documented the experiences of pachucas/os and zoot suiters, who were vilified and persecuted by police.[14] There is also a robust literature on ethnic Mexican organizing against state violence through groups such as the GI Forum, which represented veterans and their concerns, and the Community Service Organization (CSO), which mobilized multiethnic communities downtown and in the eastside districts.[15] Many of these organizations, and the scholars who study them, have focused attention on the Los Angeles Police Department (LAPD), which was then, and is still now, infamous for its racist violence.[16] As important as these studies are, they give us an incomplete picture of ethnic Mexican engagement with the state in mid-twentieth-century Los Angeles.

Ethnic Mexicans not only pursued direct actions and lawsuits to resist police brutality but also sought inclusion in the central organs of the state. They joined the city's law enforcement agencies as administrators and beat officers, and they volunteered as search-and-rescue riders. They also actively participated in the culture industries, especially film and festival, that interpreted historic and ongoing state violence in Los Angeles. Their initiatives targeted not only the LAPD, which patrols the City of Los Angeles, but also the Los Angeles County Sheriff's Department (LASD), which has jurisdiction over L.A. County—including, crucially, the unincorporated barrio of East Los Angeles, where most ethnic Mexicans lived before World War II after being expelled from the central city. For some ethnic Mexican men, as we shall see in this and later chapters, their location in the county opened up intriguing possibilities, because the county's sprawling geographies—historic home to the region's Spanish missions, Mexican ranches, and American agricultural fields—were well suited to a vision of state power and citizenship that might include the charro.

This chapter examines how diverse ethnic Mexicans used the figure of the charro to access state powers in mid-twentieth-century Los Angeles. It analyzes the work of three groups of men who mobilized the charro to assert their respectability and demonstrate their capacity for citizenship. The first is Sheriff Eugene Biscailuz, the descendant of an elite Spanish-Mexican family in "Old California" who headed the Los Angeles Sheriff's Department from 1932 to 1958. Biscailuz centered the charro in the city's public culture as a symbol of his personal heritage and civic unity, at the very same time as his office routinely persecuted Mexican laborers, immigrants, and political dissidents. The chapter then turns to a group of middle-class ethnic Mexicans who joined the East L.A. division of the Sheriff's Posse in the late 1940s and, with Biscailuz's blessing, wore trajes de charro as their uniforms. Finally, the

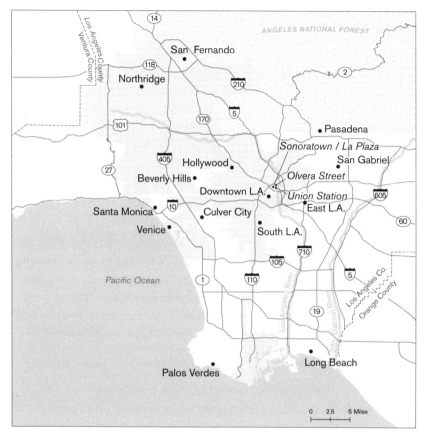

The City of Los Angeles and Los Angeles County, California. By Jennifer Tran and Alexander Tarr.

chapter explores the relationships that these East L.A. charros crafted with Mexican charros from Baja California as they worked together on *The Young Land* (1959), an influential film about state violence and vigilantism in California during the transition to American rule. After the film wrapped, these transnational relationships would support the East L.A. charros in establishing Los Angeles's first transnationally accredited charro association, the Charros de Los Angeles, in 1962.

At a time when the city was gripped by state and mob violence targeting working-class ethnic Mexicans, the charros' work was essential in allowing both middle-class and elite ethnic Mexicans to assert their respectability, their law-abiding nature, and their capacity for citizenship. Through their participation in the LASD and the culture industries that subsequently opened to them, the charros occupied public institutions and social spaces that were off-limits for many ethnic Mexicans in Los Angeles, especially those who were working class, poor, or politically defiant. In doing so, they recuperated the politics of the transitional period, when elite Mexicans had exercised significant power at the helm of the state. This work was enabled symbolically by the charro's identity as a historically conservative landowner, one who had maintained social order on the haciendas and ranchos through his benevolent but paternalistic leadership.

Despite his association with an aspirational class politics, however, the figure of the charro did not necessarily signal that middle-class ethnic Mexicans in Los Angeles were committed to cultural assimilation or political conformity in the United States. Quite the contrary: the figure of the charro allowed them to access the American state, and its capacities for both citizenship and violence, while embracing symbols of Mexican cultural nationalism and nurturing transnational networks. The charro was, in this sense, a complex and multifaceted figure—one who allowed flexibility, but also a limited form of power, in ethnic Mexicans' collective resistance to state violence and their pursuit of state power in mid-twentieth-century Los Angeles.

"THE OFFICIAL FIRST CABALLERO OF LOS ANGELES": SHERIFF EUGENE BISCAILUZ

The earliest and most influential person to integrate the charro into the city's law enforcement agencies was Eugene Biscailuz. Biscailuz led the Los Angeles Sheriff's Department between 1932 and 1958, a period of extraordinary city growth and equally tremendous violence. Biscailuz used his position at the head of the LASD to facilitate public conversations about the city's past, including its Spanish and Mexican periods, while simultaneously developing "modern" crime control policies and practices that persecuted working-class and poor Mexican laborers. Spanning past and present, he appealed to the historical agency of elite Californios, such as his own family, in the settlement of Alta California and during the transition to American rule. The figure of the charro would become a key resource for Biscailuz's multiple agendas.

Born in Los Angeles in 1883, Biscailuz fully embodied the transitional period and its politics of intercultural collaboration. His mother was also born in Los Angeles, the daughter of an interethnic marriage between an Anglo-American man from New England and a woman who descended from the last Spanish mayordomo of Mission San Gabriel. The other side of Biscailuz's family also positioned him as a "native son"—a term commonly used to refer to elites of Spanish and Mexican heritage that recognized their historic presence in California, but also obscured their roles as settler-colonizers. Biscailuz's father had been born in the elite coastal neighborhood of Palos Verdes to parents from the Basque region. His father was well connected with the city's well-to-do families through his law practice, his work editing a Basque newspaper, and a stint on the Los Angeles City Council. When Biscailuz was a child, he traveled with his father throughout the city, regularly traversing both the Anglo-dominated downtown and the Mexican-dominated plaza area. His family hosted many of the city's leading citizens, both Mexican and Anglo, at their home in Boyle Heights—not yet the industrial, working-class Mexican barrio it would become in the early twentieth century. In these ways, Biscailuz's family history epitomized the strong social ties between Anglo-Americans and elite Mexican Californians that had anchored social life in Los Angeles during the transitional period. While Biscailuz was born and reared after that period had ended, he was nonetheless socialized within its broad principles and networks.[17]

Influenced by childhood exposure to his father's legal profession, Biscailuz dedicated his adult life to law enforcement. He earned a law degree from the University of Southern California and, in 1907, joined the Los Angeles Sheriff's Department, where he rose quickly through the ranks. After a brief stint with the California Highway Patrol, in 1921 he returned to the LASD and was appointed under-sheriff. In 1932, upon the retirement of William Traeger, Biscailuz was appointed sheriff, a position to which he was elected in 1934 and continuously reelected until 1958, when he retired.[18]

Amid this transformative period in Los Angeles's history, supporters heralded Biscailuz for his ability to bridge the past with the present and future. His biographers attributed that ability to Biscailuz's ancestry among the intercultural elite in "Old California." In a 1950 biography, Lindley Bynum and Idwal Jones called Biscailuz "more than an honored law-enforcement official." He was also

> a human link connecting the historic pageantry of a colorful past with the dynamic present. He is a symbol: a man who has inherited much of the early environment of Los Angeles ... [which] gives him an old-world courtesy, a charming hospitality, a deep and sincere appreciation of friendship, a manner reminiscent of that of the old Spanish dons. To see him in a silver-mounted saddle, astride a beautiful palomino horse, riding at the head of the procession

in one of the numerous pageants which are held in this country, is to have a glimpse of the old aristocracy.[19]

Lest Biscailuz be dismissed as a quaint relic of a bygone time, Bynum and Jones hastened to add that "underneath that courteous charm is a lightning-fast mind, a steel-firm will and an intrepid personal courage."[20] For these biographers and others, Biscailuz was "the connecting link between the picturesque pueblo of the past and the great sprawling industrial center of the present."[21]

Biscailuz deliberately embraced the flexibility of his identity as both Spanish-Mexican "native son" and American sheriff. As the county's law-maker-in-chief, his closest friends were the well-capitalized white American men who ran the city's economy and culture industries. He belonged to an exclusive men's group called the Uplifters Club, which included many of the city's newspaper and bank executives as well as celebrities Will Rogers, Walt Disney, Spencer Tracy, and Clark Gable, among others.[22] Moving fluidly across Los Angeles's segregated urban geography, he was fully at home in the elite and racially exclusive westside neighborhoods of Beverly Hills, Pacific Palisades, and Santa Monica, where Biscailuz lived with his family.

Yet Biscailuz also embraced his Spanish-Mexican identity, especially cultural practices associated with the Mexican business and landed classes. For example, he enjoyed a collaborative relationship with the city's Mexican Chamber of Commerce, which sponsored benefits on his behalf and participated in his civic projects.[23] He also routinely invited ethnic Mexican singers and dancers to perform at civic events wearing Spanish or Mexican costumes. In addition, he often ventured past the westside and the central city to meet working-class and immigrant ethnic Mexicans where they were. He attended many celebrations of Mexican national holidays, such as Mexican Independence Day and Cinco de Mayo, at the plaza, Sonoratown, and East Los Angeles, and he appeared in parades and gave speeches (sometimes in Spanish) alongside the Mexican consul and visiting Mexican dignitaries.

Much of Biscailuz's persona as a bridge between Spanish past and American present, and between white and Mexican communities in Los Angeles, rested on his abilities and performances as a horseman. As a child, he had ridden horses during visits to his grandparents' property in Palos Verdes and family vacations on Catalina Island, though he had abandoned riding during the early stages of his career. One day in the late 1920s, Biscailuz was participating in a Native Sons parade while sitting atop a stagecoach. An old friend, attorney Ivan Parker, who was riding on horseback, approached him. Parker invited Biscailuz to get down off the stagecoach and go for a gallop. Though Biscailuz did not join Parker, this incident ignited Biscailuz's childhood memories of riding throughout Los Angeles County, and a week later he bought a horse, which he kept stabled at a facility in Culver City. "Thereafter," write Bynum and Jones, "he rode no more atop stagecoaches in parades, but was always seen on his arch-necked and shining mount . . . He was the official first *caballero* of Los Angeles, and horsemanship had become his minor avocation."[24] The move from stagecoach (symbol of the western frontier) to caballero (symbol of the hacienda and rancho) signaled Biscailuz's ability to straddle U.S. and Spanish-Mexican histories of the region.

Shortly thereafter, Biscailuz began to ride with an informal group of friends who dubbed themselves the "Sheriff's Posse," in implicit reference to the vigilante groups who had helped secure U.S. westward expansion and the violent conquest of Los Angeles. The posse was essentially a volunteer unit and social club composed of Biscailuz and his friends, all of whom were among Los Angeles's leading citizens and who imagined themselves much like the law enforcement of the "Old West." According to Bynum and Jones, "The posse was made up of sportsmen who liked to spend their week ends [*sic*] camping in the mountains, sleeping about the campfire, their horses dozing at the stake. They were a tanned, case-hardened crew, who could live off the country like Indians."[25] Members of the group included painter Clyde Forsyth (best known for his painting *Gunfight at O.K. Corral*); a local judge named Webster; real estate broker Ed Gerety; and actor Tom Mix, who starred in many Western films.[26] Actor Will Rogers, also known for his role in Westerns, was invited to participate, to which he jokingly replied, "Maybe I will if I don't get a better offer."[27]

After Biscailuz's appointment to head sheriff in 1932, one of his first actions was to turn the mounted posse into a rescue squad that could assist the Sheriff's Department during searches for missing persons in Los Angeles County's rugged forests and hillsides. The impetus was the 1928 disaster at Saint Francis Dam, a flood control channel constructed as part of the 1920s infrastructure-building boom, which had killed hundreds of people.[28] Thus, in 1933, Biscailuz established the Sheriff's Mounted Posse of Los Angeles County. The group was to be limited to fifty members, each of whom would provide and care for his own horse, buy his own equipment and wardrobe, pay an initiation fee of $100, and pay dues of $24 per year. Though volunteers, members of the posse were to be deputized: they were authorized to make arrests and otherwise function as fully empowered law enforcement officials.[29]

In addition to search-and-rescue work, the mounted posse was charged with appearing in parades and other civic events as representatives of the Los Angeles County Sheriff's Department. Arguably, this was its more important and visible role. The posse became a consistent feature in two of Los Angeles's most popular events: the annual Sheriff's Rodeo and the Tournament of Roses parade, both of which attracted many thousands of tourists and represented Los Angeles to the nation.[30] The posse also appeared at smaller events and festivals sponsored by local communities, and at dedications of public buildings. In 1939, for example, the Sheriff's Posse participated in "Romance of the Rails," a two-hour pageant to celebrate the opening of Union Station, which had been built in a Spanish revival style on the site of several displaced migrant communities, including the old barrio at Sonoratown. More than five hundred thousand people—one-third of the city's population—attended the event.[31]

The posse's performances at the city's Spanish fantasy sites, like Olvera Street and Union Station, impressed elite Mexican nationals traveling through Los Angeles, who believed that these sites and events—as well as Biscailuz himself—honored the Spanish and Mexican histories of the city. One of the first public appearances of the posse (which had not yet been formalized or deputized) occurred in 1931 during a weeklong celebration to commemorate the 150th anniversary of Los Angeles's founding by Spanish settlers in 1781. During the celebration, Biscailuz rode "on his creamy-maned horse and his attendant riders clanked past" on Olvera Street's recently installed cobblestones. José Palencia, who had been sent by Mexican president Pascual Ortiz Rubio, was "stirred by the display, especially the riding of the posse, [and] invited Gene to honor his country with a visit." Biscailuz, who was then still under-sheriff, explained his subordinate position and suggested that Sheriff William Traeger be invited instead. As Bynum and Jones observed, however, Traeger's "renown had not seeped over the border, and Under-Sheriff Biscailuz ... was greeted with louder cheering."[32] When Biscailuz did visit Mexico in 1936 after his election to sheriff, the governor of Mexico City, Cosme Hinojosa, thanked him for the aid he had given Mexicans in Los Angeles. Biscailuz responded to Hinojosa in Spanish: "We should all be together ... as one family in the Western hemisphere. I have always wanted to come to Mexico, and I can't believe that my dream is now being fulfilled."[33]

Yet Biscailuz's enthusiastic vision of "one family" uniting Mexico and the United States belied a hostile relationship between his department and working-class ethnic Mexicans in mid-twentieth-century Los Angeles.

During the early years of Biscailuz's tenure as sheriff, which coincided with some of the leanest years of the Great Depression, his department participated in the repatriation of nearly two million impoverished or politically radical Mexicans. More than half of those who were deported—1.2 million people—were U.S. citizens, many of them children returned to a country they had never known.[34] These raids and deportations extended the long history of state violence directed at working-class, migrant, and dissident Mexicans in Los Angeles. They key difference is that they were carried out by a well-connected Mexican American sheriff with ties to the region's Anglo-American elite, in ways that echoed the agency of elite Mexican hacendados during the transitional period a century before.

The relationship between Sheriff Biscailuz's department and L.A.'s working-class and poor Mexicans grew worse in the 1940s, amid heightened anxieties about cultural conformity and national security during wartime. During this period, law enforcement agencies in Los Angeles became obsessed with street violence among young people of color. Much of their anxiety centered on the figure of the zoot suit, which they thought signaled delinquency and flouted gender norms. They implemented strict statutes regarding curfews, street gangs, and clothing. Both the police and sheriff's departments regarded ethnic Mexican youth as "wolf packs" and deployed anti-gang squads to combat them. Arrests of young ethnic Mexicans, especially men, rose precipitously.[35]

Tensions came to a head during the Sleepy Lagoon murder trial of 1942–43 and the Zoot Suit Riots of 1943. The Sleepy Lagoon trial involved the prosecution of seventeen young ethnic Mexican men for the murder of José Díaz, who was found bleeding and unconscious close to a swimming hole near East Los Angeles after attending a family party. Local law enforcement agencies conducted sweeps of the city's Black and ethnic Mexican neighborhoods, detaining up to six hundred young people and ultimately settling on the 38th Street gang as the perpetrators. Throughout the trial, law enforcement presented no evidence but instead relied on crackpot theories about ethnic Mexican youths' supposed tendencies toward crime. During the grand jury investigation, Lieutenant Sheriff Edward Duran Ayres opined that ethnic Mexican youths exhibited a "total disregard for human life," similar to the Aztecs' use of human sacrifices, and argued that it was only through "swift and sure punishment" that they could be made to respect authority.[36] Police Chief C. B. Horrall called Ayres's testimony an "intelligent statement of the psychology of the Mexican people," and Biscailuz affirmed that Ayres's report "fully covered the situation."[37] Ultimately, nine of the defendants were convicted of second-degree murder and sentenced to San Quentin Prison. The rest were charged with lesser offenses and served shorter terms in the Los Angeles County Jail under the jurisdiction of the Los Angeles Sheriff's Department.

When a multiracial coalition of lawyers and community activists formed the Sleepy Lagoon Defense Committee to coordinate the appeals process, law enforcement agencies moved to discredit them. Captain George Contreras of the LASD—one of a handful of Mexican American officers on the beat at the time—testified to the California Senate Factfinding Subcommittee on Un-American Activities, led by state senator Jack Tenney, that the defense committee was a Communist organization. Actor Leo Carrillo—a friend of Biscailuz who also descended from a Californio family—denounced the defense committee as a group of "Communist rattlesnakes." Sheriff Biscailuz himself referred to the defense committee as anti-American rabble-rousers and provided records about the organization to Tenney's committee. Ultimately, the charges of Communism proved unsuccessful; the appellate court recognized the legal abuses that had occurred, and the San Quentin prisoners were acquitted and eventually released.[38] Nonetheless, the Sleepy Lagoon trials stirred strong anti-Mexican sentiment among much of the city's population, especially young white military men stationed in Los Angeles, which again resulted in anti-Mexican violence.

These dynamics erupted in the Zoot Suit Riots, a series of scuffles in June 1943 that traversed the city's central and eastside neighborhoods. Thousands of white servicemen descended upon ethnic Mexican neighborhoods and attacked young men, singling out those who were dressed in zoot suits. In one instance, sailors dragged two zoot suiters on-stage as a film was being screened, stripped them nearly naked in front of the audience, and then urinated on their suits.[39] As with the vigilante mobs a century before, local law enforcement and corporate media supported the attacks, describing them as having a cleansing effect. And, even though white men perpetrated the overwhelming majority of the violence, ethnic Mexicans were blamed for provoking the attacks. By the end of the melee, more than 150 people had been injured and more than 500 Latinos, mostly ethnic Mexicans, had been arrested on charges of vagrancy and disturbing the peace.[40]

Ethnic Mexicans in Los Angeles responded to the violence in a number of ways. Some protested individual cases of police brutality and pursued legal avenues for redress. Others, like the Community Service Organization, lobbied for greater Mexican American political representation within the department and the creation of citizen oversight boards to ensure police accountability. Biscailuz himself pushed for greater crime control and repression; for example, in 1947, he opened a new juvenile facility and training academy in East Los Angeles.[41] But Biscailuz also diversified his agency's officers to include more women, African Americans, and Mexican Americans.[42] And, recognizing the need for unifying symbols and a shared sense of history, he created new civic institutions that celebrated the city's layered Spanish, Mexican, and Anglo periods. Within this broad push, he turned often to the charro, which offered a moderate and revered symbol of the Spanish-Mexican past through which to unify the city's diverse constituencies around a supposedly shared rural, premodern heritage.

In 1946, Biscailuz launched the Sheriff's Rodeo. Held annually at the Los Angeles Coliseum, the Sheriff's Rodeo became extremely popular among city residents and tourists, drawing up to one hundred thousand spectators each year. The Sheriff's Rodeo was not a competitive rodeo so much as an exhibit—much like Buffalo Bill Cody's nineteenth-century Wild West Show adapted to mid-twentieth-century Los Angeles. It featured stars from the city's influential Western film and television industry as well as performances by local equestrian groups, musicians, and dancers. Crucially, Biscailuz ensured that the Sheriff's Rodeo included Mexican charros from the beginning. For the very first event, he invited charros from Guadalajara to perform and personally greeted them at Lockheed Air Terminal, alongside the Long Beach chief of police and the local Mexican consul. A reporter from the *Los Angeles Times* described the charros disembarking from the plane as a "baker's dozen Mexican horsemen and horsewomen . . . wearing their gay-colored Latin caballero costumes."[43] At Biscailuz's invitation, Mexican charros continued to participate in the Sheriff's Rodeo every year thereafter.[44] During other civic events, too, Biscailuz and other civic leaders embraced the charro as a symbol of civic and transnational unity. During the 1957 parade for Mexican Independence Day, a panel of judges from both the U.S. and Mexico awarded first prize to a float that depicted Uncle Sam clasping the hand of a Mexican charro.[45]

Thus, by the mid-1940s, in the aftermath of some of Los Angeles's most iconic and violent events—Sleepy Lagoon, the Zoot Suit Riots, World War II, and the Red Scare—civic leaders had begun to position the charro as a figure with the potential to bridge tensions and cultivate unity among city residents, in part through invocation of a ranching past associated with the Mexican elite. Biscailuz was a leader in this regard: the charro allowed him to claim legitimacy and belonging among Los Angeles's elite and to craft a unifying symbol for the city, while pursuing forms of state violence that were remarkably similar to those long used against working-class and immigrant Mexicans in the city. But elites like Biscailuz did not have a monopoly on the meaning or strategic use of the charro, especially in relation to the state. In East Los Angeles, a group of working-class but upwardly mobile ethnic Mexicans capitalized on Biscailuz's fascination with charro culture and his use of the charro as a unifying symbol to broker a more genial relationship with the Los Angeles County Sheriff's Department. In doing so, they created space for a wider cross-section of ethnic Mexican men, not just the wealthy Spanish-Mexican elite who claimed ancestry in "Old California," to demonstrate their respectability and their capacity for citizenship in mid-twentieth-century Los Angeles.

THE EAST L.A. SHERIFF'S CHARRO POSSE
AND THE CHARROS DE LOS ANGELES

Around 1947, Biscailuz expanded the mounted posse program to create district posses linked to each of the fourteen sheriff substations throughout Los Angeles County. The original main posse was retained to serve ceremonial functions representing the metropolitan region as a whole. The district posses would appear in local parades and pageants, and participate in search-and-rescue work. By 1950, nearly 560 men had joined these fifteen posses as deputized civilian volunteers.[46]

Because the sheriff's substations were located in suburbs of Los Angeles County that were overwhelmingly white throughout the 1950s and '60s, most of the people who joined the posses in this period were white, landowning suburban men. In addition, because district posse members were expected to own their own horses and trailers and to furnish their own equipment and clothing—an outlay estimated close to $5,500—posse members came almost exclusively from Los Angeles's postwar middle class.[47] For them, joining the posses was simultaneously a civic duty, a social outlet, and a way to play "cowboys and Indians" in modernizing Los Angeles. Indeed, as in earlier years, the expanded posse's activities were described as "much the same as in the days of the Old West." In addition to holding monthly meetings, each district posse participated in weekend rides through the county's mountains in which they "camp[ed] overnight with sleeping bags and a chuck wagon," fancying themselves lawmen on the old frontier.[48]

In East Los Angeles, however, the district posse took a decidedly different form: one that centered on the figure of the charro. There, in the historic barrios produced through urban renewal and Mexican displacement from the central city, a group of working-class but upwardly mobile ethnic Mexican men joined the East L.A. Sheriff's Posse. Though these men had different citizenship statuses—some were U.S. citizens, some were citizens of Mexico—all traced their presence in the United States to the mass Mexican migration of the early twentieth century. Accordingly, they drew upon both their personal histories of migration and their knowledge of Mexican ranchero-themed popular culture, as well as their experiences living and working in the United States, to negotiate a position within the city's law enforcement agencies.

The first of these men, Marcelino Rodríguez, was born in Los Angeles in 1913. He was the son of Mexican migrants: his father was from Aguascalientes, his mother from San Luis Potosí. Rodríguez's wife, Teresita, was an Apache woman from Taos, New Mexico. In the 1940 census, Rodríguez was living on Breed Street in East Los Angeles, working as a laborer in parks maintenance and making $660 per month.[49] He and Teresita also owned a small ranch, Rancho de Sany, along the San Gabriel River, where Rodríguez owned and rode horses. He frequently participated in festivals and parades associated with Mexican patriotic days while wearing a traje de charro. At that time Rodríguez was intrigued by charrería but did not know much about it, so he blended charro and cowboy styles in a way that echoed the cultural hybridity of the nineteenth-century U.S. Southwest. According to Miguel Flores, "When he mounted his horse, he dressed in the suit of the charro in his own way, without knowing which were the correct garments that he should use, so his costumes always mixed that of the charro and the cowboy."[50] Many parades awarded prizes to whoever wore the most authentic charro costume, and Rodríguez, despite his enthusiasm, was regularly disqualified. Nonetheless, Rodríguez was a skilled rider and possessed the requisite horse and equipment to join the East L.A. Sheriff's Posse, which he did in the late 1940s. By the early 1950s, he had been named captain.[51]

During a Cinco de Mayo parade in Los Angeles, Rodríguez met Carlos Valencia. Valencia was a migrant to Los Angeles who had been born in the small town of Coeneo de la Libertad, Michoacán, in 1906. Growing up in the Mexican countryside, he learned roping and riding skills from his father, who instilled in him a deep appreciation for charrería. Valencia migrated to the U.S. in 1920 and bought his first horse and traje de charro in 1938. The 1940 census records him living in Pasadena with his wife and children; he worked as a general laborer.[52] Subsequently he and his wife, María, a Puerto Rican woman, took leadership roles in cultivating knowledge of charrería among L.A.'s ethnic Mexicans. They also coordinated numerous fund-raisers, hoping to either expand the lienzo at Rodríguez's ranch or purchase a larger facility. Valencia appears to have joined the posse in the late 1940s.[53]

A third ethnic Mexican man who joined the East L.A. Sheriff's Posse in this period was John Gándara, who was born in Texas and moved to Los Angeles in 1916. In 1940, Gándara was living in East Los Angeles and working as a truck driver. He joined the Sheriff's Posse in 1947 and remained a civilian volunteer until 1975, when he retired.[54]

Upon joining the East L.A. Sheriff's Posse, these men (and possibly others who have been lost to the historical record) used the figure of the charro to nurture relationships with Sheriff Biscailuz. Gándara recalled that during one of the group's practice rides in South San Gabriel in 1949, "we invited Sheriff Biscailuz to be our guest of honor there, and he come [sic] in there and he enjoyed it very much, so much so that the following year, 1950, he designated the Sheriff's Mounted Posse of [East] Los Angeles to wear the charro outfit in all our activities ... I believe he attended two or three [charreadas] after that."[55] Thereafter, while the other district posses wore "maroon shirts, Army dress pinks, boots, 10-gallon hat, and shining badge," the East L.A. Sheriff's Posse wore their trajes de charro.[56] Staked out in opposition to the zoot suit, their trajes de charro represented a decidedly different sensibility—one that emphasized respectability, social conservatism, and moderate institutional reform, as well as their embrace of Mexican cultural nationalism.

The East L.A. Sheriff's Posse appeared at many public events, linking the image of the charro—a revered symbol of Mexican nationalism—with the power of the American state. Most of these activities were celebrations of Mexican patriotic holidays that were sponsored by ethnic Mexican civic groups and took place in East Los Angeles. In 1947, for example, the charros participated in a Cinco de Mayo parade through the community of Belvedere that ended at First and Indiana, where a new recreation center funded by the Beneficencia Mexicano de Los Angeles, a mutual aid society, was to be dedicated. Tony Sein, manager of the Hispano Broadcasting Company and parade chairman, led forty-five charros in the parade.[57] Later that year, the East L.A. charros participated in Mexican Independence Day celebrations, which consisted of laying flowers on the statue of Miguel Hidalgo de Castillo in Lincoln Park, followed by a parade through Belvedere. The local Mexican

Representatives of the Los Angeles mayor's office wait for a parade in East Los Angeles to begin. Charros on horseback, almost certainly members of the East L.A. Sheriff's Posse, can be seen in the background. The star-shaped logo on the horse trailer is that of the Los Angeles County Sheriff's Department. Don Stouffer, "East Los Angeles Parade," 1951, Security Pacific National Bank Collection, Los Angeles Public Library.

consul, as well as representatives of the Civic Patriotic Committee and Mexico's tourism department, were on hand, as was Sheriff Biscailuz.[58]

Despite their prominence in the East L.A. barrio, the members of the East L.A. Sheriff's Posse were largely excluded from the posse program writ large, whose institutional culture welcomed descendants of California's historic Spanish-Mexican elite, like Biscailuz, but not working- or middle-class Mexicans. Attendance records for the Christmas party held for members of the Sheriff's Posse each year demonstrate the class-based limits of ethnic Mexican inclusion in the police state, even for those who mobilized around the dignified and elite image of the charro. For the 1955 event, a small group consisting of Biscailuz and his close friends convened first at the Beverly Hills home of Eldred and Mary Meyer, who were described as the leading personal collectors of Californiana (the material culture of the Spanish and Mexican periods in California). The Meyers also boasted a collection of rare western-themed dime novels from the 1860s—a testament to the frequent coupling of the Spanish fantasy heritage and western frontier mythology in the city's elite social life. Afterward, the Los Angeles County Sheriff's Department held a dinner dance for all posse members at the Beverly Hills Hotel's Rodeo Room, where posse members performed their own "western"-themed entertainment. Only about 125 of the roughly 560-odd members attended this event, and all were Anglo-American men.[59] It is possible that the East L.A. posse members were not present because both events were held in the elite, racially exclusive area of Beverly Hills; nor did they participate in other posse events in similar geographies.

Partly for this reason, and partly because interest in charrería was rapidly growing in the Eastside barrios, Rodríguez, Valencia, Gándara, and others continued to ride together outside of the East L.A.'s Sheriff's Posse as part of an informal group they called the Charros de Los Angeles. Though not yet accredited by the Federación Mexicana de Charrería, this group's formation in or about 1957 signaled the members' growing autonomy from, and perhaps dissatisfaction with, the LASD posse. It also allowed a larger group of ethnic Mexicans to participate in charrería outside the institutional binds of the state.

Throughout the late 1950s and early 1960s, the Charros de Los Angeles expanded significantly. Like their counterparts who joined the East L.A. Sheriff's Posse, the men who joined the Charros de Los Angeles in this period were blue-collar workers, though many were upwardly mobile. They typically lived in the modest ethnic Mexican communities that spread across the Eastside. Most were homeowners, and some owned small ranchitos where they kept chickens, goats, and horses. Unlike the posse members, a good number of whom had been born in the U.S. and were American citizens, the members of the Charros de Los Angeles were overwhelmingly migrants with roots in the Bajío region of Mexico. Of the twenty original members of the organization, most were from the states of Jalisco, Michoacán, and Zacatecas. Only two had been born in the United States.[60]

Some of the men who joined the Charros de Los Angeles in the late 1950s and early '60s knew the arts of roping and riding through everyday ranch life in their sending communities. Others, however, had little firsthand experience and had to learn from their more experienced paisanos (countrymen). Just like their predecessors in Mexican California during the 1820s and '30s, they were limited in their access to "authentic" Mexican material goods, such as trajes and hand-tooled Mexican saddles. As a result, the burgeoning Charros de Los Angeles at first mixed cowboy and charro styles together indiscriminately, depending on what they had at hand. Mario Arteaga, a skilled charro who would later become the group's instructor, recalled, "They were all confused, so their outfits . . . were mixed, just like their regalia, some wore their sombreros backwards, others used the charro suit with a Texas saddle, others wore charro pants and cowboy boots, etc."[61]

Over time, the Charros de Los Angeles developed a more robust knowledge of charrería. They shared information, clothing, and equipment with each other and, later, they hired instructors from Mexico like Arteaga. They also obtained and studied the formal guidelines of charrería developed by the Federación Mexicana de Charrería in Mexico City. Soon, they developed a more "authentic" presentation that was sustained by transnational connections with influential Mexican citizens and Mexican organizations like the FMCH. It was this authenticity, as well as their connections with Biscailuz via the Sheriff's Posse, that earned the East L.A. charros the attention of film director Ted Tetzlaff and producer Patrick Ford (son of film director John Ford) as they prepared to film a Western titled *The Young Land* in Los Angeles during the late 1950s.

THE YOUNG LAND

Released in 1959 by Columbia Pictures, *The Young Land* examines racialized violence and the administration of legal justice in California in 1848, just after the end of the Mexican-American War.[62] Set in the fictional town of San Bartolo, which is depicted as the commercial and social gathering place for surrounding rancho society, the film engages intimately with histories of state and vigilante violence in Alta California. For its viewing public a century later, in the aftermath of Sleepy Lagoon and the Zoot Suit Riots, and during the city's anti-Communist Red Scare, the film must have raised vexing questions about the possibilities of American institutions to adjudicate racial justice in Los Angeles. In this context, the film offered the city's charros, who were cast as extras in several roles, the opportunity to depict a more inclusive history of the transitional period in California while enabling them to continue forging transnational linkages with Mexican charros and politicians.

The film's opening scene depicts a shoot-out between white American outlaw Hatfield Carnes (played by Dennis Hopper) and Mexican resident Francisco Quiroga (played by Carlos Romero) after a tussle in San Bartolo's saloon. Sheriff's Deputy Jim Ellison (played by Patrick Wayne, son of John

Wayne) arrives after hearing shots fired and demands that Carnes relinquish his gun. Carnes retorts, "Why? Because I killed a Mexican?" Ellison responds gravely, "Because you killed a *man*." Thus begins the film's effort to recuperate the humanity and citizenship of the Mexican inhabitants of historic California—an effort that was fully aligned with the inclusive project of post–World War II U.S. liberal democracy, and with the charros' own agenda.

The following scenes depict preparations for Carnes's trial. Since California is a newly acquired territory, American legal institutions do not yet exist in any meaningful way. Thus, a federal judge from New England, Millard Isham (played by Dan O'Herlihy), arrives with Deputy U.S. Marshal Ben Stroud (played by Cliff Ketchum) to administer the trial. At their first encounter, just moments into the film, Sheriff Ellison greets Isham warmly. He then reminds Isham of the region's residual Mexicanness. Speaking in both Spanish and English to those around him, Ellison tells Isham that he has not been officially deputized. Rather, he explains, he was appointed by a local ranch owner, Don Roberto de la Madrid, who "runs just about everything around here" but installed Ellison because he "couldn't handle the upscuffles anymore." In this way, the film recognizes the degree to which Californio ranchers exercised significant cultural and political influence during the transitional period. However, it also treats wealthy Mexican landowners such as de la Madrid as ultimately incompetent, and instead vests the power of the American state in the young and inexperienced Ellison.

Shortly after his arrival, the visiting judge, Isham, asks Ellison if twelve neutral men can be found to serve on the jury; Ellison replies that they can. He promises to recruit them that very night, during a birthday party for Elena de la Madrid, Don Roberto's daughter (played by Dallas-born actress Yvonne Craig), which will be attended by both Anglo-Americans and Mexican Californians. Ellison's description of the upcoming party is a clear reference to the intercultural nature of elite society that marked the transitional period, as well as an appeal to post–World War II racial liberalism. As a point of clarification, Ellison asks whether Mexicans can serve on the trial, to which Isham replies, "As long as they can understand English." During the film's trial scene, several ethnic Mexican men do in fact appear on the jury—all of them dressed in trajes de charro. Though not named individually in the credits, these actors appear to have been members of the East L.A. Sheriff's Posse and the Charros de Los Angeles, which are credited collectively in the film.

In another move to dignify and defend Mexicans in historical California, the film lays the blame for racialized violence in the conquered territories squarely on white settlers. In his testimony before the court, Ellison states that even before Quiroga's murder, Carnes had "pushed Mexicans around a lot," even though Mexicans had never shown him any hostility. A local shopkeeper who witnessed the murder testifies that Carnes had provoked Quiroga by saying, "You talk big, Mex. Let's see if you got guts enough to draw [a gun] on a white man." It is also revealed that Carnes had previously killed four other Mexicans elsewhere in the U.S. West. When Carnes himself testifies and uses the word "Mex," the judge reprimands him, saying that the Mexicans present, who make up approximately half the audience in the courtroom, would object to the word. The cumulative effect of these scenes is to depict American institutions in the transitional period as fair and just, regardless of race or nationality.

The most extraordinary (re)incorporation of ethnic Mexicans into American democratic institutions concerns the character of Don Roberto de la Madrid (played by Tijuana businessman and politician Roberto de la Madrid). De la Madrid arrives in town from his ranch just as the jury goes into deliberations. De la Madrid is accompanied by a group of his vaquero employees—played, in all likelihood, by local Mexican Americans, possibly members of the Charros de Los Angeles, though again none are individually credited. During the trial, the vaqueros cluster under a group of trees outside the courtroom. Ellison greets de la Madrid warmly in Spanish and takes him to meet Judge Isham. De la Madrid has brought an elegant lunch, which is served by a silent and noticeably dark-skinned male servant. The two elite men—one Mexican, one American—eat together while waiting for the jury to reach a decision. Their lunchtime conversation analyzes the legal rights of Mexicans in the U.S. Southwest after conquest. De la Madrid tells Isham that this case will be "the most important trial in [his] career" because it tests the veracity and strength of the Treaty of Guadalupe Hidalgo. He wonders aloud whether the jury will be as stern with Carnes as it would be with a Mexican citizen who killed an American. Judge Isham replies that he doesn't know, but hopes the jury will be fair. As a gesture of goodwill, Isham asks de la Madrid to sit next to him on the judge's bench during the reading of the verdict, so that Mexicans will know they have been fairly represented.

The jury reads its unanimous verdict that Carnes is guilty, and Judge Isham sentences Carnes to twenty-five years in federal prison. Through its depiction of this decision, the film suggests, falsely, that U.S. juridical institutions consistently held white citizens accountable for their violence toward ethnic Mexicans during this period. However, since California is in the process of transitioning to a constitutional government and doesn't possess adequate state capacity to properly imprison him, Carnes's sentence is suspended. Carnes's light sentence includes only one condition: that he not wear a firearm at any time. Carnes refuses to accept this condition. After a brief scuffle in the courtroom, he challenges Sheriff Ellison to a gun duel outside. After a classic chase scene, followed by a shoot-out on a dusty western street, Ellison shoots and kills Carnes. Afterward he proclaims, "American justice has been upheld"—presumably on behalf of Mexicans in Los Angeles and across California.

The film delivers a complex message about the legal and juridical relationships between Mexicans and Anglo-Americans in California after U.S. conquest. Parts of the narrative are indisputably progressive. The historic influence of elite Mexicans is recognized and honored throughout the film. Mexicans of middling classes are likewise depicted in humane, dignified, positive ways. The net effect is to recuperate the capacity of ethnic Mexicans for citizenship, both in the past and in the present. Other parts of the film, however, reinforce common postwar ideas about liberal progress that, in turn, echoed ideologies of U.S. manifest destiny. De la Madrid and the other ethnic Mexican characters play no meaningful role in the final conflict, and the administration of justice ultimately lies in the hands of an inexperienced white male American sheriff and an Anglo-American judge from New England. The film thus naturalizes white settlement of California and the U.S. Southwest and implies that ethnic Mexicans have peacefully relinquished political power to Anglo-American men. It also erases the agency of those elite Mexicans who actively shaped the exercise of state power in Los Angeles well into the 1870s, including through the use of violence against indigenous people, Chinese immigrants, and working-class and poor Mexicans. In these ways, the film aligned more with midcentury liberal desires to recuperate American legal and juridical institutions as fair and racially neutral than with concerns to accurately represent Los Angeles's history.

For the East L.A. charros, however, the film was far more important as a site of industrial production than historical representation. As noted, members of the East L.A. Sheriff's Posse and the Charros de Los Angeles served as extras for several key roles. They played the jurors who appear in the jury box wearing their trajes de charro, as well as the vaqueros from de la Madrid's ranch who gather outside the courtroom. Through these roles, they shaped representations of the state in Los Angeles during the transition to U.S. rule, albeit in minor ways. More importantly, the film's production gave the East L.A. charros the opportunity to connect with two Mexican nationals from

Baja California, Roberto de la Madrid and Mario Arteaga, who were not only wealthy and influential businessmen, but also skilled charros.

Roberto de la Madrid (who plays the soft-spoken hacendado of the same name in the film) held dual U.S. and Mexican citizenships, was bilingual and bicultural, and maintained a prosperous binational business career in banking and oil. Later, he would hold numerous political appointments in Baja California. An accomplished horseman, de la Madrid rode with the charro association in Tijuana, through which he cultivated relationships with Mexico's elite, including future Mexican president José López Portillo. As one of the leaders of Tijuana's charro association, de la Madrid invited Mario Arteaga, a skilled young horseman from Michoacán, to work for the Tijuana association as its instructor. Shortly thereafter, when Ford recruited de la Madrid to work on *The Young Land* as the film's technical director, de la Madrid brought Arteaga with him to Los Angeles to help prepare and train the horses. Though initially contracted to work behind the scenes, both men were soon persuaded to appear on camera. De la Madrid played the role bearing his own name, and Arteaga had a bit part as Elena's chaperone and caretaker of her horse.[63]

One can only imagine what it was like for the Los Angeles charros to work on-set with de la Madrid and Arteaga every day. We can picture de la Madrid and Arteaga telling their Los Angeles counterparts about the history and politics of charrería in Mexico, and we can speculate that the charros from Los Angeles enthusiastically told the Baja California charros about charrería's growing popularity in the United States. We can envision them practicing their roping skills during downtime between shots, making plans to ride together off-set, and hanging out socially in the evenings and on weekends. No historical records capture these activities. Still, it is clear that the practice of charrería in Los Angeles was transformed by their work together on the film. The charros from Tijuana and the charros from Los Angeles knit together a translocal relationship that was rooted in their shared appreciation for the charro and commitments to Mexican cultural nationalism.

That relationship would endure for many years after the film wrapped. Though de la Madrid returned to his business and political activities in Baja California, Arteaga remained in Los Angeles, where he continued to work as Ford's personal horse trainer. To do so, Arteaga moved to the exclusive neighborhood of Northridge, in the suburban San Fernando Valley, where many Western film and television actors, producers, and directors lived.[64] Once there, Arteaga was looped into a circle of middle-class, upwardly mobile, and politically active ethnic Mexican men, some of whom had recently moved to other neighborhoods in the San Fernando Valley. These men included brothers Henry Nava and Julian Nava, both of whom had grown up in East Los Angeles and helped found the Community Service Organization, one of Los Angeles's leading civil rights organizations for Mexican Americans. By the mid-1950s, Julian Nava had received his doctorate in history from Harvard University and moved to Northridge to join the faculty of Valley State University (now California State University, Northridge), where he became the college's first Mexican American history professor. Miguel Flores, cousin to the Navas and chronicler of charrería in Los Angeles, was also part of this group of friends. So too were the men involved in the East L.A. Sheriff's Posse and the Charros de Los Angeles.[65]

After their work together on *The Young Land* concluded, Rodríguez and Valencia invited Arteaga to serve as instructor for the East L.A. Sheriff's Posse, and he readily agreed. For the next several years, though he traveled frequently between Mexico and the United States, Arteaga guided the East L.A. charros in meeting the requirements of the Federación Mexicana de Charrería so that they could eventually become accredited. Under Arteaga's instruction, the East L.A. charros grew more knowledgeable about the performance of charrería. They also built connections with charros in Tijuana and other Mexican cities and acquired more professional equipment and clothing. These shifts all contributed to the East L.A. charros' increasing autonomy from the sheriff's department. The timing was right, too, for the fate of the East L.A. Sheriff's Posse was about to change dramatically.

MODERNIZING THE "RUSTIC COWBOY AGENCY"

In 1958, Sheriff Biscailuz retired from the position he had held for more than twenty years. Lauded as the "first caballero of Los Angeles," Biscailuz had, by the time of his retirement, made the charro a central part of his public image. For example, in 1953 he attended "A Night in Old Mexico," a fund-raiser honoring L.A.'s Mexican Chamber of Commerce, at the swanky Jonathan Club in downtown L.A., where he wore an elaborately embroidered charro hat gifted him by former Mexican president Lázaro Cárdenas.[66] In 1954, Biscailuz was honored for his forty-seven years of service to the Los Angeles Sheriff's Department in a celebration held at the Hotel Statler. Actors Leo Carrillo and Duncan Renaldo, both friends of Biscailuz, dashed through a

Sheriff Eugene Biscailuz standing with his palomino horse in the late 1950s. Photograph by Ed Clark, LIFE Picture Collection/Getty Images.

crowd of one thousand, wearing trajes de charro and firing blanks from their pistols.[67] In 1957, Captain M.J. Benjamin of the Hollywood Sheriff's Posse presented Biscailuz with a birthday cake that depicted the sheriff dressed as a charro while riding a palomino horse.[68] Then, in 1958, on the eve of his retirement, Biscailuz posed in full charro regalia with his glossy palomino for a photograph that was to be published in *Western Lithograph,* a regional magazine distributed to thirteen western states.[69]

The charro, and the moderately more inclusive vision of state power he enabled, would have little place in the regime of Biscailuz's successor. Peter J. Pitchess led the Los Angeles County Sheriff's Department nearly as long as Biscailuz, from 1958 to 1981, but with a radically different tone and agenda. For the first few years of his tenure, Pitchess reluctantly maintained some of the cowboy civic institutions that Biscailuz had established. For example, Pitchess continued to host the popular Sheriff's Rodeo at the Los Angeles Coliseum for a few years; he even invited charros from Guadalajara and other Mexican cities. But Pitchess soon disposed of these practices, which fit neither his personal identity nor the vision he wanted to implement for the department.

Instead, and like many law enforcement agencies across the country in the mid-twentieth century, Pitchess embraced the "professionalism" model of law enforcement. The professionalism model alleged that policing demanded as much expertise and deserved as much respect as professions such as medicine and law. It called for the expanded use of quantitative data, technology, and self-defined measures of "efficiency" to reduce crime.[70] Toward that end, Pitchess introduced more aggressive patrol tactics, such as the use of infiltrators and field interrogations, and equipped all deputies with billy clubs, saying they were necessary for combating juvenile delinquency. He set up the department's Special Enforcement Detail, one of the country's first SWAT teams, and he dramatically expanded the county's jails and punitive facilities. Pitchess also professionalized the figure of the deputy. He passed new policies that required deputies to have significantly more education and, once hired, they received substantially more training, as well as higher salaries and better benefits. He also changed the sheriff department's citizenship policy: all deputies, including civilian volunteers, were now required to be U.S. citizens or in the process of becoming U.S. citizens. Finally, he stripped authority from the myriad celebrities, members of the media, and civic leaders to whom Biscailuz had issued honorary sheriff's deputy badges. As part of this process, Pitchess restructured the posse program. He argued:

> Historically, reputable people from all walks of life have been called up to assist a handful of regular officers when occasion demanded it under the rule of posse comitatus. But the complexities of our modern day society require persons enforcing the law to possess knowledge, training and skills far beyond the requirements of the past.[71]

Though civilians could continue volunteering with the posse, only trained full-time deputies could wear badges and carry out law enforcement functions.

Because of these changes, Pitchess was later described as "the Los Angeles County sheriff who transformed the nation's largest Sheriff's Department from a rustic cowboy agency into a modern professional law enforcement organization."[72] Yet modernization also meant a recommitment by the city's largest law enforcement agency to the norms and practices of whiteness, and the corresponding rejection of Mexican people and cultural practices, even those widely regarded as respectable and law-abiding. This shift in the LASD's policies and practices under Pitchess's leadership echoed the historic expulsion of elite Mexicans from the centers of state power in the 1870s, and the more distinctly racialized use of state violence to discipline and harass ethnic Mexicans of all class backgrounds that followed.

Most immediately, Pitchess's changes resulted in the dismissal of many members of the East L.A. Sheriff's Posse, whose inclusion of some Mexican citizens and orientation toward Mexican cultural nationalism made them suspect under the Pitchess regime. In the early 1960s, they appeared at a Cinco de Mayo festival in the plaza, organized by the Mexican Civic and Patriotic Committee, where they were scheduled to appear in a color guard ceremony with the Mexican flag, just as they had done many times before. According to Miguel Flores, an unnamed representative of the sheriff's department coldly ordered them to roll up their flag and vacate the premises. Seeing no other choice, they complied.[73] Shortly thereafter, John Gándara, who had become captain of the East L.A. posse, called the rest of the members to a meeting. He relayed the message that any posse member who chose to associate with the Charros de Los Angeles—always the more working class and culturally nationalist of the city's two charro groups—would be expelled from the posse. He also notified them of the new citizenship policy. Several of the charros immediately resigned from the posse upon learning of these changes. One was Mario Arteaga, who, as a Mexican citizen and transnational actor, renounced his position as honorary instructor of the East L.A. posse, even though he continued to live in Los Angeles, where he worked on many renowned English-language Westerns and remained involved with the Charros de Los Angeles.[74]

It appears that at least a handful of the charros—namely those who were U.S. citizens, like Gándara—remained members of the East L.A. Sheriff's Posse, for they are reported as participants in several events during the mid-1960s. These events included the 1964 celebrations of Cinco de Mayo at the plaza, a 1965 Lion's Club parade, and a 1966 Blessing of the Animals at Olvera Street.[75] Biscailuz also participated in some of these events as sheriff emeritus; however, he did so from a position that represented the city's past, not its present or future.

Meanwhile, the Charros de Los Angeles continued to pursue greater expertise, authenticity, and transnational connectivity in their practice of charrería. In 1962, Arteaga and Rodríguez applied for and received their official federated status from the Federación Mexicana de Charrería. With accreditation in hand, the Charros de Los Angeles became the very first charro association in the United States to be formally recognized by the FMCH. Shortly thereafter, the Mexican consul of Los Angeles authorized the Charros de Los Angeles to be the official representatives of Mexico at all Mexican civic festivals in L.A.[76] The group continued riding at Marcelino Rodríguez's ranch in South San Gabriel and occasionally at another ranch in the Eastside called El Número Tres, while they pursued funding to build their own dedicated lienzo.[77]

At the same time, the city's burgeoning "Latin" entertainment industry provided fertile new ground for the city's charros—both those who called Los Angeles home and those who traveled to the city from Mexico as tourists and performers. For example, in 1967, Mexican actor Antonio Águilar staged a charreada at the Los Angeles Sports Arena with his wife, Flor Silvestre, as well as his son and approximately forty other riders—some of whom were likely members of the Charros de Los Angeles.[78] Águilar had just completed a similar run at San Francisco's Cow Palace, where the event drew more than thirty-five thousand spectators, causing Águilar to gush, "Imagine me out-drawing the great master Roy Rogers! I just can't believe it!"[79] Other Mexican legends also visited Los Angeles in the 1960s, where they performed as charros and drew large numbers of tourists. Tito Guízar—beloved Mexican singer, actor, and star of the classic ranch comedy film *Allá en el Rancho Grande* (1936)—headlined a "Viva Mexico!" celebration at Disneyland in 1969 that included a group of unnamed charros (perhaps members of the Charros de Los Angeles), five mariachi bands, and Mexican dancers parading down Main Street USA alongside Disney characters.[80] And later that year, charros performed roping tricks at Universal Studios' Fiesta Mexicana, an entertainment festival held at the studio's new "zócalo" stage.[81] All of these public events, with their corporate sponsorship and increasingly transnational orientation, certainly put charros on stage in shaping the city's "Latin" culture. However, they gave working-class and middle-class ethnic Mexicans little purchase on the reins of state power in Los Angeles, which continued to be experienced as a hostile and occupying force.

Indeed, under the renewed "modern" state led by Pitchess and his counterparts in the LAPD, ethnic Mexicans were targeted, once again, for racial violence intended to discipline their political activism and resistance to subjugation. Most famously, under Sheriff Pitchess, deputies used tear gas and deadly force to suppress the 1970 Chicano Moratorium against the Vietnam War in East Los Angeles—the largest ethnically identified antiwar protest in American history to date. Dozens were injured and three were killed, including esteemed Mexican journalist Rubén Salazar, who was mortally wounded when a tear gas canister fired by a sheriff's deputy hit him in the head. Although Pitchess maintained that "there was absolutely no misconduct on the part of the deputies involved [in the incident] or the procedures they followed," the county agreed to pay the Salazar family hundreds of thousands of dollars in compensation. The incident led to the California Supreme Court decision in *Pitchess v. Superior Court* (1974) that a defendant is entitled to obtain records of public complaints about the use of excessive force by police officers (now known as a Pitchess motion).[82] Since then, state violence against ethnic Mexicans and other people of color in Los Angeles has continued, and resistance to police brutality remains an enduring preoccupation.

Thus, at a crucial moment in mid-twentieth-century Los Angeles, marked by racial violence and the policing of dissent, diverse ethnic Mexican men tested the degree to which the charro could be brought to bear on the state and its capacity for both violence and citizenship. These contests played out unequally depending on the social class, citizenship status, and orientations toward Mexican nationalism of the people involved. For Biscailuz, who could claim a direct ancestral connection to the landed elite of Old California, the figure of the charro allowed him to claim legitimacy at the helm of the nation's largest sheriff's department, easing his path to substantial personal power, while also cohering Anglo-Americans and many ethnic Mexicans around a dignified, respectable symbol of Spanish-Mexican history. Reflecting popular perceptions of his status as "native son," Biscailuz's legacy is widely commemorated in Los Angeles's civic landscape to this day.[83]

For the working-class and middle-class men who joined the East L.A. Sheriff's Posse and transnational actors like Arteaga, the outcomes were decidedly more mixed. For a time, they succeeded in wearing their trajes de charro in public office and performing at public events dedicated to Mexican cultural nationalism. They even managed to produce representations of Mexican male power, limited though these were, through their participation in *The Young Land* and public festivals celebrating regional history. Through these activities, they performed their respectability, law-abidingness, and capacity for citizenship. However, these performances were largely confined to the East L.A. barrio; there is little evidence that they gained significant access to segregated spaces, institutions, and clubs across the full span of the city's geography in the way that Biscailuz did. Moreover, many were expelled from the posse within a decade because of their status as non-U.S. citizens, their Mexican cultural nationalism, and the perception that they were simply not professional or modern. Though their transnational networks subsequently expanded in ways that created greater opportunities for the practice of charrería, their claims to state power through the charro were sharply delimited.

TWO

Building San Antonio's Postwar Tourist Economy

IN 1946, THE PLANNING COMMITTEE FOR FIESTA, San Antonio's biggest annual party, placed an advertisement in the *San Antonio Light* inviting attendees to wear "frontier, colonial, and charro or charra costumes."[1] The message itself was not wholly unusual; dressing up as figures associated with the western frontier and Spanish colonialism had been a regular feature of Anglo-American social life in San Antonio for decades. This was especially true at Fiesta, which celebrated the 1836 U.S. victory at the Battle of San Jacinto through the massacre of more than six hundred Mexicans, in retaliation for the American defeat at the Alamo six weeks earlier. Dressing up as Spanish and Mexican characters for Fiesta, given this context, was a classic exercise in white imperialist nostalgia: celebration through mimicry of what had been vanquished. What was different, in this case, was that Mexican Americans were among the party- and parade-goers who dressed up in historical costumes, exercising their claims to civic and regional belonging via the image of the charro. Indeed, after the 1946 events had run their course, another story in the *Light* noted the participation of "Mexican charros [who] reminded spectators there were others than men from Tennessee and Louisiana who settled Texas."[2] These men were likely representatives of the Mexican Chamber of Commerce: middle-class Mexican American businessmen who used the charro to help grow the city's postwar tourism industry while recasting the racialized position of Mexican labor in South Texas.

Like their counterparts in Los Angeles, ethnic Mexicans in Texas experienced profound dispossession, economic subjugation, segregation, and racial violence after the Texas Revolution in 1835–36 and the conclusion of the Mexican-American War in 1848. Partly because the Treaty of Guadalupe Hidalgo did not guarantee the property rights of Tejanos as it did for

Mexicans elsewhere in the U.S. Southwest, Tejano land loss was widespread, except for a few communities in the Rio Grande Valley along the U.S.-Mexico border.[3] Mass displacement, in turn, dramatically reconfigured the Tejano class structure. Between 1850 and 1900, land and ranch owners declined from 34 to 16 percent of the Tejano population, and skilled laborers dropped from 29 to 12 percent. Meanwhile, the percentage of manual or unskilled laborers grew from 34 to 67 percent, concentrating ethnic Mexicans in the lowest tiers of the labor market.[4] As more white settlers migrated to the region and lobbied for segregation, ethnic Mexicans also faced segregated and unequal housing, schools, and public facilities. In San Antonio, these practices, upheld by racial violence, confined the majority of ethnic Mexicans to a barrio on the west side of the city. That barrio expanded substantially in the first three decades of the twentieth century, as tens of thousands of Mexican laborers from rural South Texas and revolutionary Mexico migrated to San Antonio in search of industrial work and political peace.[5] The concentration of racialized poverty in the westside barrio was endemic, and the city's neglect of basic services and infrastructure so severe, that the Works Progress Administration, in 1946, called San Antonio's westside barrio "one of the most extensive slums to be found in any American city"—worse than those in New York, London, Paris, and Naples.[6]

Though the vast majority—nearly 95 percent—of San Antonio's ethnic Mexican population was poor and racially segregated, there were, by the 1930s, two other distinct classes of ethnic Mexicans in the city. These groups had different but complementary abilities to challenge the subjugation of ethnic Mexicans in South Texas. The first were the ricos: wealthy, politically conservative Mexican exiles who had fled to San Antonio during the Mexican Revolution. By the 1930s, the ricos constituted less than 1 percent of San Antonio's ethnic Mexican population, but they controlled numerous media outlets and civic organizations. Among the most influential was the Spanish-language newspaper *La Prensa,* which promoted Mexican nationalism and elite forms of Mexican cultural heritage—including, as we shall see, charrería.[7]

San Antonio also had a tiny but growing Mexican American middle class composed of business owners and professionals, and it was from this class that the city's charros were drawn. In the 1930s, this group made up less than 5 percent of the city's ethnic Mexican population, but it expanded dramatically after World War II, as Mexican Americans accessed upward mobility through unionized manufacturing labor, military service, and the GI Bill.

The city's Mexican American middle class was part of what historians have called the "Mexican American Generation"—people who valued and embraced their Mexican cultural heritage but who saw their future in the United States and believed in working within the American political system in order to change it.[8]

In the postwar period, members of the Mexican American Generation organized a rich network of civic organizations that combined appreciation for Mexican culture with lobbying for moderate social reforms to American institutions. In San Antonio, these middle-class organizations included multiple chapters of the GI Forum and the League of United Latin American Citizens (LULAC), the Political Association of Spanish-Speaking Organizations (PASSO), the Pan American Progressive Association (PAPA), the Mexican Chamber of Commerce, and myriad cultural and social clubs—including, by 1955, four separate charro associations. These organizations worked on a variety of issues: school desegregation, voter registration and turnout, small business loans, access to public sector jobs, support for striking farmworkers, and more. While their ideologies, initiatives, and tactics differed, these organizations shared the goal of creating new economic pathways, opportunities, and forms of capital for ethnic Mexicans in the United States.[9] The middle-class members of San Antonio's charro associations contributed to this broad push by drawing specifically on the imagery of the charro to help reboot the city's postwar economy.

They had a unique opportunity, born of economic crisis. For even as other cities in Texas and the U.S.-Mexico border region boomed after World War II, San Antonio was in trouble. To be sure, the city's population was rapidly growing as military personnel, defense workers, and their families moved to San Antonio for training or employment at one of the city's five army and air force bases.[10] However, the city's exponential growth camouflaged deeper problems. During the 1940s, San Antonio lost its position as a regional financial center to Houston and Dallas, where civic elites had successfully crafted diversified economies based on global manufacturing, oil, and services.[11] San Antonio, by contrast, operated as a distribution and collection center for South Texas, but had no significant industrial plants or oil reserves of its own. Nor was the agricultural and ranching economy of the surrounding hinterlands financially robust any longer. Instead, San Antonio's economy had become almost completely reliant on federal largesse. With demilitarization looming in the years after World War II, San Antonio's business elite was growing anxious for alternatives.[12]

These conditions opened the doors to change, and the city's racialized power structure began to shift. New coalitions of business-oriented elites, especially San Antonio's Good Government League, replaced the old political machines at the ballot boxes by promising modernization, stability, efficiency and, most of all, economic growth. Modernization was no less entangled with racial hierarchy in San Antonio than in Los Angeles, but its implementation operated differently in San Antonio given the city's geographic and cultural position at the crossroads of American South and Mexican North. As in other impoverished southern cities, San Antonio's civic and business leadership could no longer embrace Jim Crow segregation and explicit racial discrimination if they wanted to attract investors and a middle-class, college-educated workforce. Given San Antonio's location near the U.S.-Mexico border and its strong ties to the economy of northern Mexico, modernizing racial relations was doubly important to maintain good relations with Mexican investors, tourists, and shoppers, who constituted an important market segment. For these reasons, the emerging Anglo business elite made moderate gestures toward racial inclusion during the late 1940s and '50s. They selectively incorporated a small number of middle-class Mexican Americans and African Americans, as well as elite Mexican nationals, into the local power structure. They found a special kinship with conservatives and moderates, like the city's middle-class charro-businessmen, who shared their ideologies of profit and progress and eschewed radical or confrontational forms of politics.[13]

In the postwar period, these diverse groups strategically reinvested in the only pillar of the city's economy that had remained robust since the early twentieth century: tourism. San Antonio already had a vibrant tourist industry and landscape, most of which centered on sites associated with the Texas Revolution as well as the region's Spanish and Mexican periods. From the 1910s through the 1930s, conservationists, politicians, and investors had worked to restore, expand, or create the area's four Spanish missions (including the Alamo), the Spanish Governor's Palace, La Villita, and the Riverwalk/ Paseo del Rio, among many others.[14] Yet these cultural heritage projects rested on racial scripts that were becoming increasingly unstable in the postwar period. The Alamo, for example, offered tourists and locals a rendering of Texas history in which Mexicans violently and senselessly attacked Americans, while neglecting the loyalty, participation, and death of some Tejanos in that battle.[15] Other tourist sites, like La Villita, were premised on the destruction of Mexican barrios and displacement of their residents, and traded in stereotypes of lazy and premodern—if quaint and artistic—Mexicans to entertain white residents and tourists.

With the push for modernization and the inclusion of some Mexican Americans in the postwar growth coalition, these representations could no longer stand. Instead, and with the active participation of the city's charros and other middle-class Mexican Americans, San Antonio's civic leaders reinvested in tourism in ways that showed growing (though still limited) sensitivity to the city's multiple ethnic and racial histories. They aggressively pursued federal funding to expand a tourist-oriented downtown landscape, and they provided funding and staffing for tourist-friendly civic, social, and cultural events. They were especially eager to invest in landscapes, events, and organizations that celebrated South Texas's diverse ranching and agricultural economies. For while ranching may have declined in importance economically, it remained a vital part of the region's cultural identity. As historian Char Miller explains, "to awaken the city's somnolent economy, an emerging pro-growth coalition gambled it could construct a new west out of the materials of the old."[16] In San Antonio, as in other southwestern and border cities, the materials of the old West included not just cowboys and Indians, but also charros.

San Antonio's growth interests had only to look south to Brownsville to witness the charro's power for economic development. Brownsville, a small city along the international border in the Rio Grande Valley, had begun hosting a "Charro Days" celebration in 1938 to aid economic recovery from the Great Depression. Over time, the four-day celebration, which involved growing partnerships with the Mexican city of Matamoros just across the border, came to include parades, dances, concerts, motor and sailboat races, a bullfight, and a rodeo (first American and then Mexican style), as well as appearances by Mexican charros sent by the FMCH. Charro Days attracted media attention from *Time, Life,* and *National Geographic* magazines, the Paramount and Universal Studios newsreels, and Macy's department store, all of which catapulted Brownsville into the national spotlight and attracted tourists from far and wide.[17] Other border cities like Tucson had also used charro- and vaquero-themed festivals to successfully boost their tourist industries while maintaining healthy binational business networks and smoothing U.S.-Mexico relations.[18] San Antonio's growth machine elites were keen to put their city on the map in a similar way, and the city's charro-businessmen were equally keen to help them.

During the 1940s and '50s, San Antonio's charro-businessmen capitalized on the city's pro-growth agenda and its moderate gestures toward inclusion to create new opportunities and experiences for ethnic Mexicans in the city, especially those who were middle class and upwardly mobile. They acted as what Genevieve Carpio, in her study of Mexican American real estate agents, has called "racial brokers"—people who facilitated upward mobility for Mexican Americans by navigating diverse ethnic and racial communities and a social structure built on racial capitalism.[19] San Antonio's charros were an especially effective bridge between Anglo-American growth machine interests in San Antonio, on the one hand, and elite businessmen in northern Mexico, on the other. At a time of tremendous conflict in the U.S.-Mexico border region, the city's charros used strategies of negotiation, collaboration, and persuasion—rather than direct action or militant resistance—to nurture relationships between these groups.

The charros' ideological commitments to growth and profit, and their strategies of friendly collaboration with elite businessmen, might be interpreted as less radical, or perhaps less significant, than other Mexican American political action at the time. But interpreting the charros in this way would miss the larger context—and, thus, the stakes—of their work. For decades, ethnic Mexican workers in South Texas had faced rampant violation of their labor and human rights, including extremely low wages, underpayment, and wage theft; inadequate food, water, and shelter; and racial discrimination in housing and public accommodations. Economic subjugation had long been intertwined with the policing of migration in ways that racialized ethnic Mexican workers as "illegal aliens" or "wetbacks." Employers capitalized on these constructions—literally—when they called immigration officials to conduct a workplace raid before payday or to deport workers who resisted or fought back.[20] Employer mistreatment of ethnic Mexican workers was so extreme and so widespread that during negotiations over the Bracero Program, the contract labor program administered jointly by Mexico and the United States beginning in 1942, the Mexican government at first refused to authorize contracts in Texas.[21] Economic exploitation and state harassment of Mexican workers in Texas continued throughout the 1950s, as Border Patrol agents rolled out a new tactic for apprehension of undocumented Mexican workers: aggressive targeting of ethnic Mexicans at the workplace, followed by mass deportations to the Mexican interior. This strategy, dubbed Operation Wetback, was first tested in the Rio Grande Valley towns between Harlingen and Brownsville; by 1952, it had been adopted by virtually every Border Patrol station across the U.S. Southwest, including field offices in and around San Antonio.[22] Though resistance certainly fomented in the fields and factories, Mexican labor remained violently subjugated across South Texas and beyond.

In this context, the work of San Antonio's charros to help build the city's postwar economy takes on greater significance. San Antonio's charro associations drew upon the historic figure of the charro—the autonomous, land-owning, highly skilled, and defiant Mexican horseman—to present ethnic Mexicans as economic actors with dignity. This was a radical departure from prevailing representations of ethnic Mexican workers at the time. Thus, though the charros' tactics may have been moderate, even conservative, their message was not. Equally important, their use of the charro's imagery was not only symbolic or performative but also resulted in substantial new opportunities for ethnic Mexicans in San Antonio. As we shall see in this chapter, San Antonio's charros successfully integrated some political and economic institutions, occupied exclusive physical spaces, and produced new urban landscapes in the image of the charro and the hacienda in the two decades after World War II. To be sure, they were confined to a limited terrain that hinged on the charros' willingness to support the city's economic development agenda without pressing for a more substantive distribution of resources. Even so, the charros effectively challenged the ongoing alienation of ethnic Mexicans from their land and labor in South Texas, while claiming a place for Tejanos and their historic ranching culture at the center of San Antonio's postwar economy.

SAN ANTONIO'S CHARRO ASSOCIATIONS: MEMBERS, NETWORKS, VISIONS, AND SPACES

Middle-class Mexican American men in San Antonio established four charro associations in the late 1940s and early 1950s. The San Antonio Charro Association and the Charro Riding Club were both founded in 1947 and merged to become one organization, which retained the name of the San Antonio Charro Association, in 1950—by far the most active of the city's charro groups. A third organization, Los Dorados Riding Club, was established in 1950; and a fourth, the Charros de Bejar, was formed in 1955.[23] Hundreds of men joined these four charro associations in the decades after World War II. These were family affairs: the charros' wives joined the ladies' auxiliaries, their sons joined junior charro groups, and their daughters competed as queens and, later, escaramuzas. Thousands more ethnic Mexicans,

José Chavarrí, a Spanish-Cuban tailor, sews custom trajes de charro for members of the city's charro associations, 1949. Courtesy of University of Texas at San Antonio Special Collections/Zuma.

including migrant workers traveling through the city, attended the charro associations' events as spectators. Other Latin Americans in San Antonio, though small in number, also participated in shaping the city's charro culture. For example, Spanish-Cuban tailor José Chavarrí designed and made custom charro suits from his shop on North Flores Street in the westside barrio.

The members of the charro associations were drawn almost exclusively from San Antonio's small but growing Mexican American middle class. They were not necessarily elite, but they were, without exception, businessmen and professionals. They also represented well the central characteristics of the Mexican American Generation. While a few had been born in Mexico and migrated to the United States as children, most had been born in Texas to Mexican immigrant parents. They were U.S. citizens, and they spoke both English and Spanish with equal facility. Some lived in the historic westside barrio, but others lived in majority-Anglo neighborhoods across the city, including the neighborhood of Alamo Heights, where many of the city's most influential power brokers lived. All of the charros were high school graduates, and most had undergraduate or even graduate degrees—an exceptional fact in a city where less than 15 percent of ethnic Mexicans graduated high school.[24] Most of the city's charros were also members of the city's other middle-class Mexican American organizations, such as the Pan American Progressive Association and LULAC, and most belonged to one or more of the city's middle-class ethnic Mexican social clubs with their wives and children.[25] Like other members of the Mexican American Generation, especially in Texas and cities across the U.S. South, they generally opposed radical tactics and direct action, preferring instead to use negotiation, strategic collaboration, and institutional reform.[26]

Because the charro associations were composed overwhelmingly of businessmen, their members were especially well represented in the city's Mexican Chamber of Commerce. Like LULAC, the Mexican Chamber of Commerce was established in 1929, with different but complementary aims. The Mexican Chamber supported ethnic Mexican–owned businesses and crafted strategic collaborations with the city's "main"—that is, Anglo—Chamber of Commerce, around the shared goal of growing the city's economy. The Mexican Chamber was especially focused on cultivating international tourism and trade. As a former president explained, the Mexican Chamber's initial purpose was "to promote more tourists to San Antonio from Mexico and South America and to try and help the city of San Antonio. We also work with the Armed Forces in this area, and we work most definitely with the San Antonio Chamber of Commerce. We want to work with them. Businessmen realize that their business is helped by our activities."[27]

As both businessmen and leaders in the ethnic Mexican community, the members of the charro associations were well equipped to aid with economic development. José R. Núñez, who served as the first president of the San Antonio Charro Association, was a veteran of World War II and owner of the Casa Blanca Restaurant. While serving as president of the charro association, throughout the late 1940s and early '50s, he was simultaneously the first vice president of the Mexican Chamber of Commerce of San Antonio, vice president of the Mexican Chamber of Commerce of the United States, and president of the Pan American Progressive Association. Located in the heart of the westside barrio, on a block studded with Mexican-owned doctor, dentist, and law offices, his restaurant was a regular meeting place for members of these organizations and San Antonio's Spanish-speaking middle class more broadly. Another early member of the San Antonio Charro Association,

José Núñez, president of the San Antonio Charro Association, at his Casa Blanca Restaurant in 1949. Russell Lee Photograph Collection, e_rl_14646_0161, Dolph Briscoe Center for American History, University of Texas at Austin.

Fortunato de los Santos, owned a furniture company and served as chair of the Mexican Chamber's board of trustees in the 1950s.[28] Leopoldo Garza, who was vice president of the San Antonio Charro Association throughout the 1950s and remained involved in the group until he was quite elderly, was also a member of the Mexican Chamber of Commerce. So too was Joe Casanova, a beer distributor and sales agent for Falstaff Brewery.[29] Other charro association members were doctors, real estate agents, insurance salesmen, and publishers who were involved with the Mexican Chamber.[30]

The charro association was especially effective in creating social opportunities for the city's diverse economic growth interests to come together. This was especially true of two annual events: the installation ceremonies for the newly elected board of directors and the charro queen's coronation ball. The 1950 events are illustrative. After restaurateur José Núñez was elected president of the San Antonio Charro Association, the association held a gala at the Gunter Hotel to celebrate and confirm his presidency and the newly elected board. An elite space dominated by Anglos, the Gunter Hotel had long been a hub for business networking and tourism. Nevertheless, Núñez and other ethnic Mexicans—both middle class and elite, and from both sides of the border—regularly occupied the exclusive hotel for charro association functions like this one. Carlos Barrera, representing the Charro Riding Club (which would merge with the San Antonio Charro Association later that year), and members of the Charros Del Rio Bravo, from Nuevo Laredo, Mexico, attended Núñez's installation. At the gala, the association elected Ruth Hernández, a sixteen-year-old alumna of Horace Mann High School, as its first queen. The association also awarded a trophy for civic activity to Roberto Cruz, who had coordinated fund-raising activities in the ethnic Mexican community for the city's recent March of Dimes campaign.[31] Events like this allowed participants to nurture personal and professional networks simultaneously, in locations that were otherwise off-limits to most ethnic Mexicans in the city.

The charro associations accessed other important social spaces in San Antonio, too, including the "Spanish fantasy" sites created by Anglo-American businessmen, politicians, and conservationists. The charro associations frequently held parties and fund-raisers, for example, at La Villita and the Spanish Governor's Palace. These events were attended mostly by ethnic Mexicans, but always included at least a few Anglo businessmen or cultural conservationists. The charros also occupied mainstream civic spaces, not visibly marked as "Spanish," that were in the throes of desegregation in the 1950s, such as the city's largest and most central parks. In addition, they occupied spaces that had been constructed specifically to support the city's postwar economic modernization, such as the Bexar County Coliseum, which was built in 1948 to host the city's new Livestock Exhibition and Rodeo. Performing cultural activities associated with the Tejano ranching class in these diverse urban spaces, they counteracted—even if temporarily—the displacement of Mexicans from the land and their segregation in the westside barrio. Instead, they used the figure of the charro and the practice of charrería to reclaim a Mexican presence in the heart of the modern city and its economy.

At the same time, the charro associations produced new urban landscapes in the image of the rancho and the hacienda. In the first few years of their existence, the city's charro associations did not have regular access to a dedicated space of their own, so they held their events at public parks in the central city. In October 1948, *La Prensa*'s César Serrato reported that the association had met for the second time at Brackenridge Park and that more than twenty people had attended.[32] At the end of 1949, however, with fund-raising assistance from the newly organized Mexican American Youth Association (MAYA), the San Antonio Charro Association began leasing the former "Buck a Boo Ranch," presumably owned by an Anglo rancher, on the south

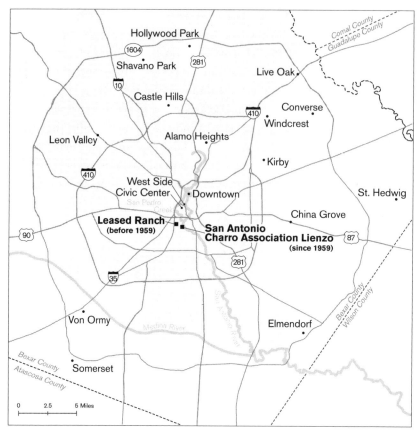

The City of San Antonio and Bexar County, Texas, with the locations of the San Antonio Charro Association's first leased ranch and their contemporary lienzo. By Jennifer Tran and Alexander Tarr.

side of the city near the intersection of Mission Road and East Sayers Avenue.[33] At the time, this was a predominantly Mexican area, but it was still relatively remote. Located several miles south of the westside barrio as well as La Villita and the other "Spanish" tourist destinations in central San Antonio, its location was, in fact, approximate to the historic Tejano ranches that had surrounded San Antonio in the 1820s, just after Mexican independence.[34]

A semipermanent physical space allowed the charro association to expand and promote its activities. They began sponsoring charreadas and other events at their leased ranch nearly every weekend. They raised money for institutions, such as the San Fernando Cathedral and the Stella Maris Clinic, that served the ethnic Mexican community and the poor living in the west-side barrio, and they occasionally held fund-raisers to support wounded Mexican American veterans returning home from war.[35] They also sponsored charitable events on behalf of Mexican nationals, such as a 1955 benefit for flood victims in Tampico featuring Mexican film star Pedro Armendáriz and a 1956 fund-raiser for orphaned children in Monterrey.[36] When the charro association was not hosting its own rodeos, social events, or charitable causes, it often allowed its leased ranch to be used for activities sponsored by the city's other ethnic Mexican clubs and organizations.[37] Through activities such as these, which responded to the practical needs of ethnic Mexicans on both sides of the border, the San Antonio Charro Association built on a long legacy of barrio-based mutual aid organizing in the United States.[38] But they also demonstrated the economic capacity of ethnic Mexicans in San Antonio—their ability to raise money and contribute to local, regional, and transnational economies—through both the figure of the charro and the spatiality of the modern hacienda and rancho.

CRAFTING STRATEGIC RELATIONSHIPS WITH THE ANGLO-AMERICAN GROWTH MACHINE

The charros and their supporters were most visibly concerned with preserving a form of Mexican culture they saw as valuable, while extending its popularity among working-class and transnational Mexicans in San Antonio. At the same time, however, their performances and place-making practices served to remind city leaders, and the Anglo-American public more broadly, of ethnic Mexicans' historic presence in San Antonio, as well as their ongoing claims to the region and its economy. San Antonio's charros were quite deliberate in using the figure of the charro this way. Throughout the late 1940s and '50s, they built strategic relationships with the city's economic elites, urban planners, and middle-class conservationists. These growth machine interests, who were almost exclusively Anglo, came to depend on the charros to generate "local color" for tourists and white suburbanites. For this reason, they often included the charros in mainstream institutions, generated favorable press coverage for their events, and helped to coordinate auspicious real estate deals. These were two-way relationships that benefited both groups, albeit in different ways.

For one thing, the charro associations had Anglo-American members from their inception. Larry Mazer, a lifelong resident of San Antonio and owner of a tailor shop, was one of the founding members of the San Antonio Charro Association and served as its executive secretary in the early 1950s. At that time, he was also involved with the Mexican Chamber of Commerce as well as several Jewish organizations. Likely because of his devotion to the city's ethnic Mexican community, Mazer was elected the very first "Rey Feo," or ceremonial king presiding over festivities, of LULAC's Feria de las Flores in 1951.[39] Other Anglo men were not only members of the charro associations but also served as its leaders. In 1960, for example, Peter Reed, whose company invented the tall glass novena candle featuring images of Catholic saints, was elected president of the San Antonio Charro Association, while Carol Walker was elected vice president; in this year, therefore, the top two leadership positions were both held by Anglos (although Reed's parents, both Irish, had lived in Mexico for some time).[40] Anglo-American men were also sometimes mentioned in the press as being members, though their degree of involvement seems minor. For instance, Ed Stolle, a candidate for the Texas State Legislature in 1965, was listed as being a member of an unspecified "Mexican Charro Association" as part of his candidate profile.[41] Such figures likely affiliated themselves with the charro associations in order to build relationships with the city's ethnic Mexican middle class, whose voting and purchasing power was clearly growing. For the charros, Anglo membership was also important because it kept open the lines of interethnic collaboration that were essential to their vision of racial progress and a more equally shared economic prosperity.

For similar reasons, and much like their counterparts in Los Angeles, the San Antonio charros nurtured congenial relationships with the city's law enforcement agencies. The charros and the city's sheriff and police departments frequently appeared as partners in public events, and they worked together on civic causes. In 1950, for example, the San Antonio Charro Association participated in a historical pageant, alongside the Bexar County Sheriff's Posse and the San Antonio Conservation Society, to celebrate the reopening of the Menger Hotel —another exclusive downtown hotel—after an extensive renovation.[42] The following year, when the Sheriff's Posse barns were destroyed by fire, Los Dorados Riding Club held a benefit charreada at Brackenridge Park to help them rebuild.[43] A few years later, in 1953, the San Antonio Charro Association and the San Antonio Police Department cohosted famous local charro José Díaz in a demonstration of roping skills, with proceeds to benefit that year's March of Dimes campaign.[44] Beyond fund-raisers and celebrations, charros and law enforcement officers competed in friendly riding matches, too. For Labor Day 1953, the San Antonio Charro Association sponsored a competition between what it characterized as two different schools of the equestrian arts: the jaripeo mexicano, represented by the charro association, and American-style rodeo, represented by the Bexar County Sheriff's mounted patrol.[45] Beyond the networking that these partnerships facilitated, they had an important political effect: they positioned the charros as moderates, not radicals—people who could be trusted with the responsibilities of democratic citizenship and economic leadership.

In a similar vein, San Antonio's charros worked to build bridges with influential Anglo-American politicians. Not bound to any one group, party, or cause, they worked strategically and flexibly with a wide range of elected officials. They consistently invited the mayor of San Antonio, at that time always an Anglo-American businessman, to their events, and they publicly supported candidates for local, state, and federal office.[46] As part of these efforts at political networking, the San Antonio charros engaged in practices of strategic gifting. That is, they gave politicians sombreros, spurs, and other charro regalia to express their support, while signaling that they expected the candidate or politician to serve their needs and interests. During President Harry Truman's visit to San Antonio in 1948, for example, the president of San Antonio's Mexican Chamber of Commerce, Ramón Galindo, presented Truman with a charro hat from Mexico City.[47] The following year, when Texas governor Allan Shivers attended San Antonio's Black and White Ball, the governor of Mexico City likewise gave him a charro hat.[48] A few months later, in 1950, the San Antonio Charro Association presented Governor Shivers with a set of spurs, meant to complement the hat, at the city's very first Stock Show and Rodeo, held at the brand-new coliseum.[49] Through these practices of gifting, the San Antonio charros reasserted their status as Texas's "original cowboys," gently reminding recipients of their role in the creation of regional ranching history and their continued influence on the city's traditions, public culture, and economy.

The effectiveness of these strategies was uneven. While such gifts may have earned the charros visibility among Anglo elites, they usually failed to make a meaningful dent in whitewashed renditions of the Texas cowboy and the frontier. As a potent example, in 1951, Governor Shivers led the opening-day parade for the city's annual Livestock Exposition and Rodeo mounted on a horse named Rainbow that local charro Antonio Pérez had lent him. The San Antonio Charro Association and Los Dorados Riding Club participated in the parade alongside other mounted units, including the Sheriff's Posse, with which they had a friendly relationship. But the governor himself was, in the words of the *San Antonio Express,* "escorted by an honor guard of mounted Texas Rangers"—descendants of the vigilante group that had terrorized ethnic Mexicans in the border region since the 1820s. The newspaper then emphasized that "the touch of *real* western atmosphere will be provided by the Fiesta San Jacinto Association with a stage coach entry."[50] The Fiesta San Jacinto Association (later renamed the Fiesta San Antonio Association) had primary responsibility for organizing Fiesta, the city's annual celebration of Anglo-American heroes at the Battles of the Alamo and San Jacinto. At best, then, it seems the charros' enthusiastic participation and practices of gifting added some local color to violent settler narratives of the cowboy, the Texas pioneer, and the western frontier. At worst, and accurately or not, it suggested ethnic Mexicans' acquiescence to those processes.

But cosponsorship of events and gifting were not the charros' only strategies for forging relationships with Anglo investors and politicians. Another, arguably more effective, strategy was the deliberate use of charro queens and other female royalty (princesses, duchesses, and so forth) to build patriarchal networks between Anglo and Mexican businessmen in ways that served the wider project of economic growth. Queens had not existed in Mexican ranching society, but they were part of the colonial project in New Spain under the Spanish Crown, and they had become widespread in elite and middle-class American culture, including in San Antonio, by the early and mid-twentieth century.[51] Following suit, beginning in the years after World War II, virtually all the Mexican American social, cultural, and recreational clubs in San Antonio, including the charro associations, elected queens to represent them.

Mexican American queen contests across the United States, including San Antonio, were (and are) complicated social and cultural arenas. On the one hand, they promised significant material and symbolic rewards to their female participants. Queen contests affirmed that Mexican American women possessed beauty, talent, intellect, and bright futures—affirmations that were too often absent in other dimensions of their lives. The charro queens circulated within a network of middle-class ethnic Mexican families and organizations, in both the U.S. and Mexico, that generated opportunities for marriage, education, and professional development. Queens and other royalty also won prizes such as clothing, jewelry, and trips.[52] But these rewards were premised on young women's willingness and ability to participate in distinctly gendered spheres centering on beauty, fashion, and the transmission of elite and respectable forms of Mexican culture. Always in their late teens or early twenties, queens were and are usually the daughters or nieces of one of the male members of the associations. They were required to be unmarried, chaste, and wholesome. Contestants had usually been extensively involved in charitable work on behalf of the ethnic Mexican community, where they developed community leadership skills. They (and their mothers) were expected to devote significant time and money to sewing costumes and preparing their physical appearance.[53] And, once elected, queens played no role in the actual governance of the charro associations and had no decision-making powers; their role was (and remains) decorative and symbolic.

For the men who led the charro associations, the queen contests served a more clear-cut and uniformly positive purpose. In their eyes, the queens represented ethnic Mexican gender roles and family structures positively to outsiders, allowing Mexican American men to forge a patriarchal brotherhood with elite Anglo and Mexican men around their shared sense of raising beautiful, respectable, service-oriented young women. This brotherhood was most tangibly on display during the queen's annual installation ceremonies, which were always held in tandem with celebrations of Mexican Independence Day. The first such celebration, in 1950, began with a group of mariachis playing in front of La Villita, followed by the coronation of the queen by the city's mayor, Jack White. The queen and the mayor then traveled together to the Municipal Auditorium in a carriage escorted by the charros, where the queen delivered a Mexican flag to the city's Mexican consul. The consul then gave the grito de independencia (shout of independence) before they all returned to La Villita for the remaining festivities.[54] Versions of the same event were held annually throughout the 1950s and always included a predictable set of cultural rituals performed by the charro queen in conjunction with the Mexican consul, the city's mayor, and San Antonio's charro-businessmen—representatives of the city's increasingly diverse postwar growth coalition.

These same patriarchal business networks could also generate new forms of economic opportunity. The charro associations frequently sent their queens to participate in binational economic development initiatives meant to further develop tourism and foreign trade between South Texas and northern Mexico. In September 1950, Ruth Hernández of the San Antonio Charro Association and Shirley Morin of the Charro Riding Club rode together in the parade for Pan American Friendship Week, an event organized by Anglo-American civic boosters and businessmen. The event also included a "Good Neighbor Convention" and dedication of the foreign trade zone by Governor Allan Shivers.[55] Activities like these were powerful opportunities to nurture both personal and professional relations among the city's diverse pro-growth coalition. As binational, bilingual actors committed to a growth agenda—that is, as racial brokers—the city's charros exercised a unique form of power to bring these constituencies together. The charros were especially well positioned to cultivate networks with elite businessmen from northern Mexico, tying together a borderlands economy.

TRANSNATIONAL NETWORKS WITH ELITE MEXICAN BUSINESSMEN

Like middle-class ethnic Mexicans in other border cities at the time, San Antonio's charros saw transnational business and tourism as a viable and pragmatic way to pursue Mexican American civil, economic, and cultural rights. Accordingly, the San Antonio charros knit together a thriving transnational economy, rooted in charrería and other forms of ranchero culture, with elite Mexicans and their commercial enterprises. This charro-led cultural economy coexisted with the "Spanish"-themed tourism and trade promoted by San Antonio's Anglo civic elite, but it was organized through markedly different networks and served substantially different purposes: namely, the creation of a transnational Mexican business class in which San Antonio's Mexican Americans played both anchoring and bridging roles.

Beginning in the early 1950s, the city's charros traveled frequently to Mexico for meetings, competitions, and performances. In July 1951, for example, Mexican charros affiliated with the FMCH invited the San Antonio Charro Association to Mexico City, where they were treated as guests of honor and hobnobbed with high-ranking Mexican political officials and investors. Among the highlights of the trip were a competition at Rancho La Tapatía between two charro associations, La Metropolitana and La Nacional; another charreada at Rancho del Charro, home of the oldest charro association in Mexico; a visit to the home of former Mexican president Manuel Ávila Camacho, who gave them a tour of his stables and offered his moral support; and benediction from the Archbishop of Mexico, Luis María Martínez, who wished them luck and told them that he had, in his youth, been a charro too. During a visit with Mexico City's city council, council members passionately reminded the San Antonio charros that "the Mexican charro is the authentic representative of the most beautiful and romantic

traditions of our country" and conveyed their respect and admiration for the
visiting charros. José Núñez responded that the council's recognition of their
work would motivate the San Antonio charros to continue elevating Mexico
and the image of the charro back in the United States.[56]

Affirmed and motivated by their time in Mexico, the San Antonio Charro
Association soon reciprocated by inviting Mexican charros to visit San
Antonio for a charreada that September. *La Prensa* emphasized that this
would be the first "international" charreada in San Antonio and the entire
United States, because it would feature competition between the San Antonio
Charro Association and the charro association from Tepatitlán, Jalisco. *La
Prensa* stressed that the visit by the Jalisco charros was especially significant
because, although the residents of Aguascalientes, Guanajuato, and Michoacán
were also excellent horsemen, those from Jalisco simply rose to the top. The
Jalisco charros, accompanied by a band of mariachis, traveled to San Antonio
on board a luxury bus donated by La Línea de Autotransportes de Los Altos,
whose president and two young daughters also came along for the trip.[57]

Eager to honor the visiting charros and businessmen as enthusiastically as
they had been received in Mexico, the San Antonio Charro Association
planned several days of activities. These included a banquet and dance at La
Villita organized by Club Reynero, an official welcome by mayor and hotelier
Jack White, and a dinner with civic leaders, both Anglo and Mexican
American, at the home of the Mexican consul. The visit also included a public festival at Pablo's Grove, a gravel pit-turned-public park near Lackland Air
Force Base on the west side of the city. To its San Antonio–based audience,
the association promised that one of the festival's greatest attractions would
be a demonstration of classic roping technique by professional charro Martin
Díaz, who would then compete against Aureliano Reyes, a renowned charro
from Aguascalientes, in the manganas, followed by demonstrations of the
coleadero by Leopoldo Franco from Mexico City.[58] These activities were
much like those that the San Antonio charros regularly cosponsored with
Anglo politicians and business elites, but foregrounded the performance of
Mexican cultural heritage, via charrería, in service to the economic needs and
cultural interests of the Mexican business class.

Cross-border visits and competitions like these endured throughout the
1950s and well beyond, enabling the constant fertilization of networks that
served business, personal, and cultural purposes simultaneously. In March
1952, for example, the San Antonio Charro Association sponsored a bar-
beque and charreada at their ranch on behalf of representatives from the

Estrella de Oro line of buses, who were visiting San Antonio to purchase modern equipment. This was a clear instance of the San Antonio charros brokering a transnational economic deal that benefited two local businesses: one in San Antonio, another in Mexico City.[59] Later that year, the San Antonio Charro Association invited Mexican charros from Jalisco, Zacatecas, Querétaro, and Nuevo León to celebrate the completion of their new lienzo on the leased land at Mission Road. Leaders from Mexico's banking, industrial, and commercial sectors attended and offered their blessing.[60] Throughout the 1950s, the charro association continued to host visiting Mexican businessmen to their ranch for meetings, charreadas, and barbeques that were attended by a wide cross-section of San Antonio's community. Their labor affirmed the importance of Mexican cultural heritage to San Antonio's historic development, while signaling the openness of the city's postwar economy to ongoing Mexican investment.

By the mid-1950s, the San Antonio Charro Association had secured a position as a highly regarded and politically moderate bridge between the business classes of northern Mexico and South Texas. This position allowed them to weigh in, though indirectly, on immigration and border policies that affected the lives of border residents, workers, and travelers in this period. For Labor Day 1952, the San Antonio charros sponsored a charreada at the recently completed Bexar County Coliseum, where they competed against an association of charros from Nuevo León. In their publicity, the charro association noted that this would be the first charreada in San Antonio that would feature all nine traditional events, which would be performed by seven champions brought from Mexico. Organizers expected to pay more than $10,000, including travel costs for the Mexican participants, rental fees for the coliseum, the costs of leasing high-quality cattle and horses from a Mexican stock contractor, and publicity. This was quite a sum, indicating that the San Antonio charros had significant capital at their disposal. But both the charros and *La Prensa,* mouthpiece of the elite ricos, argued that the expenses were more than worth it because the event promised to improve fraught relations between the U.S. and Mexico, especially the growing use of workplace raids and deportations to police Mexican labor.[61]

Three years later, the constant threat and practice of deportation still loomed large, and came to the fore at another charro event. For U.S. Independence Day in 1955, the San Antonio Charro Association sponsored a bullfight featuring a competition between Mexican national Mario Garza and "el guerito" John Short, an American bullfighter. During the bullfight,

John Short fought the first bull, which refused to charge the red flag and kept fleeing from him. From the stands, the audience shouted, "Talk to him in Spanish, he's Mexican!" and "He's running from you because he doesn't have a passport!" The city's Mexican consul and representatives of city government were present, as were newspaper reporters from San Antonio, Dallas, and several Mexican cities.[62] Thus, before an elite and binational audience, the charros facilitated ethnic Mexican laborers' playful response to a very serious issue: the Border Patrol's use of deportation to terrorize undocumented Mexicans, as well as the harassment and violence that Mexican workers in South Texas experienced at the hands of employers and the state every day.

For the most part, however, the charros positioned themselves as cultural and economic organizations, not political ones, and they focused on moderate cultural initiatives that contributed to the city's pro-growth economic agenda. Through their procedural activities, cosponsorship of fund-raisers and benefits, and strategic use of gifts and female royalty, they built diverse networks that would allow them to create stronger business opportunities, as well as a more inclusive public sphere, for ethnic Mexicans in San Antonio. Their approach largely worked, though in ways fractured by social class. By the mid-1950s, the San Antonio Charro Association was one of the few Mexican American organizations that could count on consistent, if limited, access to the centers of political and economic power in San Antonio. This sense of respect and high regard resulted in a number of cultural, structural, and spatial gains for the charro associations and the Mexican American middle class from which they were drawn—though not, by and large, for the city's working-class and poor Mexicans.

FRACTURED GAINS

During the mid-1950s, San Antonio's elite increasingly recognized the charro association as a valuable contributor to the city's cultural heritage and social life. In 1957, during a banquet held at the Spanish Governor's Palace, the San Antonio Conservation Society (SACS)—one of the city's oldest and most influential preservation groups—made a series of awards to recognize individuals and organizations that had contributed to the public life of the city. SACS recognized the San Antonio Charro Association for "preserving the techniques and traditions of Mexican horsemanship." Out of dozens of awards, the charro association was the only group representing people of Mexican descent to be honored.[63]

In addition, the marriages, travels, and other activities of charro association members were regularly included in the society pages of the city's two English-language newspapers, the *Express* and the *Light*, alongside those of Anglo-American heritage groups such as the Daughters of the Confederacy, the Daughters of the Republic of Texas, and the San Antonio Conservation Society. In many instances, the marriages reported were interracial marriages between ethnic Mexican women—often the queens of the charro associations—and Anglo-American men, usually local businessmen or veterans.[64] Stories like these demonstrated that the professional and business networks nurtured by members of the charro associations also had an impact on their personal lives, resulting in upward mobility and interethnic relational power for some ethnic Mexicans. The pattern of favorable press coverage was especially significant given that English-language media coverage of ethnic Mexicans otherwise focused almost entirely on discussions of criminality and depravity.

Buoyed by these indications of respect and recognition, the charros used their growing power and influence to support up-and-coming Mexican American politicians in the 1950s. Most notably, the charros supported several campaigns for Henry B. González, the first Mexican American in memory to win a seat on San Antonio's city council (in 1953) and then the Texas State Legislature (in 1956). In August 1956, during González's legislative campaign, the charros sponsored a dinner dance at their ranch in his honor, to which they invited leading members of the city's banking and business sectors as well as elected officials and the city's "best social and civic clubs." During the dinner dance, the charro association awarded González honorary membership and presented him with an elegant sombrero, much as they had done a few years before with politicians like Harry Truman and Allan Shivers.[65] Later that fall, the charro association sponsored a bullfight in González's honor featuring bullfighters from Mexico City, San Luis Potosí, and San Antonio.[66] At this point in his career, González—the descendant of a wealthy Mexican family that had fled to San Antonio during the Mexican Revolution—was best known for helping to found the Pan American Progressive Association, to which many of the city's charros belonged, and for successfully prodding the San Antonio City Council to desegregate public facilities. Later, when he was a state legislator, his politics would become more contentious and complicated. But in the mid-1950s, when the charros threw their weight behind him, González was simply an upper-middle-class, politically moderate Mexican American man like them, working to advance ethnic Mexicans' civil, economic, and cultural rights in San Antonio through collaboration and persuasion.[67]

Within this context of widespread public recognition and growing influence, 1959 represented a banner year for the city's charros. First, the San Antonio Charro Association applied for and was granted nonprofit status by the state of Texas. The documents drafted in this period illustrate the association's dual commitments to uphold Mexican cultural nationalism and to promote San Antonio's economic development, especially through tourism. In its constitution, the organization described its aims:

1. To maintain and perpetuate the glorious traditions of the Mexican sport of "Charrería" in its purest form.
2. To cooperate with the authorities in general when the services of the organization are solicited for community and charitable activities which are in accord with the principles of the organization.
3. To procure by means of this sport more color and Mexican atmosphere for the city of San Antonio in order to develop tourism and increase prosperity.
4. To organize, promote and compete in events appropriate to the nature of the organization if approved by the Executive Committee.[68]

Other policies adopted at this time reflect a similarly middle-class, pro-business orientation. Membership in the association was restricted to men over age eighteen who were "engaged in legitimate business activities" and had never been convicted of a felony. All members were required to pay initiation fees and dues. The adult membership was limited to one hundred men, with vacant positions to be filled as follows: first preference to sons of active charros; second, to members of the junior charro group when they became eighteen years old; third, to sons of formerly active charros; and fourth, to new applicants "possessing the high character and integrity of spirit and mind."[69] These policies promoted a politics of middle-class respectability that appealed to Anglo-American politicians and businessmen as well as elite Mexican nationals. But they also recast the racial position of Mexicans in the regional economy, from unskilled and vulnerable stoop labor to upstanding, respectable, and autonomous businessmen.

The charros' effectiveness as racial brokers also resulted in a significant spatial gain: the ability to purchase a valuable piece of downtown real estate and to construct a permanent lienzo charro. In 1959, members of the San Antonio Charro Association met with benefactor and conservationist Elizabeth Graham to talk real estate. Graham was the past president of the San Antonio Conservation Society and, like so many middle-class Anglo-Americans at the time, she was fascinated with Spanish and Mexican "folk" cultures. During her visits to Mexico in the early 1940s, she had become enamored with charrería, which she regarded as a dignified and colorful expression of Mexican masculinity. According to biographer Marilyn Bennett:

> She enjoyed the easy feeling of the *charros*, Mexican cowboys, riding their horses along the river banks on Sunday afternoons. They were handsomely dressed in their traditional style of sombreros, crisp dress shirts with bright colored ties, intricately embroidered chaps, and boots with spurs attached. Their courtly air made a great impression of fine horsemanship, discipline, and tradition. Graham's thoughts went to her own city's river life and how natural it would be to see charros riding alongside the San Antonio River . . . [she] returned to San Antonio intent on finding a way to bring charreada to the city.[70]

Apparently, Graham was unaware that the San Antonio charros had organized their association more than a decade prior and had been hosting extremely popular events in San Antonio since then, albeit on leased land. In her account, Bennett emphasizes that "various charreadas were being held ad hoc on Sunday afternoons"—clearly an understatement, given the records of their activities in *La Prensa*—but that "what the association really wanted was a dedicated space to preserve and promote charreada in its fullest cultural and historical form and thus enrich and promote the city's Mexican American traditions."[71]

Toward that end, Graham offered to sell twenty acres of her property to the San Antonio Charro Association under conditions that, while certainly favorable to the charros, were also intricately linked to the city's postwar economic development agenda. Graham's offer was part of an urban redevelopment project called the Mission Area Plan, which proposed to connect the region's historic Spanish missions, by this time well preserved, in the service of tourism and economic growth. The project, more than six miles in length, would stretch from Mission Concepción, just southwest of the downtown Alamo district, along the San Antonio River south to the Missions San José, San Juan, and Espada. The missions would be interwoven with parks and linked by a grand green parkway. The property that Graham proposed to sell to the San Antonio Charro Association was one of those parks. A two-page spread in the *San Antonio Light* penned by urban planner S. B. Zisman outlined the city's vision. Zisman enthused that by the time of its projected completion in 1980, the project would be "one of the most fabulous cultural developments in the U.S." Zisman ruminated that the historic irrigation system of the acequias, some of which were still in use, was to be part of the "great living museum to which visitors will come in ever greater numbers." The article later describes the city's cultural and historical inheritance as making it unique for urban redevelopment: "This enrichment of the new by the old is the great cultural contribution of San Antonio, unmatched by any other city in the whole Southwest."[72] Graham's offer, then, was not merely an isolated benevolent action, but rather part of a long history in which San Antonio's growth machine had embedded the Spanish fantasy past in the city's physical landscape for tourist consumption. The difference, in this case, was that the space would be owned and controlled by Mexican Americans themselves and that the landscape constructed there would celebrate— indeed, reterritorialize—the historic and enduring Mexican contribution to Texas's ranch culture and economy.

The charro association purchased twenty acres from Graham at 6126 Padre Drive, on the far south side of the city and not far from their formerly leased ranch, for $15,000. The land was made exempt from city and county property taxes, with the understanding that the space would be used only to host charreadas or other equestrian events.[73] Charro association members envisioned building a grand equestrian club complete with lienzo charro, swimming pool, outdoor terraces, and a banquet hall with dance floor—a projected investment of $75,000 to $80,000. This landscape, which charro association members hoped would be complemented by other "Spanish"- themed architectural relics in the surrounding area, was meant to reflect the grand spatiality of the hacienda under Mexican rule of the region.[74] Not until many years later were the members of the San Antonio Charro Association able to clear the land of its brush, install new grandstands, and create a park- like setting—an effort that involved much saving, fund-raising (including taking out a hefty loan), and the contribution of their own labor and personal resources.[75] Even so, the eventual completion of the facility demonstrated their vitality as economic actors—their ability to maintain good credit, access stores of financial capital, and contribute their own skilled labor. These qualities signaled a radically different racial and economic position for ethnic Mexicans in postwar San Antonio. The San Antonio Charro Association retains the same parcel of land to this day, where it stages numerous char-readas and other events. As in years past, some of these contemporary events are held in service of the city's ethnic Mexican community, while others are targeted at tourists and businesspeople from both the U.S. and Mexico.[76]

The charro association's purchase of the land and construction of a perma-nent lienzo emerges as even more significant given the destruction of working-class and impoverished Mexican barrios through urban renewal during the same period. As historian Robert Fairbanks observes, "What started . . . as a focus on slum clearance and providing adequate housing for the poor became much more centered on preserving downtown and promoting economic growth" in San Antonio, chiefly through tourism and the construction of interstate highways connecting the downtown core to the suburbs.[77] Of the nineteen "slum" zones identified by the city's urban renewal board between the 1950s and '80s, only three of the redeveloped areas contained housing roughly equivalent to what was destroyed. One major urban renewal project, Rosa-Verde, displaced 1,700 people from the westside barrio in order to make improvements to the hospital district and create a public market for tour-ists.[78] But the most egregious was the Civic Center Project, which evicted nearly 1,600 people, mostly low-income ethnic Mexicans, from the central business district. Renewal authorities built a convention center, performing arts facilities, a sports arena, hotels, and restaurants on the site. They also developed cultural amenities such as the Texas Institute of Cultures (an anthropological museum and historical archive) and the Tower of the Americas. Renewal authorities planned for these buildings to initially support HemisFair, the world's fair held in San Antonio in 1968, and then catalyze the city's tourism industry for many years to come.[79] The net result of these postwar projects, when added to the tourist assets created by groups like SACS in the 1930s and '40s, was an enormously profitable tourist land-scape—one that netted an annual economic impact of $13.4 billion to the city of San Antonio and Bexar County by 2013.[80] Though only a modest contributor to that sum, the charro association's lienzo is a vital part of the city's tourist landscape and economy.

Many of the projects created in this period appeared to include, even cel-ebrate, the city's diverse communities. Yet they also laid bare the fractured gains of San Antonio's ethnic Mexican community, along the lines of social class, in relationship to the tourist industry. As noted, many new tourist projects in the central-city area were premised on the displacement of working-class and poor ethnic Mexicans to the western, southern, and eastern parts of the city, far from the tourist gaze, even while they were expected to toil in minimum-wage service-sector jobs in the central-city tourist industry.[81] The charro association, by contrast, benefited from its relationships with diverse power brokers to occupy a new physical space where they could celebrate the legacy of the Mexican ranching economy in South Texas for perpetuity. Their spatial victory was rooted in the symbolic power of the charro as a representation of elite Mexican cultural heritage and skilled, dignified Mexican labor, as well as the San Antonio charros' use of moderate and nonconfrontational tactics to nurture diverse economic networks across local, regional, and transnational space.

In the ensuing years, the charros continued to draw on these moderate, conciliatory strategies to shape the tourist economy. Part of this labor has involved staking greater claims to Fiesta, the city's premiere tourist attraction, as a way to continue dismantling San Antonio's prevailing racial scripts. As we saw at the beginning of this chapter, individual ethnic Mexican men, such as those belonging to the Mexican Chamber of Commerce, wore charro suits to participate in the annual Fiesta parade beginning in the 1940s. After the San Antonio Charro Association formed in 1947, these same men continued to participate in Fiesta parades, but now as an organized group.[82] However, the association's own charreada was not included on the program as an official Fiesta event until the early 1970s. At that time, the city's Chicano and Black Power movements were demanding that Fiesta become more inclusive, and Fiesta's internal leadership was plagued by factionalism. In this volatile context, San Antonio's charros once again embraced a politics of polite negotiation, rather than confrontation, to secure a greater role in Fiesta. Socrates Ramírez, a longtime member of the San Antonio Charro Association, invited his friend, retired Colonel Davis Burnett—who was also executive director of the Fiesta San Antonio Commission—to a breakfast meeting at the Menger Hotel, where the charro association had by now become a consistent presence. During their meeting, Ramírez persuaded Burnett to include the association's charreada as an official Fiesta event. They also struck an agreement whereby Fiesta's primary royal figure, King Antonio, would ride at the head of the charros alongside the charro association's queen. The following year, King Antonio would return the favor by inviting the charro association's queen to ride in his river parade. Assessing these changes, historian Laura Hernández-Ehrisman has argued that "the San Antonio Charros were the first men to intrude on the cavaliers' masculine space in the 1970s, but they did not offer a parallel role within Fiesta."[83] Even so, the expanded inclusion of the city's charros in Fiesta was a welcome departure from years past, and it built on familiar tactics that the charros had used successfully in many other contexts.

At a time when most ethnic Mexicans in San Antonio were subject to labor exploitation, political marginalization, state surveillance and deportation, and ongoing displacement by urban renewal, San Antonio's charros invoked a radically different image and position for ethnic Mexicans in relation to the city's postwar economy. They did so by drawing on the charro's symbolic power as a representation of skilled, landowning, and dignified Mexican masculinity, and by using collaboration, negotiation, and persuasion to nurture relationships with the elite business classes of both San Antonio and northern Mexico. Those networks and tactics resulted in some important victories: new business opportunities, support from elected officials, interethnic friendships and marriages, organizational autonomy and recognition, and a permanent physical space in which to practice charrería and nurture their cultural heritage. To be sure, those victories primarily benefited the middle-class and elite members of San Antonio's ethnic Mexican community. Nonetheless, they fundamentally recast the image of ethnic Mexicans as workers and consumers—that is, as vital and contributing members of the economy—and enabled some ethnic Mexicans to access the full sweep of the city's geography, including some of its most important social and cultural spaces. Equally important, their accomplishments laid the groundwork for the more expansive—and often more militant—civil rights and racial justice initiatives pursued by later generations.

THREE

Creating Multicultural Public Institutions in Denver and Pueblo

IN THE LATE 1960S AND '70S, ethnic Mexicans established dozens of new charro associations in the United States. The expansion of charrería at this time reflected a newly politicized racial identity, most visibly associated with the Chicano movement, as well as Mexican Americans' upward mobility and their growing access to homeownership, especially in suburbs. By March 1975, there were fifty-eight U.S.-based charro associations formally affiliated with the Federación Mexicana de Charrería (FMCH), prompting the FMCH to appoint a special executive assistant to the United States for the first time.[1] The charro associations of this era worked primarily in the service of creating more responsive public institutions and integrating or reclaiming public spaces for the exercise of cultural citizenship.

The U.S. charros who mobilized in this period worked within a dramatically different political landscape than their predecessors—one marked by the desegregation of public institutions, new federal protections on voting and against discrimination, and the implementation of affirmative action, equal opportunity, and War on Poverty programs. It was a hard-fought and hard-won political order in which American institutions were expected to not only reflect the diversity of the U.S. population but also right historic wrongs. New and expanded public programs promised to redistribute social and economic resources through the intentional, proactive inclusion of Mexican Americans and other people of color. While public memory tends to focus on the era's social movements, much of this broad shift proceeded through the arduous—and much less visible—work of building and transforming public institutions from within. As in other communities of color, civic-minded Mexican Americans filed lawsuits, joined human relations committees, conducted research, put individual and collective pressure on their employers, and lobbied elected officials to ensure that ethnic Mexicans could fully access the new slate of public resources.

These shifts in the political landscape corresponded to, and also propelled, a seismic shift in the ways that charros and ethnic Mexicans more broadly understood and articulated their racial identity in the United States. As the previous two chapters showed, the charros who mobilized in the 1940s and '50s subscribed to a politics of respectability that rested, in part, on demonstrating Mexican Americans' proximity to whiteness. They cultivated interpersonal relations with Anglos and used tactics of negotiation and persuasion to access white institutional power, whether the police state in Los Angeles or the economy in San Antonio. With the advent of civil rights laws and the expansion of redistributive programs, claiming whiteness or demonstrating respectability was no longer the most obvious strategy for redress. Instead, it became necessary to articulate a coherent identity as an oppressed group—to shift, as historian Nancy MacLean has argued, "from pursuing whiteness to claiming brownness."[2] Thus, it was in this period that Mexican Americans began to articulate more forcefully their distinct experiences of racialization: conquest, displacement from the land, economic subjugation, and ongoing discrimination on the basis of language, culture, and heritage. They lobbied for redistributive and compensatory programs that addressed their specific needs and experiences, such as bilingual education and publicly financed celebrations of Mexican heritage. Increasingly, they could count on the support of Latino public officials, elected in the wake of civil rights laws and voter registration drives, rather than making overtures across racial lines to politicians who were almost exclusively white, as in years past.

All of this work relied on cultivating a shared racial identity within often-fractured ethnic Mexican communities, and the charro provided important grist for the mill. This was especially true in Colorado, the subject of this chapter, where ties to Mexico were much weaker than in the border states of Texas, California, and Arizona, and where disparate racial identifications among Spanish-speaking peoples had long impeded their political mobilization. By the 1960s, much of the ethnic Mexican population of Colorado identified as "Hispano," not Mexican, and many did not identify with the histories of racialization espoused by the Chicano movement, especially when emanating from places with large populations of Mexican immigrants and their children. Instead, they traced their origins to what historians have called the Hispano homeland—an interconnected web of rural villages, sheep-based economies, and mining towns established during the first push of Spanish

The "Hispano homeland," featuring places of origin and urban destinations for many of Colorado's Hispanos/ethnic Mexicans in the 1970s. By Jennifer Tran and Alexander Tarr.

colonial settlement northward in the sixteenth and seventeenth centuries. Though the Hispano homeland later expanded and evolved through regional migration, it remained both spatially and culturally isolated from Mexico, and Hispanos were more likely to identify with Spanish histories of settlement and baroque forms of Spanish culture than anything related to Mexican nationalism.[3] It was only in the early twentieth century, when Hispano villagers migrated farther north into Colorado for wage work in railroads, steel mills, coal mines, cattle ranches, and sugar beet fields, that they interacted with Mexican migrant laborers and Mexican culture more regularly.[4] Yet the number of Mexican migrants to New Mexico and Colorado was small compared to other states, even at the height of the Mexican Revolution, and Mexican cultural nationalism in popular culture never took hold in Colorado to the same degree as it did in places like California or Texas.[5] As a result, there was little sense of a shared identity *as* Mexicans, and little political movement in the name of a coherent ethnic or racial community.

This began to shift in the years after World War II, as both Hispanos and Mexican migrants moved to Colorado's cities in large numbers. By the mid-1950s, Hispanos were leaving the rural villages of their historic homeland in ever larger numbers, seeking work in Albuquerque, Española, Santa Fe, Phoenix, Denver, Pueblo, and other regional cities. At the same time, migration by Mexican nationals to Colorado's cities also increased, spurred by shifts in seasonal farm labor and the expansion of urban manufacturing and public services.[6] By 1980, there were thirty-eight thousand Hispanos in Denver, making them 7.7 percent of the city's total population, while in Pueblo, 15 percent of the population identified as Hispano and another 17 percent identified as Mexican.[7] In both cities, ethnic Mexicans' political turnout was low, in part because of long histories of disidentification among those who identified as Hispanos, Spanish Americans, and Mexicans.[8] Still, as all these groups urbanized in Colorado, their specific origins mattered less than the conditions they now shared: de facto segregation in public schools, inadequate representation in state and local politics, discrimination on the basis of language and cultural heritage, and exclusion from public art and history institutions, to name just a few.[9]

In this context, Hispano and Mexican leaders turned to the charro as a vehicle for forging a shared racial identity, with the goal of building a more inclusive and responsive urban public sphere. Focusing on the cities of Denver and Pueblo, this chapter examines some of their initiatives. After giving an overview of the Pueblo and Denver charro associations, it explores how they pursued more equitable forms of representation in Colorado's public education, history, and art institutions. The first initiative was a 1973 curriculum guide about charros and vaqueros composed by Lena Archuleta, a Hispana educator from rural New Mexico, which was meant to be used for bilingual education in Denver Public Schools. The chapter then considers efforts by charros in Pueblo to craft more inclusive public history through a sister city partnership with Mexican cities, integration of the Colorado State Fair in Pueblo, and expanded Hispanic participation in Pueblo's celebrations of the American Bicentennial in 1976. Returning to Denver, the chapter closes by considering the effort among Hispano and Chicano legislators to diversify public art at the state capitol through their proposal for a bronze charro statue, which failed to materialize.

Not all of these initiatives succeeded, to be sure, but the charro's flexibility as a symbol of economic autonomy and Mexican cultural nationalism was essential to their gaining traction at all. The charro provided a shared reference point, rooted in agrarian histories and cultures, that could motivate and give meaning to ethnic Mexicans' struggles for full participation in urban public life, even though diverse Spanish-speaking peoples related to and made meaning of the charro's symbolism in different ways. Among Hispanos, who otherwise lacked meaningful attachment to Mexican cultural nationalism, the charro nonetheless resonated, both because he allowed them to express their longing for rural heritage amid rapid urbanization and because he represented histories of land ownership at a time when Hispanos were struggling to hold on to their village and grazing land.[10] Among those who identified as Chicanos, the charro fit neatly within the Chicano movement's embrace of icons associated with the Mexican Revolution, such as Pancho Villa and Emiliano Zapata, both of whom are remembered and valorized as charros. For more recent generations of Mexican migrants, the charro was a direct symbol of Mexican identity and Mexican nationalism that assuaged the poverty, exclusion, and dehumanization they too often experienced. For all of these groups, the charro represented highly valued connections to rural land and skilled labor that had been disrupted by persistent displacement, labor migration, and urbanization, whether in the U.S. or Mexico—processes that defined a shared ethno-racial identity across time and across borders. On this basis, he represented a powerful source of unity through which to participate in American public life.

THE PUEBLO AND DENVER CHARRO ASSOCIATIONS

By 1978, there were six charro associations in Colorado: three in Denver, two in Pueblo, and one in Gunnison.[11] The leaders of these charro associations were actively involved in the movement to transform urban public institutions and access public resources on behalf of *all* ethnic Mexicans, whether they identified as Hispanos, Spanish Americans, Chicanos, Mexican Americans, or Mexicanos. This chapter focuses on the Denver and Pueblo charro associations because they often worked together as one unified bloc, but also because their work illustrates well the divergent racial and urban geographies of those two cities.

Colorado's first charro association, the Pueblo Charro Club, was founded in 1967 and received accreditation from the FMCH two years later, at which point they changed the group's name to the Asociación de Charros de Pueblo/ Pueblo Charro Association.[12] The Pueblo Charro Association was an indisputably Hispano organization. Its founders and members all had roots in those industries and institutions—mining, mills, and the military—that had drawn Hispanos into southern Colorado's urban industrial economy since the early twentieth century. Many came from Hispano villages across New Mexico and Colorado, then served in the Navy or Marines during World War II or the Korean War. As adults, nearly all worked at either Colorado Fuel and Iron (CF&I) or the Pueblo Army Depot, the major local employers of Hispanos and Mexicans. They were pro-union and pro-American, with pride in their rural Hispano roots. For example, cofounder Miguel "Torro" Torrez served in the U.S. Marine Corps during the Korean War and then worked for Pueblo's CF&I Coke Plant for thirty-five years. Ron Codina, who joined the association in 1973 and served as its president from 1979 to 1985, grew up riding horses in Walsenburg and Avondale (both small towns in southern Colorado), and worked at the Pueblo Army Depot for most of his life. Member Leonel "Leo" Arthur Romero served in the U.S. Navy and Seabees, then worked at the Pueblo Army Depot for twenty-eight years. Another early member, Francisco Manuel García, was born in Las Vegas, New Mexico, in 1939, served in the U.S. Navy for six years, and later worked as a mechanic in Pueblo. While most of the founders and members were Hispanos who had been born and raised in the villages of Colorado or New Mexico, a handful of Mexican migrants joined the group as well. Usually, though, they had migrated as children and came of age entirely in the United States. For example, founder John Delgado Guerrero was born in Guanajuato, Mexico, in 1915 and migrated to the United States with his parents when he was four years old. After a short stay in Kansas, he spent the rest of his life in Pueblo, where he worked at CF&I for forty years. In the organization's early days, there were as many as forty-two members with profiles similar to these: roots in the rural villages of the Hispano homeland evolved into adult lives as urban industrial workers in Colorado's mining, manufacturing, and military industries.[13]

Given their rural roots in the villages and ranches of New Mexico and Colorado, most of the men who joined Pueblo's charro association in the 1970s and '80s were avid outdoorsmen. However, as people removed from more recent histories of Mexican immigration or Mexican cultural nationalism, they did not have firsthand experience with charrería—they had to learn it. Manuel Gallegos, the organization's first president, grew up riding horses and helped his father raise cattle and sheep, but he, like the other men who formed the association, was not exposed to charro culture until he was an adult. He recalled that when the group first started, they used western saddles and American cowboy gear, knowing little about the proper charro dress and equipment, much like their counterparts in Los Angeles a generation before. Gallegos explained: "When this started we had an instructor come from Mexico. He showed us what was right and what was wrong."[14] As they became more skilled and knowledgeable, the Pueblo Charro Association worked to socialize their children and other participants into the norms and regulations of charrería and Mexican cultural nationalism writ large. As Gallegos reported, "We've had 36 or 38 families at one time involved in the association. We teach them the culture, the dress, and how to take care of their horses."[15] By teaching other Hispano families how to dress and perform as charros, Gallegos and leaders of the Pueblo Charro Association inculcated an expanded sense of Mexican origins among people who otherwise had little inclination to identify as such.

A few years after its founding, and after extensive fund-raising, the Pueblo Charro Association purchased a twenty-acre site on Thirty-Third Lane, just south of Highway 50 and nine miles east of central Pueblo. There, they constructed their own lienzo for practices and training. The lienzo was located near the village of Vineland, home to just a few hundred people, and surrounded by a rural area inhabited and worked primarily by Hispanos and Mexicans. The lienzo thus established the charros' presence within the Hispano homeland's traditional rural, village-based geography. At the same time, however, the Pueblo charros also sustained an urban presence, maintaining an office and conference room inside the Irish Pub at 108 Third Street in downtown Pueblo. The Irish Pub was a dynamic hub of social and political networking, owned and operated by charro Ted Calantino, which brought Hispanos together with the city's substantial population of European and Mexican immigrants.[16] Stretched across the interconnected rural and urban geographies of the Hispano homeland, the Pueblo Charro Association thus provided and maintained a multitude of physical spaces in which a shared racial identity could be forged around the practice and celebration of charrería.

In May 1972, with help from the Pueblo charros, Dave Pino and Tony López formed the Denver Charro Association. They immediately sought recognition from the FMCH, which they received in 1973. As with their Pueblo counterparts, most of the Denver charros had been born in Colorado or New Mexico, not Mexico, though some had moved periodically with their

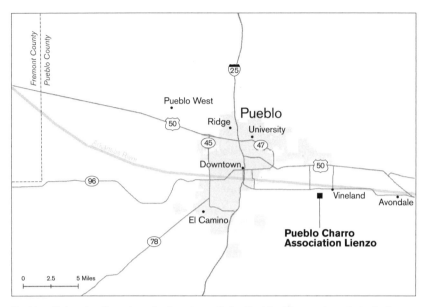

Pueblo, Colorado, featuring the location of the Pueblo Charro Association's lienzo.
By Jennifer Tran and Alexander Tarr.

families across the U.S. Southwest to follow work opportunities. As adults,
reflecting Denver's greater industrial diversity and sharper class inequality
compared to Pueblo, they worked in a range of occupations, both blue collar
and professional. Denver Charro Association founder Tony López was born
in 1924 in the "two-lane village" of Rodey, in southern New Mexico, and
moved to Denver with his mother when he was a child. He served in the U.S.
Army during World War II and won thirteen war medals, including a Bronze
Star and a Purple Heart, yet struggled to find steady work upon his return to
the United States. Eventually, he took a course in auto transmissions and
opened a repair shop, which he ran until his retirement. He helped form the
charro association after achieving economic stability as a small business
owner.[17] The Denver Charro Association also had several middle-class professional members, some of whom were the first to integrate the public institutions for which they worked. A notable example is Lena Archuleta, a
Hispana woman from rural New Mexico who became the first Latina principal of Denver Public Schools. Even more so than her husband Juan, who
was also a member of the Denver Charro Association, Lena became an
important spokesperson for charrería in Colorado, as we shall see later in this
chapter. Another professional member was Frank Carrillo, who served as the

The Denver Charro Association, 1972. Photograph by John Beard for *Denver Post*/Getty Images.

Denver Charro Association's secretary in its early years. Carrillo was born to parents from La Junta, Colorado—a major crossroads for Hispano ranching in the nineteenth and early twentieth centuries—who later moved to Pueblo, then Denver, where he worked for the Colorado State Patrol and the Adams County Sheriff's Office for forty years.[18]

In November 1972, approximately six months after its founding, the Denver Charro Association held its first charreada. Due to weather, the event had to be moved indoors to the Jefferson County Fairgrounds, and several events had to be abandoned because the space to which they relocated was too small. Nonetheless, the charreada was very well attended, with approximately 1,500 participants and spectators. For Hispanos, the event was clearly an opportunity to express pride in their cultural heritage. One attendee, Rebecca Sandoval Griggs, told a reporter from the *Rocky Mountain News,* "It's about time you started reporting about some of our cultural events. We're proud that someone is finally taking notice of our culture." Her sister, Felima Sandoval Kulinsky, chimed in, "We want other people to know that we're a happy people." But it was not only Hispanos who cohered in the celebration of charrería. The reporter described the audience as "a motley mix

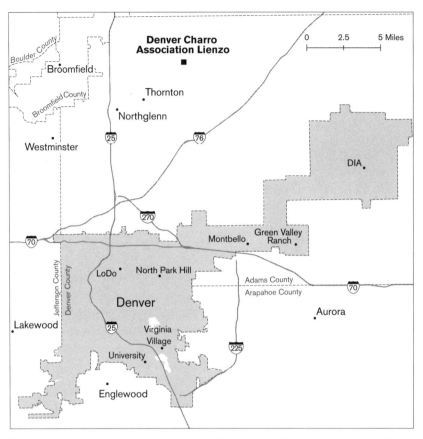

Denver, Colorado, featuring the location of the Denver Charro Association's lienzo. By Jennifer Tran and Alexander Tarr.

of mustachioed Chicanos, cowboy-hatted rural folk, and lollipop-wielding kids."[19]

Using the proceeds from this and other events, the Denver Charro Association purchased property on East 128th Avenue in Adams County, almost twenty miles north of central Denver, to build their own lienzo. At the time, Adams County was still largely agricultural, but real estate developers had begun carving farmland into subdivisions, creating suburban communities such as Northglenn and Thornton. By the early 1970s, these far-flung suburbs were becoming popular destinations for working-class whites, as well as some Hispanos and Mexicans, who sought affordable homes and high-quality schools within commuting distance of Denver.[20] The location of the Denver charros' lienzo was thus substantially different from its counterpart in Pueblo: whereas the Pueblo lienzo was located within a prototypically village-based Hispano geography, the Denver lienzo was located within an emerging hub of white and brown suburban flight, with little history of Hispano ranching. Indeed, through their decision to build the lienzo in Adams County, the Denver charros helped to launch a Mexican presence in suburbia, a process that will also be seen in Los Angeles in the next chapter.

Located in suburbia but with roots in Denver's urban Mexican communities, the Denver Charro Association enjoyed the support of a broad cross-section of the Denver community. The program for a 1973 charreada, for example, featured numerous advertisements by the Spanish-surnamed owners of restaurants, bakeries, and food wholesalers, as well as auto dealers, mechanics, and parts shops in central Denver. The Denver Charro Association also reached out to professional Mexican Americans and the new cohort of Chicano and Latino politicians, as well as elite Anglo-Americans, through their practice of naming "honorary members." In 1973, the association's honorary members included Governor John Love, state senator Roger Cisneros, Spanish-language radio station owners Andrés Neidig, George Sandoval, and Jesus Pineda, and Forrest F. Hammes, owner of a local advertising firm and past secretary of the Arapahoe County Fair.[21] In pursuing this form of outreach, the Denver charros—like their counterparts in San Antonio a generation before—nurtured local and regional networks with a broad range of influential leaders in the name of creating more open and responsive urban public institutions. Unlike their predecessors in the post–World War II period, however, most of their relationships were now with civic leaders who identified as Hispanos or Latinos.

Reflecting their personal backgrounds in the military and unionized industry, Colorado's charros expressed full faith in the power of American public institutions to facilitate opportunity for ethnic Mexicans in the United States. As the Denver charros explained, their primary motivation was to "represent the Mexican-American people of Colorado with pride and dignity."[22] At the same time, they believed that charrería could be a powerful way to improve racial and ethnic relations in Colorado. They were committed to "promoting goodwill among all Americans at every opportunity" and creating "a bridge for better understanding in the greater cosmopolitan Denver area."[23] For them, it was clear that these bridges should be built in the public sphere. Thus, almost immediately after their inception, the Colorado charro associations focused on creating more equitable racial relations within the public education, history, and art institutions of Denver and Pueblo.

Much of the Colorado charros' energy focused on the empowerment of Hispano and ethnic Mexican youth, both inside and outside formal educational settings. As Ron Codina later recalled, the founders of the Pueblo association "got it going as a way to promote pride in the heritage; they were trying to teach the kids about something that's been going on in Mexico for 400 years, to teach the kids a little discipline."[24] Their goal was "to instill in youth a true spirit of horsemanship with respect for their country [presumably the United States] and pride in their ancestry [presumably Mexican]," so that ethnic Mexican and Hispano youth could become better citizens and professionals.[25] But even while they focused on equipping individual children with the behavioral qualities and modest financial resources they deemed necessary for success, Colorado's charros were not naïve about the conditions of profound inequality that plagued ethnic Mexican youth. Indeed, discrimination and de facto segregation in public schools had been driving forces in the racialization of ethnic Mexican children in Colorado (and elsewhere) for decades.

Educational inequality had been a major concern for Hispanos and Mexicans in Colorado since at least the 1920s, when sugar and mining companies systematically recruited migrant laborers from southern Colorado and northern New Mexico as well as the interior of Mexico. Agricultural employers paid extremely low wages and provided substandard housing; migrants faced conditions of desperate poverty. To make ends meet, whole families, including young children, worked in the fields up to fourteen hours per day in intense heat. It was virtually impossible for Hispano and Mexican children in agricultural areas to get a decent education.[26] Conditions in urban public schools were scarcely better. As Hispanos and Mexican immigrants urbanized in large numbers during and after World War II, urban school districts across Colorado implemented segregated classrooms and, eventually, segregated schools that were not mandated by law, but rather enshrined in social practice. Dropout rates among Spanish-speaking students in some urban school districts were extraordinarily high; in Denver, fewer than 10 percent of Spanish-speaking students graduated from high school throughout the 1940s.[27] For these reasons, education was a persistent focus for Hispanos and Mexican Americans in Colorado, especially in the years after World War II.[28]

By the late 1960s, educational inequality still had not improved to any meaningful degree. In 1968–69, the U.S. Civil Rights Commission conducted an extensive study of public education in the U.S. Southwest. The commission reported severe segregation, underrepresentation of Mexican American teachers and administrators and their concentration in majority-Mexican American schools, underfinancing of schools with predominantly Mexican American students, teachers shunning or ignoring Mexican American children, and the suppression of Mexican American culture and the Spanish language. While these conditions prevailed across the U.S. Southwest, they were especially acute in Denver.[29] Thus, educational justice remained a key priority for both Hispano leaders and the Chicano movement in Denver. The Crusade for Justice, led by former boxer Rodolfo "Corky" Gonzáles, organized walkouts from Denver public high schools and established an autonomous community school, La Escuela Tlatelolco. Meanwhile, Hispanos and Mexican Americans continued their efforts to integrate and transform the city's public schools from within.[30]

In response to pressure from activist groups and the embarrassing findings of the U.S. Civil Rights Commission, state and federal legislators in the late 1960s and early '70s passed a series of laws meant to dismantle conditions of educational inequality. While national in reach, these decisions disproportionately targeted conditions in the U.S. Southwest. In 1968, Title VII of the Elementary and Secondary Education Act (known as the "Bilingual Education Act") recognized the special educational needs of children who spoke limited English and stipulated that the federal government would provide financial assistance for bilingual programs. By 1978, thirty-four states had repealed their English-only laws and enacted bilingual education.[31] Also in 1968, Congress authorized the creation of National Hispanic Heritage Week, which called upon educators to observe one week in September with appropriate ceremonies and activities.[32] In 1973, the U.S. Supreme Court decided the landmark case *Keyes v. School District No. 1*, which ordered the Denver school district to implement a mandatory desegregation plan—the first "northern" city so ordered, and the first where Hispanics were explicitly considered as a separate class for purposes of desegregation.[33] And in 1974, the Supreme Court in *Lau v. Nichols* affirmed the importance of bilingual education even in desegregated schools, stating that "there is no equality of treatment merely by providing students with the same facilities, textbooks, teachers, and curriculum; for students who do not understand English are effectively foreclosed from any meaningful education." To be sure, these decisions did not create wholesale educational equality. But they did create important openings for ethnic Mexican educators, parents, and allied activists in Colorado and across the nation to create public schools that better served their children.[34]

In numerous cases, they turned to the charro as an instrument of educational justice. Throughout the 1970s, the Denver and Pueblo charro associations partnered with the Latin American Education Foundation to host public charreadas, with proceeds dedicated to college scholarships for "Latin American" students—the identity they often embraced as a unifying label, rather than "Mexican" or "Hispanic."[35] On another occasion, the Denver Charro Association gifted twelve-year-old John Pineda, a Walsenburg boy detained at the Colorado Boys Ranch, with a Black Angus calf named "Charro" that he was to raise. When the animal reached maturity, John would be allowed to sell it, and he could apply the proceeds toward a college education.[36] Innovators in multicultural and bilingual education likewise viewed the charro as a source of cultural pride and racial uplift for ethnic Mexican students, as well as a way for Anglo-American students to learn about the nation's diverse cultural histories. Throughout the 1970s and '80s, multicultural education companies produced books, musical albums, and videos that used the charro to represent a colorful and honorable Spanish and Mexican past.[37]

Lena Archuleta, member of the Denver Charro Association and Hispana educator, wrote one such text. The daughter of a World War II veteran and shoe repairman, Archuleta had grown up in rural New Mexico. The valedictorian of her high school class, she attended the University of Denver, where she majored in Spanish with a minor in education. Thus, Archuleta was one of the very few Hispanos who graduated high school and obtained a college degree in the years before World War II. Afterward, she taught at schools in New Mexico until 1951, when she and her husband, Juan Archuleta, returned to Denver. There, she worked as a teacher and librarian at schools with substantial numbers of Spanish-speaking students before becoming the principal of Fairview Elementary School in 1974, making her the very first Hispano/Latino principal in the Denver Public School district. Through this work, Archuleta nurtured relationships with diverse ethnic Mexican leaders from across the political spectrum, cultivating a shared racial and cultural identity in the name of creating more inclusive and just urban public schools.[38]

To guide this work, Archuleta embraced the Mexican ranching past and its diverse cast of characters, especially the charro, which she saw as a unifying symbol for Hispano, Chicano, and Mexican immigrant children in south-western schools. In 1973, she authored a curriculum guide titled "The Rodeo and Cattle Industry: Its Rich Spanish-Mexican Heritage," which explores the history of charros and vaqueros to empower Hispano and ethnic Mexican students in the Denver Public Schools. In its distinction between charros and vaqueros, and inclusion of them both, her guide recuperates the agency of workers and indigenous people in the making of ranch cultures and econo-mies. Archuleta composed the guide using social studies and foreign lan-guage materials, as well as contributions from people she knew in the Denver and Pueblo charro associations. In writing the guide, she wanted to help teachers create a culturally responsive curriculum as Denver rolled out deseg-regated classrooms and bilingual education during the 1970s.[39]

Archuleta's curriculum guide makes a strong claim for the Mexican ori-gins of rodeo—that charros and vaqueros, whether in New Mexico or "Old" Mexico, were the "original cowboys." This claim is anchored in the title of the guide itself, which explicitly argues for the "rich Spanish-Mexican heritage" of the rodeo and cattle industry. She elaborates this central idea throughout the guide, challenging the racialization of cowboys and rodeo as white in American popular culture. Her guide claims: "The 'vaquero' was the earliest American horseman to work with cattle, the *first American cowboy* [emphasis added]." She elaborates: "The vaquero plied his trade in Mexico during the sixteenth century, and his methods and equipment were adopted and adapted by both the California vaquero and later by the Texas cowboy." Notably, too, in this sentence she redefines the word "American" in a transnational sense, to include Mexicans as inhabitants of the Americas, in a way remarkably similar to certain wings of the Chicano movement.[40] Later, the guide shows that virtually all of the elements that would come to make up American-style rodeo had their origins in Mexican practice. "The [western] saddle as we know it today is a Mexican invention," she writes.[41] Thus, though personally identified as Hispana, Archuleta demonstrated a commitment to cultivating a shared Spanish-Mexican identity, via the figures of the charro and the vaquero, among the diverse children and parents with whom she worked in Denver's public schools.

Reflecting Archuleta's commitments to bilingual education, the curricu-lum guide also devotes a great deal of space to etymology. It highlights the many Spanish-language words related to ranching that were incorporated into the English language during U.S. colonization. For example, in her dis-cussion of the animals that Spanish colonists brought to the "New World,"

Archuleta notes that the tough, hardy horses "were called *mesteños,* which means wild horses. Later, of course, the *Americanos* called these horses mustangs."[42] Her use of the Spanish-language "Americanos" subtly situates Anglo-American settlers as foreigners within the region, while asserting Hispanos' and Mexicanos' longer historical presence. In a gentle appeal to Denver students who might be struggling to learn English, the guide also highlights Americans' historic difficulties in learning Spanish as they moved west. For example, Archuleta writes, "[American] cowboys had difficulty in saying 'chaparreras', so they called these leg coverings 'chaps.'"[43] She lists many other words that "became the basis for American-English words" with only minor variation, such as la reata (lariat), cincho (cinch), jáquima (hackamore), bandana (bandanna), botas (boots), lazo (lasso), guitarra (guitar), and rancho (ranch).[44] Finally, she inscribes a persistent Spanish-Mexican linguistic influence on the physical landscape by showing how Spanish-language words were incorporated into the region's topography. She writes: "The Spanish *vaquero* (cowboy) used many words that are now in the English language such as: *mesa, canyon* (cañon), *sierra, arroyo.*"[45] Archuleta's guide thus marked the region's Spanish speakers as not only long established in the region but also as having inscribed meaningful place-names upon its landscape and contributed in valuable ways to its culture.

Drawing from the era's growing emphasis on experiential education, Archuleta's guide suggests many hands-on activities. These activities centered histories of Mexican ranch life, creatively adapted to urban life in Denver, as a source of pride and mobility for Hispano, Chicano, and Mexican students. For students in primary grades, the guide suggests that the teacher plan excursions to the annual stock show, city zoo, or historical museum; lead students in singing songs about ranch life in English and Spanish; stage make-believe rodeos or charreadas; and teach the students about farm animals, their products, and the Spanish names of both. For students in intermediate grades, the guide encourages students to conduct original research, build dioramas, dance "La Vaquerita," or use tape recorders to prepare a broadcast of a make-believe charreada. For students in the upper grades, the guide suggests that students make a giant mural with labels in Spanish, or that the teacher invite members of the Denver Charro Association to do demonstrations and talk about the various events of the charreada.[46]

Archuleta's guide also incorporated popular education techniques that valued learners' existing culture and knowledge. These same convictions were embedded in the Chicano movement's educational campaigns, including the pedagogical practices used at the Crusade for Justice's autonomous school, the Escuela Tlatelolco. In a similar spirit, Archuleta's guide emphasized the value of students' familiarity with and knowledge of the Spanish language, as well as charrería and sheep ranching. Thus, despite tactical and ideological differences among Chicano and Hispano activists, both turned to popular education techniques to counteract the dehumanization of Hispano, Chicano, and Mexican immigrant children in Colorado's public schools. In the guide's introduction, Archuleta advises teachers to conduct additional research as they are able, and she provides lists of potential resources, including contact information for the Denver Charro Association (which was her own phone number and address). But she also writes that "pupils will have much to add to the information as they participate in the various learning activities," and encourages teachers to see their students as active producers, not just consumers, of knowledge. In these ways, Archuleta built upon the very recent advances of federal legislation relating to bilingual education, while responding to the principal findings of the Civil Rights Commission's 1968–69 study: namely, that Mexican American children were rarely being drawn into classroom discussions, that their knowledge and potential contributions were consistently overlooked, and that they were punished for speaking Spanish.

In all these ways, Archuleta's curriculum guide centered Hispanos' and Mexicans' historical contributions to the making of southwestern ranch culture as the basis for a shared racial and cultural identity through which children could experience an empowering education. Centering principally on the distinct issues of language, culture, and heritage through which ethnic Mexicans had long been racially subjugated in the United States, the guide inverted the power dynamics bound up in Colorado's struggles for desegregation and bilingual education during the 1970s. These choices positioned the guide, and Archuleta herself, as an important bridge between the radical activism of the Chicano movement and efforts to integrate and hold accountable powerful public institutions like the Denver Public Schools from within. Her efforts, not only through the curriculum guide but also throughout her career, complemented the exhaustive labor performed by Hispano and Latino educational activists in the 1970s—and ever since.

It is difficult to know how teachers, students, and parents actually engaged Archuleta's curriculum guide, or the kind of impact it made upon their individual and collective understandings of the U.S. Southwest's history and culture. What *is* clear is that the demands and strategies for desegregation, bilingual education, and multiculturalism that Hispano and Latino activists pursued during the 1960s and '70s largely failed to significantly change patterns of educational inequality—not because of shortcomings or ideological fractures within the movement, though these were real, but because of demographic, spatial, and legislative shifts under way across Colorado. Already by 1973, when the *Keyes* decision was handed down, white families and some Hispano and Latino families were moving to the suburbs—including places in Adams County, location of the Denver charros' lienzo—where they found more affordable homes and hoped to avoid mandated school busing. Then, in 1974 voters passed the Poundstone Amendment to the state constitution, which prohibited the incorporation of surrounding suburban communities into the Denver school district, severely limiting the reach of the desegregation order wrought by *Keyes*.[47]

Isolated and segregated in Denver's older schools, Latino students continued to exhibit staggeringly high dropout rates. They remained subject to the same forces that had long been at play: the undervaluing of the Spanish language and Mexican culture; too few Latino teachers and administrators; the tracking of ethnic Mexican students into vocational, remedial, and English-language learner classes; and districts' refusal to apply for federal funding to create support services for Hispanic students.[48] Even so, in 1995 the court allowed Denver Public Schools to terminate its mandatory desegregation plan, arguing that the district had achieved all practicable results. As the court acknowledged, the widespread effects of suburbanization, coupled with the Poundstone Amendment, made higher rates of integration between Latino, Black, and white students not just unlikely, but virtually impossible to achieve. Thus, public education remained a primary site of struggle among Hispanos, Mexicans, and other Latinos in Colorado.[49]

SISTER CITIES AND FIESTA DAYS

One hundred miles south in Pueblo, a smaller city with deeper ties to the Hispano homeland, Hispanos and Chicanos were also battling for a more just city through boycotts, direct action, and lawsuits.[50] The members of the Pueblo Charro Association were central to this collective effort, focusing on the transformation of public institutions devoted to heritage and culture. Throughout the 1970s, they worked to center figures associated with Hispano and Mexican ranching histories in the city's public art landscape and its public history institutions. Through these efforts, they built bridges between Hispanos and members of the city's robust Chicano movement, but they also developed meaningful ties with people and places in central and western Mexico, where relatively little connection had existed before. These enhanced local and transnational connections generated a more coherent racial identity as Mexican Americans, rooted in a newfound sense of shared history in the rural ranching societies of what Alan Eladio Gómez has called "Greater Mexico."[51]

In this last respect, the Pueblo charros had a key ally in Henry Reyes, a Spanish-language radio broadcaster and local politician. The U.S.-born son of migrants from Puebla, Mexico, Reyes sought to promote Mexican culture, especially Mexican histories of ranching and rural life, in southern Colorado. He knew a great deal about charros and charrería, and he enjoyed collegial relationships with members of the Pueblo Charro Association, whose events he sometimes attended. As a local Chicano activist later recalled, "I was impressed with Henry's thorough knowledge of the events of the charreada. He was like a living history book and shared his knowledge with the audience at each performance of the charros."[52] For a decade spanning the mid-1960s to the mid-1970s, Reyes launched numerous initiatives that centered the charro and other ranchero cultural forms in Pueblo's urban public sphere. His efforts buttressed the charro associations' own activities and pushed them toward an increasingly transnational orientation that united Hispanos more firmly with Mexican migrants.

In the mid-1960s, Reyes was the driving force behind the creation of Fiesta Days as part of the Colorado State Fair. The Southern Colorado Agricultural and Industrial Association—a private organization of wealthy white businessmen—had established the Colorado State Fair in 1872 as a way to draw tourists, investors, and settlers to southern Colorado. For nearly a century, the Colorado State Fair celebrated Anglo settler histories of ranching, riding, and mining in southern Colorado. Attendance by Hispanos and ethnic Mexicans had always been low.[53] All of this troubled Reyes deeply. In promoting the idea of Fiesta Days, Reyes wanted to celebrate southern Colorado's Hispanic heritage and draw more Hispanos and Mexican Americans to the state fair. He knew that such an effort would require a more inclusive vision of the state's ranching history—one that encompassed charros, vaqueros, and shepherds. Yet Reyes remembers how difficult it was trying to persuade the Colorado State Fair Commission to include even one day in the fair's schedule:

There was an attitude from some officials that we didn't need to be attracting more Mexicans to the Fair . . . they couldn't even pronounce charros or mariachi. They wanted more Roy Rogers-type cowboys. But I told them that thousands of Hispanics will come to the Fair if you give us a day to celebrate our culture. And that turned out to be right.[54]

In 1966, Reyes capitalized on the appointment of Don Svedman, the new state fair manager, to make Fiesta Days a reality. Svedman was looking for ways to make the fair more profitable, and Reyes had plenty of ideas. Reyes learned that Svedman had recently seen a Thanksgiving Day performance by Mexican entertainer Antonio Águilar and his wife, Flor Silvestre.[55] Popularly known as "El Charro de México," Águilar had become instrumental in popularizing charrería among U.S. audiences. His show, a four-day "Mexican Festival and Rodeo," had been touring the U.S. for ten years by the time Svedman saw it.[56] When Reyes learned how much Svedman had enjoyed Águilar's performance, he convinced Svedman to create something similar for the Colorado State Fair.

Owing largely to Reyes's influence and Svedman's support, the Colorado State Fair governing board created the Fiesta Committee in 1966. Henry Gurule, Francisco Gallegos, and Florinda Gallegos—all Hispano members of Pueblo's charro association—served on the Fiesta Committee from its inception. The first Fiesta Days were held in 1967 and featured a performance by Águilar, who brought "his trained horses to acquaint people with the Mexican Cowboy—El Charro Mexicano."[57] Fiesta Days also included "Noche de Fiesta" as well as a Catholic Mass, a parade, and musical performances. Reflecting the charros' enduring interest in education, proceeds were contributed to Hispanic student scholarships.[58] A full charreada, performed by the Pueblo charros in competition with another team, was added to Fiesta Days in the early 1970s. At that time, the Pueblo charros began to lobby state senator Paul Sandoval, the first Hispanic senator on the Colorado State Legislature's Joint Budget Committee, to create permanent funding for the event. Senator Sandoval promised his support and said he would try to line-item the money in the fair's budget. A complete charreada has been a fully funded and very popular feature of Fiesta Days and the Colorado State Fair ever since.[59]

Building on his success with Fiesta Days, as well as his popularity in regional Spanish-language radio, Reyes campaigned and won a position on the Pueblo City Council in 1969. He then served two four-year terms, including a stint as city council president in 1976–77. Reyes's election and long service was significant because Pueblo's Hispano and Mexican community, though numerically large, had long struggled to elect a co-ethnic representative because of the city's system of at-large elections and low voter turnout, as well as disidentification among Hispanos and Mexicans.[60] During his tenure on the city council, Reyes became a key advocate for the celebration of Mexican ranching cultures, including the charro, in Pueblo's public institutions. He also served as architect of the transnational social networks that would allow charrería to flourish in southern Colorado during the 1970s.

One of Reyes's first actions as city councilman was to build a sister-city partnership between Pueblo, Colorado, and Puebla, Mexico (his father's hometown). President Dwight Eisenhower had launched the sister-city program, which was intended to reduce global conflict through the development of personal relationships across national borders, in 1956. Southern Colorado State College (now Colorado State University–Pueblo) already had a long-standing partnership with the Universidad Popular Autónoma de Puebla. The president of SCSC, Victor Hopper, reached out to government officials in Puebla to initiate a sister-city partnership. Those officials in turn invited Hopper and a delegation, which included Reyes, to visit Puebla. Afterward, Reyes took the lead in developing the program.[61]

Reyes acknowledged that the main goal of the sister-city partnership was to bolster international relations, but an equally important goal for him was improving relationships among Anglos and ethnic Mexicans in Pueblo. He explained, "We were having problems with the Anglo community. The Anglo community was having trouble accepting things we stood for."[62] Reyes believed that exposure to elite forms of Mexican culture like charrería could help alleviate Anglo discrimination against Hispanos and Mexican Americans at home in Colorado. He also hoped that cultivating relationships with Mexican nationals might prove beneficial to ethnic Mexicans' struggles for more responsive and inclusive public institutions in Pueblo.

Toward that end, the trips that Reyes coordinated were lavish by design. The first delegation of 150 persons was greeted with decorated buses, banners, and balloons, and enjoyed numerous banquets and receptions. The 1973 delegation, which included 163 Puebloans, traveled on a Boeing 707 airplane chartered by Reyes and his radio station co-owner George Sandoval.[63] Similar trips that ultimately involved over three thousand people occurred annually until 1997, when Reyes stepped down as organizer of the collaboration. Reflecting on the importance of the exchanges, Reyes said: "Everything we've been told about Mexico many times is embarrassing, just negatively critical. But when [sic] we went there and found wonderful friendships and they treated us well. They took us into their homes which were beautiful and treated us like we were family; people [Puebloans] just couldn't believe it."[64]

The expanded transnational relationships that Reyes and others helped to build soon imprinted on Pueblo's physical landscapes through the creation of new public art. In 1973, Puebla officials donated a sculpture crafted by renowned Mexican artist Jesús Corro Ferrer, which sits prominently in front of Pueblo's city hall in the Sister Cities Plaza. The sculpture depicts an eagle made of steel plate mounted on a white concrete pedestal, with the seal of Pueblo and the coat of arms of Puebla on painted tile just below the eagle's talons. Notably, the city seal of Pueblo highlights the area's rural, agricultural features: it features a cow standing in a grassy field next to the Arkansas River, with the Sangre de Cristo Mountains and Old Fort Pueblo, the area's first permanent structure, in the background; an ear of corn and bushel of wheat are prominently depicted in the foreground. In this way, ranching was situated alongside agriculture and military exploration as emblems of the area's heritage, in ways that were simultaneously urban and transnational—thus providing a shared sense of origins for Hispanos, Chicanos, and Mexican immigrants in Pueblo.

The local, regional, and transnational networks cultivated through Fiesta Days and the sister-city program laid the foundation for the Pueblo charros' most ambitious vision yet: hosting the first International Charro Congress and Competition as part of celebrations of the bicentennial of the American Revolution in 1976. In doing so, they centered Mexico's national sport within celebrations of the American birthday party, while cohering and galvanizing Hispanos, Chicanos, and Mexicans to participate fully in the U.S.'s premiere public history event of the decade.

THE BICENTENNIAL CHARRO

The evolution of bicentennial celebrations illustrates powerfully the multi-cultural opening of U.S. public institutions in the 1960s and '70s. Bicentennial preparations were initially carried out by the American Revolution Bicentennial Commission (ARBC), which Congress created in 1966. The ARBC had advocated holding the national birthday party, which was expected to cost more than $1.5 billion, in just one historic city—either Philadelphia or Boston. However, after significant public pressure, in 1973 the ARBC was dissolved and replaced by the American Revolution

Bicentennial Administration (ARBA), headed by John Warner, who had served as secretary of the U.S. Navy during the Vietnam War and would later become the U.S. senator from Virginia.[65]

Under Warner, the new organization infused the Bicentennial with a multicultural and populist spirit. Although the agency was still headquartered in Washington, D.C., Warner created new regional and statewide commissions to coordinate day-to-day planning. Instead of one central theme, ARBA identified three: (1) *heritage,* which honored not only the "founding fathers" and the "three great documents" but also forgotten people and places; (2) *festival,* which embraced the richness of U.S. diversity and promoted positive international relations through dance, drama, music, and the arts; and (3) *horizons,* which encouraged civic and social improvement, including initiatives that might benefit indigenous communities, immigrants, and communities of color.[66] Warner created a national advisory council of representatives from multiple ethnic, religious, geographic, and occupational groups, whom he charged with promoting a broader diversity of perspectives and strengthening public investment in the Bicentennial. Many state and regional commissions, including the one in Colorado, likewise created ethnic advisory committees or review boards to ensure diverse participation.[67]

Reconstituted in this way, the ARBA, like many other public agencies, provided significant institutional support for the "ethnic revival" that flourished in this period. As historian Matthew Jacobson has shown, the ethnic revival was especially popular among white Americans, for whom identification as Italian, Polish, Greek, or some other European ethnicity was one way to negotiate critiques of white supremacy emanating from the era's civil rights and Black Power movements.[68] In Colorado and other states of the U.S. West, these impulses translated into bicentennial projects that celebrated the white settler experience via histories of European and immigrant westward migration as "pioneers." White (or white-dominated) communities and organizations used the ARBA's institutional structure and financing to preserve pioneer villages, commission public artworks, and create local history museums that memorialized the white settler experience in the landscape. Yet people from historically marginalized communities, especially Chicanos, African Americans, and indigenous groups, also benefited substantially from the ARBA's newly inclusive vision. With federal and state support, they succeeded in adding to the archive, creating history and art museums, and preserving and celebrating aspects of their cultural heritage. In many cases, they secured access to public institutions, organizations, and physical spaces previously denied them.[69]

Colorado's charros were among them. The Pueblo Charro Association earned bicentennial sponsorship and financing to host the first International Charro Congress and Competition in Pueblo in 1976. The Pueblo charros' bicentennial vision was grand and ambitious. They hoped "to reintroduce a rediscovered cultural heritage of the Southwest; promote the 'Charrería'; to enhance the relationship between the U.S. and Mexico; to provide an opportunity for future participants in the sport and to expose contributions of the Mexican-American in the development of the Southwest." These goals clearly illustrate the Pueblo charros' multiple interests in empowering local people of diverse origins, rewriting regional history, and cultivating transnational relationships. To achieve these goals, they planned to invite twenty charro teams, from both the United States and Mexico, for a full week of competitions, meetings, parades, dinners, and dances in Pueblo. They also intended to establish a permanent lienzo, riding school, and cultural center with research facilities that would support the practice of charrería in Colorado well after the Bicentennial's conclusion.[70]

Preparations began as early as 1971, when members of the Pueblo Charro Association joined the Pueblo Chamber of Commerce's newly formed Centennial-Bicentennial Task Force. The chamber—an organization dominated by real estate developers, small business owners, and media companies—appears to have been enthusiastic, because coverage of the charro association and its bicentennial vision appeared frequently in the chamber's newsletter. The Pueblo Charro Association, in turn, formed a centennial-bicentennial subcommittee charged with coordinating the planning. Members included a diverse set of Hispanos from the charro association, as well as Mexican Americans who held positions within related public institutions in Pueblo. Thus, in addition to Henry Gurule, Ted Calantino, Phil Martínez, and Frank Guerra from the charro association, Douglas Patino, vice president for student affairs at Southern Colorado State College, also joined the committee.[71] Over the next few years, diverse representatives from the FMCH, the Pueblo City Council, and the Colorado Centennial-Bicentennial Committee (CCBC) also joined in the planning.[72]

In early June 1974, the charro association formally submitted its application to the CCBC. The application's first stop was the Colorado Multi-Ethnic Committee, a statewide body akin to the national advisory council created by John Warner as part of the multicultural reorganization of the ARBA; its members included many of Colorado's most notable Black, Hispano, and indigenous leaders.[73] The Multi-Ethnic Committee's primary role was to review and endorse applications for ARBA recognition and funding. At its very first meeting in August 1974, the Multi-Ethnic Committee endorsed the International Charro Congress and Competition as an official bicentennial event and sent the proposal up to the CCBC for state approval.[74]

The Pueblo Charro Association's proposal was embraced in part because it offered a clear opportunity to nurture positive international relations—a crucial goal for the nation's top brass given widespread discontent with the aggressive military and diplomatic interventions of the U.S. in Southeast Asia, Latin America, and elsewhere in the early 1970s. Cognizant of that fact, the Pueblo Charro Association framed their bicentennial project as an exercise in international friendship and goodwill. In the fall of 1974, while their application to the CCBC was still under review, the Pueblo Charro Association sponsored a trip to Guadalajara, Jalisco, to participate in that year's National Charro Congress and Competition.[75] While competitive trips like this would normally be attended only by charros and their family members, in this case the Pueblo charros invited a broad cross-section of Pueblo delegates to attend. In preparation for the trip, the Pueblo Charro Association distributed an information packet that declared to the delegates: "Your visit to Guadalajara, Jalisco is an important contribution in international relations. We hope that each one of us will return to Pueblo having established a friendship with a person from Mexico."[76] On the eve of the trip, Takaki, acting in his capacity as president of the Pueblo City Council, formally proclaimed the first week of November 1974 to be "International Charro Week" in Pueblo because "the Charro has contributed greatly to the socio-economic and cultural development of the Southwest" and because "the friendship of the United States of America and the United States of Mexico is of great significance to the Western hemisphere." Takaki also noted that the states of Jalisco and Colorado were taking steps to become "sister states," a higher-scale partnership akin to the sister-city program between Pueblo and Puebla.[77] In this way, Takaki and the Pueblo charros situated the charro at the center of a budding transnational friendship with diplomatic as well as cultural significance. Equally important for race relations back home in Pueblo, the trip served to educate Hispanos and others about a Mexican ranching tradition to which many had had little exposure. Leopoldo Trujillo and Henry Gurule, two members of the Pueblo Charro Association who joined the delegation to Guadalajara, explained, "The trip was not only a rewarding experience in international relations, but also a significant learning experience in preparing for the 1976 event in Pueblo, Colorado."[78]

One of the lessons they surely learned was that charrería in Mexico was an extravagant affair associated with the Mexican political and economic elite. On their first day in Guadalajara, the Pueblo delegates listened to a speech by Jalisco governor Alberto Orozco Romero. There were multiple luxurious banquets, dances, and award ceremonies. Douglas Patino, for example, was honored for his work promoting charrería in the U.S. and given the Silver Spur award, one of the FMCH's highest honors. In accordance with the congress's theme, "La Mujer/The Woman," an entire day honored the queens of Mexican and U.S. charro associations, including Ruby Tafoya, queen of the Pueblo Charro Association. Women also attended a special reception hosted by the governor's wife, where the world's leading female bullfighter, Conchita Cintrón, was honored as a special guest. Upon their return to the U.S., the Pueblo Chamber of Commerce reported that "the lavish dinners, colorful entertainment, ceremonial presentations and exciting charreada (Mexican rodeo) were a royal treat to Charro members who had worked diligently to snare the top honor." The chamber's newsletter then issued a friendly challenge to its readers: "How are you going to top all that, Pueblo?"[79]

"Topping all that" required, first and foremost, official ARBA endorsement, which came through in March 1975, a few months after the delegation's return from Guadalajara. Acting upon the endorsement of Colorado's Multi-Ethnic Committee, the CCBC approved the International Charro Congress and Competition as an official centennial-bicentennial activity. The CCBC also awarded the Pueblo Charro Association $10,000 in public funding, with the requirement that they locate matching funds.[80]

With official endorsement and partial funding in hand, the hard work of planning and fund-raising accelerated. That spring, U.S. and Mexican charros engaged in near-constant transnational activity to coordinate and promote their bicentennial events. José Islas Salazar, president of the FMCH, visited Denver on May 1, 1975, for a meeting. Four days later, a delegation from Pueblo visited Puebla for another sister-city exchange, this one timed to coordinate with Cinco de Mayo, where they presented a fringed ARBA flag and five ARBA pins to Mexican president Luis Echevarría Álvarez.[81] Extensive cross-border visits like these persisted throughout the duration of bicentennial planning and beyond. These visits, much like their counterparts in San Antonio a generation before, built upon and solidified the networks that Reyes and others had established through the sister-city and sister-state partnerships. They also linked southern Colorado's Hispanos, who previously had only weak relationships with Mexicans and Mexican nationalism, more firmly to the world of transnational cultural production associated with charros and charrería. Notably, too, these transnational relationships were increasingly structured by U.S. public institutions, like the ARBA, rather than solely through interpersonal or business networks, as in years past.

Next was the issue of preparing the physical space. Under the direction of secretary Ted Calantino, the charro association began working on architectural plans for the lienzo and related facilities. The vision was to include an arena, park, baseball field, parking lot, and horse stables, all of which would be open to the general public; the cultural center with research facilities seems to have been scrapped.[82] The association also ordered a bicentennial flag, featuring the ARBA logo, to fly at the lienzo alongside the other flags they regularly displayed (presumably an American flag and a Mexican flag, and perhaps a Colorado state flag as well).[83] Still, while qualifying competitions would be held at the lienzo, the Pueblo charros always hoped to hold the final competition as part of Fiesta Days. They determined that the county fairgrounds, where Fiesta Days was held, would not only accommodate far more spectators but also signal the full rights of Hispanos and Mexican Americans to occupy and use that symbolically important location in the city's cultural life. Thus, in late December 1975, the Pueblo Charro Association made a formal presentation to the Colorado State Fair Commission requesting that the final two days of the international charro competition be included as part of Fiesta Days 1976. Their request was granted.[84]

As noted, paying for the charros' expansive bicentennial program would require $10,000 in matching funds. Association members attended a CCBC seminar meant to help applicants find appropriate financing for their events.[85] In addition, they planned a slew of fund-raisers that targeted local Hispanos and Mexicans for support, often through the celebration of both Hispano and Mexican cultural forms such as Hispano music, ballet folklórico, and tamale sales.[86] But the Pueblo charros' fund-raising strategy mostly rested on applying for special federal funds for groups who were planning inclusive bicentennial programs, especially those likely to appeal to underrepresented communities or to cultivate international relations. The bicentennial charreada promised to do both.

In April 1975, shortly after learning that their event had been approved as an official bicentennial event, the Pueblo Charro Association made a new grant application to the ARBA in which they showed how their event met the four criteria required of organizations seeking supplementary funds. Their application demonstrates their sophisticated understanding of the newly multicultural political landscape created by the ARBA and other institutions, as well as how they might position charrería to create new opportunities for ethnic Mexicans in Colorado. First, the applicants argued that the International Charro Congress and Competition was a project of *special international significance* because it "fosters international friendship by matching youthful competitors from both Mexico and the United States in sports of skill and talent. The friendship of the United States and Mexico has great significance to the Western Hemisphere and the magic and excitement of the charrería can only cement these bonds."[87] This claim built upon and cemented the work that Reyes, the Pueblo charros, and others had been doing to develop transnational ties between southern Colorado and Mexico; it also signaled a stronger sense of shared cultural heritage among Hispanos and Mexicans.

Second, the applicants noted that the international charro competition would encourage an *overall balanced bicentennial program* that would not be centered solely on the Atlantic seaboard, but across the continent. They asked Warner and his staff to honor "the many Hispanic people who contributed to this nation's birth and development." They observed that charrería was an integral part of the lives of Hispanic people in the Southwest and argued that ARBA's financial support would broaden the reach of the bicentennial commemoration to their region.

Third, the applicants claimed to meet the requirement of *emphasizing ideas associated with the revolution* by framing U.S. independence as only one event within a global struggle for freedom during the eighteenth and nineteenth centuries, in which Mexico had also participated. They wrote:

> The struggle for freedom did not begin or end with the American Revolution, but it was merely an episode in an epic, universal struggle to eradicate tyranny and autocracy. The concept of government by consent of the governed was a dream that our neighbors to the south shared with America's founding fathers. Mexico and the United States share a heritage filled with the ideals and dreams which spawned a revolution, and it was the charros, cowboy/cavaliers, who helped free the Mexican people to self-government.[88]

By situating the charro as a freedom fighter akin to Boston's Tea Party patriots, the Pueblo Charro Association drastically simplified the charro's historical roles in both the war for independence from Spain and the Mexican Revolution: charros had actually fought on both sides, and after the revolution, they were responsible for elevating a tradition associated with the conservative landed elite to the status of national sport.[89] Nonetheless, the Pueblo charros' claim resisted the nationalist impulse of American bicentennial celebrations. Instead, and quite remarkably, they used the charro to show that struggles for freedom and democracy were not, and had never been, exclusive to the United States.

Fourth, the applicants noted that charrería was popular among a wide cross-section of ethnic Mexicans in the United States and would therefore satisfy the requirement that funded projects *encourage maximum participation and interest by citizens.* In particular, they claimed that charrería was "especially relevant to youth, women, minority, ethnic groups, and Native Americans." While they did not elaborate this claim for women or indigenous people, they did note that charrería had become increasingly popular among Hispanos, "who have started to discover this rich heritage and with pride."[90] The ARBA apparently found all of these statements compelling because the Pueblo charros' request for supplemental funding was approved, allowing the International Charro Congress and Competition to proceed with almost all of its funding coming from public agencies.

For a time, the association's officers shouldered the planning and fundraising work. However, in late 1975, the Pueblo Charro Association hired two staff members: Toby Madrid, former secretary-coordinator for the city's Chicano Planning Council, and Elisa Cortinas, a former outreach worker for Headstart.[91] These appointments suggest, first, that the Pueblo Charro Association had at least some financial resources at its disposal to hire staff. Second, they show that ethnic Mexican people with a range of racial identities as well as political and ideological affiliations—from the Chicano movement to War on Poverty organizations like Headstart—were invested in using charrería to create more responsive public institutions in urban Colorado.

As the International Charro Congress and Competition loomed nearer, the Pueblo and Denver charro associations committed to extensive public appearances at both "western" and "Mexican" events across Colorado. In January 1976, both associations participated in the National Western Stock Show at the Denver Coliseum, itself an official bicentennial event.[92] The Pueblo and Denver charros also worked to extend charrería to surrounding towns, suburbs and cities, including those places where ethnic Mexicans were few in number or poorly represented in local politics.[93] These appearances promoted charrería among both Anglo-American and Mexican audiences, while inserting the charro into whitewashed histories of cowboys, ranching, and rural life in Colorado. In addition, the associations continued their weekly competitive charreadas. Rotating between the lienzos in Pueblo and Denver, these Sunday afternoon competitions helped the charro teams practice for the international competition later that year. But they also built a fan base among the region's Hispanos and Mexicans, many of whom—like the charros themselves a decade earlier—knew little or nothing about charrería and the Mexican nationalist tradition from which it developed.[94]

Finally, in late August 1976—well after the official bicentennial weekend in early July had ended, but while the region was still fully aglow with the "spirit of '76"—the much-anticipated International Charro Congress and Competition took place. In an article in the *Pueblo Chieftain* announcing the week's events, journalist Ron Martínez trumpeted, with no small amount of hyperbole, "Not since the arrival of the horse to the Americas via the Spanish conquistadors has there been an event as spectacular and historic as the upcoming International Charro Competitions here this week." Martínez justified his over-the-top enthusiasm: "Why so? Because it was the introduction of the horse as a work animal by the Spaniards and perfection given to the art of horsemanship by the Mexican-Indian and mestizo that gave birth to the Mexican jaripeo. It was also this beginning that provided the foundation for American rodeo and cowboy lore."[95] Thus, like other ethnic Mexicans and Hispanos in Colorado and elsewhere, Martínez claimed that charros were, in fact, the "original cowboys." But he did so through subtle references to both the Spanish origins of the sport—thus appealing to Hispanos—as well as its "perfection" by Mexican-Indians and mestizos—racial identifications that would resonate with Chicanos.

As planned, the activities coincided with Fiesta Days at the 1976 Colorado State Fair, which had come to attract more than forty thousand people since its creation by Reyes a decade prior, making it the most popular day of the fair. The charros' opening event was a parade that wound through the streets of downtown Pueblo; it included a diverse set of Hispano, Chicano, Mexican American, and Mexican representatives. The parade's grand marshal was Paul Sandoval, state senator from Denver and part of the much-celebrated cohort of Chicano politicians who took office in Colorado during the 1970s, who was escorted by members of the Pueblo Charro Association riding as his "guard of honor." A delegation of sister-city participants from Puebla also participated in the parade. So did numerous queens representing local Mexican American organizations, including the Pueblo chapters of LULAC and the GI Forum, and visiting female royalty from cities and towns across the region that were racially marked as both Anglo and Hispano.[96] Subsequent activities, spread across six days, included a meeting of the U.S. Congress of Charro Associations, multiple Catholic Masses, barbeques and cocktail parties, a queens' ball, and, of course, daily competitions between charro associations from the U.S. and Mexico. Most of these activities were held at the Pueblo Charro Association's lienzo on Thirty-Third Lane, the Sangre de Cristo Arts Center in downtown Pueblo, or the state fairgrounds.[97]

Eight teams (down from the original vision of twenty) were scheduled to compete: four from the U.S. Southwest, and four from Mexico. The U.S. teams hailed from Pueblo and Denver, whose members rode as a combined Colorado team, as well as from Sonol, California; Del Rio, Texas (the reigning U.S. champions); and Phoenix, Arizona. The Mexican teams were to come from León, Guanajuato (the reigning Mexican champions); the sister city of Puebla, Puebla; and two teams from Ciudad Juárez, Chihuahua. As the events neared, however, the Juárez teams telegrammed to announce they were unable to cross the border due to quarantines on their horses imposed by Mexico.[98] Thus, competitors were reduced still further to six teams, including just two from Mexico. Audiences were relatively small at the daily events, never numbering more than 150 persons. Yet Mexican and U.S. dignitaries and businessmen were consistently among them. Finally, after several days of competition, the Phoenix team, apparently to everyone's surprise, emerged as the victors. The Phoenix team defeated not only the Colorado and California teams, but also the reigning Mexican champs from Guanajuato and those from Texas, who were characterized as being "over-confident."[99]

The Pueblo and Denver joint team scored low in the competitions, which they attributed to the youth of their organizations as well as the unavailability of year-round instructors from Mexico. Yet they believed they had made a "respectable showing" and earned the respect of their Mexican peers. They chalked up the experience as a crucial opportunity to learn about charrería from teams across the U.S. Southwest, including places like California and Texas, where charrería was more established, and especially from the Mexican teams who had crossed the international border to compete. Pueblo association member Gabby Granillo reported: "We learned more about charreada tonight from Puebla and León that we couldn't have learned in 50 years by ourselves." He remained optimistic that the Pueblo charros would continue to improve: "Pueblo will close the gap with the Mexican teams. We will be able to compete on the same level next year."[100]

The International Charro Congress and Competition of the bicentennial year was a landmark achievement in other ways, too. It succeeded in shifting southern Colorado's prevailing public history narratives to include the charro and the vaquero. It also united Hispanos with Chicanos, Mexican Americans, and Mexican immigrants in ways that would have been highly unlikely just a decade before. The Pueblo charros thus successfully cultivated a stronger sense of shared cultural heritage and shared racial identity to guide ethnic Mexicans' pursuit of a more inclusive and equitable American public sphere.

A FAILED BRONZE

In Denver, a city with longer and more deeply entrenched histories of white supremacy, the charro was less successful as a unifying figure for accessing public institutions, at least with regard to the transformation of public art. This became apparent in the failed effort, led by Hispano and Mexican American politicians, to install a bronze charro statue on the state capitol grounds at Denver's civic center. The project struggled not only with funding and the lack of material support from public agencies, but also because of the fraught nature of political relationships between Hispanos and Chicanos, who disagreed on tactics for transforming urban public life.

In 1981, state senator Polly Baca Barragán, a Democrat representing the Adams County suburb of Thornton (near the Denver charros' lienzo), and state representative Richard Castro, a Democrat representing Denver's Westside, cosponsored a senate resolution allowing for the installation of a charro statue on the capitol grounds as a tribute to the state's Hispanic people. Both Baca Barragán and Castro traced their roots to the Hispano homeland and were well connected with members of the charro associations. Baca Barragán, for example, grew up in Weld County, Colorado, and was a descendant of Spanish colonists; she had served on the board of directors for the Latin American Research and Service Agency (LARASA) alongside Lena Archuleta. Castro grew up in Walsenburg, Colorado, and worked as a migrant laborer before moving to Denver for college and community service work. Both Baca Barragán and Castro had also been affiliated with and influenced by Chicano movement politics, though both eschewed militant tactics of direct action and instead valued working within institutions in order to transform them. Over the years, these positions had put them, especially Castro, at odds with more radical factions of the movement.[101] In this context, they saw the charro statue as a unifying symbol around which Hispanos, Chicanos, and Anglos in Colorado might cohere. The twenty-foot bronze was to be installed on the state capitol grounds, on the block between Colfax and Fourteenth Avenues bounded by Lincoln and Broadway Streets. Their resolution passed both houses unanimously, though no public funding was provided.[102]

A committee headed by Denver businessman Gary Archuleta selected local artist Emanuel Martínez to create the sculpture. By the time of the commission, Martínez had become well known for his artistic contributions to the Chicano movement and the vernacular landscapes of Denver's Chicano and Black neighborhoods. He, too, had deep roots in the Chicano movement: he had produced pamphlets, flyers, and logos for the Crusade for Justice, the Chicano movement organization led by Corky Gonzales, and had filled the walls of that organization's Denver headquarters, as well as numerous other city buildings, with murals. Martínez had also organized with Cesar Chavez in California and traveled to Mexico to study with renowned muralist David Alfaro Siqueiros. By the time of the commission for the charro sculpture, however, Martínez's relationship with the movement had become strained. Despite his artistic and organizing contributions, Martínez remained persistently poor, a fact he could not reconcile with the movement's stated goals of economic justice and the exalted nature of many of his male colleagues. After a lawyer stole the commission for one of his paintings, Martínez stepped back from the movement and entered an "entrepreneurial period," investing in real estate as well as several businesses. He worked on the charro statue during this period of reassessment and reinvention.[103]

Martínez's approach to the charro statue reflected his changing understanding of Chicano identity politics and his growing reluctance to produce art on behalf of the movement. Martínez deliberately chose to cast an anonymous charro, noting: "Emiliano Zapata was one of the best charros around. But I didn't do Pancho Villa or Zapata because it would become a political thing."[104] Surely part of Martínez's design choice derived from his alienation from the Chicano movement. But he may also have been referring to the controversy that had erupted earlier that year in Tucson, when a professional association of Mexican journalists gave a fourteen-foot statue of Pancho Villa, mounted on a horse, to the city. Many in Tucson's Mexican American community, especially immigrants and working-class people, welcomed the Villa statue. But civic elites and business people—both Anglo and Mexican American—were loath to center a revolutionary working-class Mexican hero in downtown Tucson's public art landscape. Tucson's business elite commissioned a second—and much larger—statue of the Spanish Franciscan missionary Eusebio Kino, which they installed just a few miles away from the

Villa statue in 1989. The affair exposed the economic and ideological fault lines among ethnic Mexicans in Tucson, especially in relationship to histories of Spanish colonialism and Mexican migration, which were in some ways remarkably similar to those in Denver. Surely Martínez was aware of this fraught political climate when he chose to cast an anonymous charro for the Colorado state capitol.[105]

Despite Martínez's artistic renown and his attempts at political neutrality, the Colorado charro statue was never built. Certainly, there were initial steps forward. Martínez worked on the statue throughout the summer and fall of 1981, and in September, as part of the kickoff for that year's Hispanic Heritage Week, he unveiled a two-foot model during a short ceremony at the capitol building.[106] However, Martínez never had a chance to complete the full-scale statue. The primary issue seems to have been funding. The statue was estimated to cost $125,000, which was to be funded entirely through private contributions; the state made no investment of public funds, and private donors did not support the project. Perhaps the effort was not well organized or publicized, or perhaps Colorado's economic decline in the mid-1980s made money tight for working families. Or maybe the figure of the charro simply did not resonate with enough of Denver's ethnic Mexican community, who remained fractured in their ethnic identifications despite the hard work of the charro associations and other civic leaders to unify them. Regardless, when the money failed to materialize, the charro statue was abandoned.

Just a few years later, another statue honoring Colorado's Hispanic peoples was successfully installed in the very same location once reserved for the failed charro statue. This statue, which was also crafted by Emanuel Martínez, honored Joe Martínez, a Mexican American World War II hero from Denver. Unlike the charro statue, the Joe Martínez statue benefited from ample public investment. It was coordinated and partially funded by the Denver Commission on Cultural Affairs, a public agency, and another public agency, the Denver Parks and Recreation Department, allocated another $10,000. Private corporations and organizations known for their conservative, promilitary policies also donated generously: the Coors Brewing Company gave $14,000, and the Latin American Law Enforcement Association and the Hensel Phelps Construction Company both gave large donations. The rest came from small private donors.[107] Erected in July 1988, the finished statue depicts Joe Martínez in uniform, running with a Browning automatic rifle in his hands. Thus, the Mexican American military hero—not the charro— became the more effective means of unifying Denver's diverse ethnic

Mexicans and appealing to the state's business interests in order to create a more inclusive urban public art landscape.

The failure of Denver's charro statue reflected a broader issue: the decline of charrería in Colorado. Throughout the 1970s and early '80s, members of the Pueblo and Denver charro associations continued to travel across the U.S. Southwest and Mexico for competitions and performances, and in 1983, the Pueblo Charro Association again secured a major achievement when it hosted the U.S. National Charro Championships.[108] But by the mid-1980s, Colorado's charro associations were struggling. As many of the founders became elderly and died, few young people stepped in to take their place. The demise of the most visible aspects of the Chicano movement, which had centered land struggles and Mexican culture, was partly to blame, as was the fragile attachment to Mexican history and cultural nationalism in a region still dominated by U.S.-born Hispanos.

Economic changes in Colorado also played a role. Ron Codina, who served as president of the Pueblo Charro Association from 1979 to 1985, attributed the decline of his organization to economic restructuring in Pueblo. The city's largest employer, Colorado Fuel and Iron (CF&I), made many layoffs and closed numerous plants during the 1980s. Although these processes impacted the entire region, they were especially hard-hitting in southern Colorado and among the firm's ethnic Mexican unionized workforce. In Pueblo, two-thirds of the CF&I workforce, or roughly 3,500 people, lost their jobs; many of those workers were members of the charro association, "It ended about the time the mill went down," Codina recalled. "Some of the guys had to go out of town to work. It's an expensive sport."[109] Although Pueblo attracted some new industry, including light manufacturing and tourism, the Hispano and Mexican American men and women who had worked at the plant, some for decades, had to reinvent their livelihoods, families, and communities wholesale, including through regional migration.[110] For Codina, the loss of the area's charro association was palpable. "I do miss those days," he told a reporter from the *Pueblo Chieftain*. "There was a camaraderie. Birthdays, anniversaries—we'd celebrate them at the arena on 33rd Lane; we'd have a barbecue. There's not much left there now."[111] Not until the early 2000s, when Mexican migration to Colorado expanded, would charrería experience resurgence in the state.[112]

Even so, the charro associations in Denver and Pueblo made important inroads as they worked to create a more equitable public sphere in Colorado during the 1970s and '80s. They did so in ways that honored the homegrown cultural geography of the region—its status as a dynamic, constantly evolving

Hispano homeland—while also nurturing workable relationships with members of Colorado's Chicano movement and new forms of transnational connectivity with Mexico. Though structural inequality and segregation remained pervasive, especially in Denver, the cumulative effect of their labor was the creation of a moderately more inclusive public sphere in the realms of education, history, and art. Their counterparts in Los Angeles were working toward similar ends, with a focus on the claiming of suburban public space and the transformation of racial geographies.

FOUR

Claiming Suburban Public Space and Transforming L.A.'s Racial Geographies

FOR RENOWNED CHICANO FILMMAKER Moctesuma Esparza, it was only logical to include a charro in *Cinco Vidas* (1973), his Emmy award–winning documentary about Mexican American life in Los Angeles. The son of a Mexican migrant who came to L.A. at the height of the Mexican Revolution, Esparza devoted his life to transforming media representations of Chicanos, often through direct involvement with the Chicano movement.[1] The charro was an important tool in his artistic lexicon. *Cinco Vidas* (Five Lives), which Esparza completed for his master's thesis in film studies at UCLA, profiles two of the city's newest charro associations as they prepare for an upcoming charreada. The film features an extended interview with charro Tom Cruz, who explains: "Charrería has changed my family a lot as far as coming closer to the culture of Mexico . . . I think we have gotten away from this, and I think it's a great thing for any individual to practice their culture."[2] The film then illustrates the involvement and labor of all members of Cruz's family, in ways structured by patriarchal gender roles. While Cruz's sons, including a four-year-old boy, are shown riding and competing, Cruz's wife and daughters clean the home, prepare and serve food, and help their father and brothers get dressed. Thus, filmmaker Esparza—like Chicano activists, social service workers, and cultural producers across the U.S. Southwest during the 1970s—depicts the charro as a powerful representation of Mexican cultural nationalism, and the rightful patriarch of household and land.

The film is also notable for documenting the spread of charrería into the suburbs. Cruz's home and ranch were located not in East L.A., but in Los Nietos, a suburban community eleven miles east of downtown Los Angeles. Cruz had first been exposed to charrería as a child, when he worked at a pony ranch in another suburban community, Pico Rivera. As an adult, while

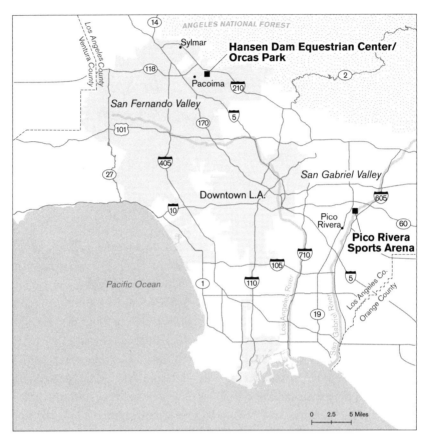

Suburban Los Angeles, featuring the locations of the lienzos in the San Fernando Valley and the San Gabriel Valley. By Jennifer Tran and Alexander Tarr.

running a small landscaping business, Cruz bought two horses and cofounded the Charros La Alteña, with members drawn from communities across the suburban San Gabriel Valley, to the east of the city. The other charro association profiled in the film, the Charros Emiliano Zapata, had also recently formed in the suburban San Fernando Valley to the north. During the 1960s, '70s, and '80s, these suburban valleys became favored destinations for upwardly mobile ethnic Mexican homeowners in Los Angeles, as well as prime organizing sites for Mexican American civil rights.

This chapter shows that the performance of charrería and associated practices of Mexican ranch life was integral to both processes. The establishment of charro associations, the construction of suburban lienzos, and the performance of mariachi and norteña music were routinely deployed in the service of Mexican American suburban place-making and identity formation. Through these activities, ethnic Mexicans demonstrated that they adhered to American suburban norms relating to private property, the nuclear family, and a politics of respectability—all while upholding their Mexican cultural heritage. Put differently, charreando in the suburbs allowed ethnic Mexicans to claim a rightful place in suburbia *as Mexicans*. But the use of charrería to claim a suburban Mexican presence had an even greater subversive potential: to reterritorialize the landowning, ranchero class of elite Mexicans dislocated by U.S. conquest. Thus, the suburbanization of charrería allowed ethnic Mexicans to resist—indeed, to reverse— one of the most important processes through which they had been racialized in the United States: their persistent, often violent displacement from the land.

While these processes of racialized displacement have been described in previous chapters, it bears emphasizing again here that the uprooting and removal of Mexicans from the Southern California ranchos was foundational to the production of L.A.'s suburban geography as white settler space. Mexican ranchland in the San Fernando and San Gabriel Valleys, itself a colonial spatial production resting on indigenous dispossession, was transferred en masse to Anglo settlers after U.S. conquest, then subdivided as corporate farms for white growers in the late nineteenth and early twentieth centuries. While some ethnic Mexicans remained in the valleys, laboring in the fields and packinghouses and residing in semi-rural colonias, most became urbanized, industrialized, and segregated in the main barrio of East Los Angeles.[3] A generation later, as the agricultural empires of the San Fernando and San Gabriel Valleys were carved into residential subdivisions for middle-class homeowners, many new suburban communities were named after the region's historic Spanish missions (e.g., the cities of San Fernando and San Gabriel) and its Mexican ranches (e.g., the communities of Verdugo, Azusa, Duarte, and Brea). Homebuilders adopted Spanish and Mission Revival architectural styles to cultivate a distinctive regional identity for Southern California's growth machine and a cohesive community identity for incoming white suburbanites.[4] These place-naming and aesthetic practices reflected an imperialist nostalgia, spatialized in the suburban landscape. While such practices appeared to honor Spanish and Mexican histories of landownership, they rested on a legal and fiscal structure of racial exclusion. Ethnic Mexicans and other people of color could not live in most of Los Angeles's new suburban communities because widespread use of redlining, restrictive covenants, alien land laws, and property owners' associations limited purchase and occupation to whites.[5]

It was only after World War II that ethnic Mexicans in Los Angeles and across the U.S. Southwest began returning to the suburbs in large numbers, shifting the contours of the region's metropolitan racial geographies. Like so many other American populations, ethnic Mexicans took advantage of the passage of fair housing laws, upward economic mobility enabled by federal policies like the GI Bill, and the simple fact that most new housing was being constructed in suburbs.[6] In Los Angeles, some moved from the central East L.A. barrio, while others moved from the demolished agricultural colonias into the tract homes that took their place.[7] Similar processes of outward mobility were occurring in other cities across the U.S. Southwest, where charro associations also helped launch an ethnic Mexican presence in suburbia, as the previous chapter demonstrated for Denver and Pueblo. Indeed, wherever ethnic Mexicans had once been landowners and ranchers, and in some places where they had not, the reclamation of suburban space promised to transform the racial geographies produced through U.S. conquest. The figure of the charro—a Mexican nationalist icon who represented power and agency—signaled ethnic Mexicans' ongoing contestation of the region's histories and geographies, this time in the battle for suburban space.

Many studies of ethnic Mexican suburbanization in the post–World War II period focus on the transformation of residential space, using rates of private homeownership by ethnic Mexicans as an index of their integration. Yet private homeownership tells us little about whether ethnic Mexicans were able to claim a sense of belonging in their new suburban communities or challenge the spatial contours of the existing racial order. Public, rather than private, space is the more salient battleground for these questions. It is in public space that normative conceptions of a people—of who belongs to the collective and who doesn't—are most clearly negotiated. Public space is also the arena in which marginalized groups develop cultural citizenship—a sociopolitical consciousness informed by embodied cultural and spatial practice—and make claims upon the wider society.[8] And it is in public space that, in some places and under some conditions, the historical exclusions of U.S. suburbia may be challenged and a more inclusive and expansive "right to the suburb" articulated.[9]

Through the stories of the Charros Emiliano Zapata and the Charros La Alteña, the two suburban charro associations profiled in *Cinco Vidas,* this chapter investigates ethnic Mexicans' claims to suburban public space in Los

Angeles. After situating each association in the context of its localized racial geographies, the chapter examines each association's work with public agencies to secure access to public space. This process required the charros to not only broker relationships with public officials, like their counterparts in Texas and Colorado, but also to become experts in complex legal and fiscal matters related to land acquisition, real estate development, and finance. As we shall see, the suburban charros faced numerous bureaucratic hurdles along the way, such as signing leases and subleases, taking out property and equipment loans, hiring attorneys and accountants, and filing corporate and property taxes. While these processes could be complicated and expensive, they also offered opportunities to tell new stories about regional history—stories in which charros, and ethnic Mexican landowners more broadly, had played powerful roles in the making of metropolitan space.

The chapter then considers how these opportunities, born of the legal and fiscal processes necessary for suburban land acquisition and use, shifted in the 1980s as California's Proposition 13 (which slashed property taxes), deindustrialization, and the turn toward neoliberalism decimated public space and public services. For charros from Colorado to California and many places in between, the promises of expanded public life that had seemed so bright in the 1960s and '70s became increasingly difficult to achieve. Instead, with the gutting of the public sphere, a new entity began to absorb the labor necessary to produce spaces for the exercise of Mexican cultural citizenship. These are charro-entrepreneurs—ethnic Mexican small businessmen who plan and promote charreadas and other ranch-themed entertainment, but under deeply precarious financial circumstances once shouldered more fully by the public sector. These shifts in Los Angeles's constantly evolving racial and colonial geographies have created new challenges for the use of charrería as a reclamation of Mexican American power. As a result, as we shall see in this and the following chapter, U.S. charros have become economic and political actors of growing sophistication in their ongoing work to contest the Southwest's racial geographies.

THE CHARROS EMILIANO ZAPATA
IN THE SAN FERNANDO VALLEY

The northeast corner of the San Fernando Valley, where the Charros Emiliano Zapata formed in 1970, was marked by long histories of segregation, racialized poverty, and the political disenfranchisement of people of color. Before World War II, the vast majority of ethnic Mexicans in the San Fernando Valley lived in one large agricultural colonia centered on the historic Spanish mission at San Fernando and the adjacent neighborhood of Pacoima. Most colonia residents worked in the fields and packinghouses owned by white "gentleman farmers" and corporate agribusiness elites—people and companies that acquired the land through dispossession and displacement following the Mexican-American War. Mexican laborers in the San Fernando Valley colonia were paid poverty wages and lived in meager conditions, often lacking basic infrastructure and services. Though strikes and protests were violently rebuked, over time they began to accumulate limited economic and political power.[10]

After World War II, like their counterparts across the region, upwardly mobile ethnic Mexicans began to move outward from the San Fernando–Pacoima area to the nearby neighborhoods of Sylmar, Arleta, and Sun Valley. These were the only neighborhoods in the San Fernando Valley where people of color could own property. By the 1950s, these northeastern neighborhoods had become racially mixed communities of ethnic Mexicans, African Americans, and Japanese Americans, while the rest of the San Fernando Valley was racially restricted to white homeowners. In 1962, nearly fifty thousand Spanish-surnamed individuals (6 percent of the valley's total population) lived in these neighborhoods, and the San Fernando–Pacoima area constituted the second largest concentration of ethnic Mexicans in Los Angeles, second only to East L.A.[11] However, in 1960, no other part of the San Fernando Valley had a nonwhite population larger than 1 percent.[12] Despite the upward mobility of some, the San Fernando–Pacoima district was also the poorest in the San Fernando Valley. Ethnic Mexicans there had far less education, lower incomes, and lower representation in white-collar and professional work than ethnic Mexicans in the city as a whole.[13]

Ethnic Mexicans in the northeast San Fernando Valley were also poorly represented in municipal politics—a problem shaped by their location in the City of Los Angeles rather than Los Angeles County or a smaller autonomous city. The vast, heterogeneous political structure of the City of Los Angeles has long relied on very large city council districts, meaning that the Black, Latino, and Japanese American residents of the northeast San Fernando Valley shared Los Angeles City Council District 1 with their wealthier and more influential white neighbors. As a result, many ethnic Mexicans in this part of Los Angeles did not invest their trust or hopes in local government, and did not participate in municipal politics. According to a profile in the *Los Angeles Times,* District 1's minority populations were considered "political throwaways" because they rarely voted or donated to electoral campaigns.[14] To be sure, the Chicano movement had made some inroads: the Chicano Community Center and the Coalition of Chicano Community Workers both operated briefly there; La Raza Unida Party ran several candidates for the city council of San Fernando, an independent city; and Mexican American students at Valley State College—now California State University, Northridge—joined a multiracial coalition to successfully demand the creation of California's first Chicano studies program (as well as a Black studies program) in 1969.[15] Still, movement activity in the San Fernando Valley was less robust than in other parts of Los Angeles, especially compared to the large urban barrio of East Los Angeles, and ethnic Mexican residents and other people of color struggled to articulate their needs in a suburban space dominated by white homeowners.

As a result, throughout the 1960s and '70s, white residents of District 1 bolstered their historic racial and class advantages by means of the city's zoning and land-use processes. For example, they created "horse-raising" zones that sanctioned and subsidized horse-keeping on large, private lots with minimum lot sizes, thus enhancing property values in white communities. They also participated in community planning processes that rejected multi-family, industrial, or commercial zoning. The result was to embed Anglo-American histories of ranching and whitewashed histories of cowboys in the American West in the suburban landscape via municipal zoning and planning codes. These were implemented at the moment of desegregation, to the enduring material benefit of white suburbanites.[16]

Similar processes played out in the northeast San Fernando Valley's suburban public spaces. In a small city park called Orcas Park, white homeowners repeatedly hosted community celebrations that celebrated American westward expansion, U.S. conquest of indigenous and Mexican land and people, and whitewashed renditions of the cowboy and the frontier. For example, the Lake View Terrace Improvement Association sponsored a "Frontier Days" celebration in 1968 to commemorate the suburban community's founding twenty years earlier. The event included a parade, horse and pony rides, a country store, sack races, and a "whisker contest."[17] Another suburban organization, the Chuck Wagon Trailers—whose purpose was to "preserve the Old West" and which counted among its membership "motion picture actors, stuntmen, cowboys and Indians"—held numerous events at

Orcas Park throughout the 1970s. Among these was their annual "round-up," which featured square dancing and country western music provided by Bob Faith and the Country Ramblers.[18] The Lion's Club of San Fernando also sponsored a San Fernando Valley Rodeo annually at Orcas Park, which drew local students from nearby Pierce College as well as rodeo amateurs and professionals from across the region.[19] In these ways, social and cultural life in the northeast San Fernando Valley anchored memories and reenactments of the white settler West in suburban public space, reproducing the racial geographies of earlier eras in everyday suburban culture.

The work of the San Fernando Valley charros was to test whether these whitewashed narratives of cowboys, ranching, and the frontier—which had always falsely represented the social history of ranching—could be made to include ethnic Mexicans once again. It was the Charros Emiliano Zapata who led the charge. The Asociación de Charros Emiliano Zapata del Valle de San Fernando (hereafter Charros Emiliano Zapata) formed as a loose group in the northeast San Fernando Valley in 1970. It incorporated in 1973 and received its accreditation by the Federación Mexicana de Charrería that year.[20] At the time of its founding, the Charros Emiliano Zapata was the only charro association located in the City of Los Angeles; the rest were located in Los Angeles County or smaller, independent cities. As we shall see, this geopolitical condition would affect the association's engagement with the state and its access to suburban public space. By 1976, the association had twenty-two members, all of whom lived in the communities of San Fernando, Pacoima, and Sun Valley, clustered around the historic Spanish mission and the former agricultural colonias of the northeast San Fernando Valley.[21]

Like earlier charros in Los Angeles, the members of the Charros Emiliano Zapata were blue-collar men who labored in manufacturing, agriculture, and the building trades. Daniel Robles, for example, spent his childhood as an agricultural laborer, following the crops with his family through Central and Northern California; as an adult, he worked at a lumber company in the San Fernando Valley. Roofers, gardeners, hospitality workers, and security guards were also well represented among the membership.[22] Through participation in charrería, they could transcend their humble economic stations and win recognition and respect for their skillful riding and roping. Member Julian Nava recalled that "Beto Cueva, our close friend, was *un charro completo*— that is, he had a national championship in each of the nine events. Every Mexican horseman I ever met knew about Beto and spoke of him with reverence, even though Beto was simply a night watchman at a movie studio."[23]

For men like Beto Cueva, charrería offered an opportunity to earn respect and admiration that might otherwise be denied them in the blue-collar workplace or the segregated and disenfranchised suburban neighborhood.

One of the most influential members of the Charros Emiliano Zapata was Julian Nava. Nava was a historian, educator, and diplomat who was well connected within L.A.'s ethnic Mexican community. Born in Boyle Heights in 1927 to Mexican immigrant parents, Nava was politicized at a young age through his family's experiences with repatriation during the Great Depression (they were spared deportation only because Nava, a U.S. citizen, suffered a health condition). After his military service during World War II, Nava attended college on the GI Bill and earned his doctorate in Latin American history from Harvard University in 1955. He was then hired by Valley State College (now California State University, Northridge) in the suburban San Fernando Valley, where he later became instrumental in the hiring of Rudy Acuña to head the university's new Chicano studies program. Nava was influential in K-12 education as well. In 1967, he was elected to the Los Angeles Board of Education as its first Mexican American member. His tenure on the board overlapped with the East Los Angeles Walkouts of 1968—the events that would catalyze filmmaker Moctesuma Esparza and so many others. He also oversaw the introduction of bilingual education and efforts toward school integration, much like his counterpart Lena Archuleta in Denver.[24]

As a scholar of Mexico, Nava was intimately aware of the significance of charrería to Mexican cultural nationalism; as an upwardly mobile suburban professional with roots in the East L.A. barrio, he equally understood how charrería might be mobilized in the service of Mexican American civil rights and suburban place-making. A decade earlier, as we saw in chapter 1, he and his brother, Henry Nava (cofounder of the Community Services Organization), had guided Tijuana charro and actor Mario Arteaga around the San Fernando Valley during Arteaga's work on *The Young Land*. His cousin, Miguel Flores, was also a charro in Los Angeles and had authored an amateur history on the city's charros, *El Charro en U.S.A.,* based on oral histories he conducted with his friends. By the 1970s, Julian Nava had become a charro in his own right. As one of the founders of the Charros Emiliano Zapata, and the association's only professional member, Nava became a key advocate for ethnic Mexicans' efforts to access and use public space in the suburban San Fernando Valley.

In June 1974, the Charros Emiliano Zapata proposed to sublease a portion of land at Hansen Dam, a flood control channel and recreation area constructed by the U.S. Army Corps of Engineers and operated by the City of Los Angeles, where they intended to host charreadas. The charros had hoped to purchase their own land but had not yet found an appropriate site. They believed the sublease was a good holding action until the right permanent site could be found.[25] The city's Recreation and Parks Commission allowed its Equine Advisory Council and representatives of a local equestrian group called Equestrian Trails Inc.—both composed of white homeowners from the northeast San Fernando Valley—to review the charros' proposal. Both organizations, as well as Los Angeles City Council representative Louis Nowell from District 1, endorsed the sublease, which was signed in June 1974.[26]

While municipal officials and local equestrian groups were generally supportive, the conditions of the sublease required the charros to finance and construct the lienzo entirely on their own. In this way, the arrangement planted the burden of producing the physical space necessary for charrería firmly upon individual ethnic Mexican suburbanites, rather than city or federal governments. Much like the failed charro statue in Denver, the lienzo charro in the San Fernando Valley gained symbolic support from public agencies, but no public money. Thus, as soon as the agreement with the city was approved, the Charros Emiliano Zapata and their families took to the task of building the lienzo themselves.

The construction project allowed for the collective invocation of Mexican histories of ranchland and labor, while reterritorializing those histories in the suburban present. As Nava recollected, "Among the *charros,* we had every skill needed to do the enormous job," a tribute to the blue-collar status of most of the charros.[27] His recollection also captures the ways in which the making of the lienzo imported the patriarchal gender roles of the historic rancho and hacienda into contemporary suburban space:

> Over many weekends, entire families contributed to building the stadium and network of corrals. The men worked with tractors and hand tools, while women and children cheered us on. During Mexican meals prepared by the women, there was always someone to play a guitar. The rest of the time, pickup doors were opened wide and *norteñas*—Mexican songs—blared out.[28]

Nava also used his professional connections to secure salvage bleachers from the Los Angeles Board of Education's surplus materials department at discounted cost, which the charros paid themselves from their working-class salaries.[29] Because these bleachers would hold fewer than 150 people, the members of the association went nearly $15,000 into debt (to be repaid, with interest, over a five-year period) with a private vendor to purchase additional bleachers that would seat nearly a thousand people.[30]

Upon the lienzo's completion, the Charros Emiliano Zapata staged charreadas nearly every weekend at their new facility, which was widely considered among charros to be the best in the state. According to Nava, "In time, huge crowds came to see *charro* competitions that lasted all day Sunday."[31] The organization's events initially included the charreada's traditional nine suertes, as well as dancing and music. These events appear to have been extraordinarily popular. Photographs in Nava's archival collections at UCLA show the bleachers packed with ethnic Mexican men, women, and children observers, with competitors perched on top of the rails surrounding the arena.[32]

Thus, ethnic Mexicans—sometimes thousands of them—succeeded in claiming significant suburban public space in the northeast San Fernando Valley, where they celebrated and performed the Mexican ranching past in the suburban present through charreadas, norteña music, mariachi suits, and ballet folklórico. In performing these expressions of Mexican cultural nationalism, they challenged dominant ideas about American suburbia, especially how people of color and immigrants should behave, and reclaimed a Mexican presence on the outskirts of Los Angeles. Nevertheless, in light of ethnic Mexicans' geographic and social isolation in the San Fernando Valley and their lack of political representation, the Charros Emiliano Zapata and their supporters were neither able nor willing to defy local suburban norms and racial geographies completely. To the contrary, they creatively adapted their activities to the local context.

One crucial way they did so was by emphasizing how the history of charros as landowners in California predisposed ethnic Mexicans to be good suburban neighbors. In 1973, the organization invited media personalities and elected officials to celebrate the installation of the association's new officers. The event announcement, likely written by Nava, gave a lengthy description of charrería that emphasized the charro's personal characteristics of honor, respectability, and hospitality:

> In the early days of California, the Charro emerged out of the heart of Mexico to meet the challenge and outcrying demands of rural ranch life in a raw frontier. The Charro played the role of the family man, Vaquero, guardian, militia, and Good Samaritan. The philosophy of that era was: Mi Casa Es Su Casa (my home is your home). We are endeavoring to carry on this heritage by accommodating it to todays [sic] living ... [The organization is] made up

of family men of all ages; men who see the need to form and keep alive, in a positive manner, the cultural aspect of the Mexican Charro (cowboy).[33]

This language positioned members of the Charros Emiliano Zapata as worthy, respectable members of suburbia—as hospitable family men who were committed to private property, family, and the greater good of the neighborhood. It also claimed a historic role for the suburban charros' ethnic ancestors, real or imagined, in creating a settler civilization in Southern California well before Anglo-Americans came along. Predicated on indigenous dispossession as the foundation for their own historical empowerment, this was both a claim to origins and to renewed possession.

In other ways, too, the Charros Emiliano Zapata took pains to ensure that association members and spectators would uphold the charro's reputation as honorable family man and upstanding suburban neighbor. Members of the board of directors were required to sign an agreement that they would "abide by a code of ethics to protect the Emiliano Zapata Corporation," including honesty, courtesy, courage, patriotism, and devotion to charrería.[34] Failure to abide by these characteristics resulted in expulsion from the organization. Similar commitments—as well as a short haircut—were required of all those who participated in the association's events, whether or not they were members.[35]

The Charros Emiliano Zapata also found creative ways to bridge charrería with American-style rodeo. Their 1975 event schedule shows two different kinds of events that were to take place on alternating weekends: "charriadas" [sic] and "charrodeos," which were characterized as "Charro & Western Rodeo Exhibition/Competitions."[36] Presumably, the "charrodeos" were intended to be welcoming to local Anglo-American riders and ranchers, of which there were many in nearby neighborhoods, as well as audiences who might simply be more familiar with American-style rodeo.

Additionally, in August 1975, the Charros Emiliano Zapata sponsored the International Horsemanship Exhibition, which featured costumed riders demonstrating Arabic, Chilean, American Indian, Spanish, Mexican, American Cowboy, and English horseback riding traditions. The Charros Emiliano Zapata clearly saw this event as a way to promote charrería among a wider, multiracial audience. Their media outreach targeted English-language publications with primarily Anglo readerships, such as *Horse and Rider, California Horseman's News, California Horse Review,* and the *Western Horseman,* and featured Mexican American television personalities from both English- and Spanish-language networks. Several political representatives, including Mayor Tom Bradley, Congressman James Corman, and Senator Alan Robbins, were on hand as honored guests.[37] Tony Kiss, a reporter from a local paper, the *Foothill Record-Ledger,* was captivated. He described the event as

> the most beautiful and colorful event this area had seen in a long time. A true fiesta spirit prevailed, under deep blue skies without smog. It was a hot day but there were improvised tents, parasols, and plenty of cervesas [*sic*] and tecates [*sic*] to keep one cool under the blazing August sun. Of course, what you gained by the cooling effects of ice cold drinks you lost right away looking at the galore of pretty senoritas, with castanetas [*sic*], and scarlet roses in their shiny black hair. What a colorful crowd, from old Mexico, Chile and Peru. It was an event rarely seen here, with the fast paced or romantic melodies by Mexican musicians. It was pageantry at its best.[38]

Kiss's language could have been lifted from a 1920s program for the fiestas in San Antonio, Santa Barbara, Los Angeles, or other southwestern cities. It echoes almost verbatim the language of the Spanish fantasy heritage that shaped the U.S. Southwest's public culture and landscape for decades. Much like their counterparts in San Antonio a generation before, the Charros Emiliano Zapata participated in these enduring depictions of the Spanish fantasy past to build support for their events among a broader suburban public. After all, they were dependent on attracting large audiences, including white homeowners from the surrounding neighborhoods, to recoup the extensive costs involved in building the lienzo.

They were, for a short while, successful: the Charros Emiliano Zapata hosted events like these on their subleased land for nearly a year without incident. However, in the summer of 1975 they faced a major hurdle. Upon receipt of a permit for a charreada to be held in September, they found that two new conditions were attached: first, that the cola, or tailing of the bull, and the manganas, or roping the front legs of a horse, were prohibited; and second, that a veterinarian must always be in attendance.[39] Because no restrictions existed on the cola and the manganas elsewhere in the U.S., including Los Angeles County, and because similar events were held at American-style rodeos without restriction, the charros saw prejudice at the heart of these conditions. They hired an attorney, Eugene Schwartz, and secured a hearing before the city's Department of Animal Regulation in late January 1976.

At stake in the hearing was not merely the specific issue of whether the Charros Emiliano Zapata could host the full schedule of events in charreadas, but also the larger question of how the region's history—specifically its Mexican past—would be interpreted and brought to bear upon the present. These questions were negotiated at every step of the bureaucratic process. In advance of the hearing, the presiding officer of the Los Angeles Department of Animal Regulation, Bob Rush, sought advice about the laws regulating charreadas in the city. Rush asked how regulation of charreadas compared with those governing American-style rodeos, because American-style rodeos had been grandfathered into municipal code in 1957 as exceptions to animal-cruelty laws on account of their historic nature. The city attorney responded that in order for charreadas to be banned while rodeos were allowed to continue, the city would need to show two things: first, that the charreada events in question were not prevalent historically in California before 1957, and second, that the charreada events posed greater risk of harm to the animals than did comparable events in American-style rodeo.[40] With these two issues established, the charros had an opportunity to assert their centrality to the making of ranching culture in the United States, as the original cowboys.

At the hearing, Julian Nava addressed the first concern by providing an extensive summary of historical charreadas in the U.S. Southwest, Mexico, and the entire Western Hemisphere. After establishing his credibility as a professional historian through reference to a "voluminous literature" documenting the practice of charrería since about 1900, Nava noted that both of the events in question were frequently mentioned in the travel diaries and journals of Americans moving across the U.S. Southwest in the late nineteenth and early twentieth centuries. Tracing the events that would become charreadas back to the Spanish Empire, Nava argued that the phenomenon was not unique to Mexico, but rather existed across much of New Spain, including Chile and Argentina.[41] In this way he recast the origins of ranching beyond America to the *Américas,* simultaneously refuting the U.S. nationalism undergirding the cowboy as white American hero and reclaiming Latin American horsemen, including the charro, in the making of hemispheric ranch cultures.

Nava then argued that charros were not only as old as American-style rodeo cowboys, but in fact were the "original cowboys." Pointing to the similarity of events and equipment in both rodeos and charreadas, and to the linguistic resemblances between words, Nava argued that Anglos had borrowed heavily from Mexican charros and vaqueros on the western frontier and suggested that Americans were indebted to Mexicans for many elements of western heritage. Echoing the arguments made by Lena Archuleta in her Denver curriculum guide just a few years before, he declared: "Virtually every single item of use that we find in the so-called western cowboy saddle and tack is a direct adaptation from the Mexican." Appealing to emergent notions of multiculturalism, he continued, "The words are often the very same words or a misspelling or a mispronunciation as part of the general process by which we, in America, have absorbed and adopted things from every people and every culture that has come to our shores."[42] Throughout the region that became the U.S. Southwest, he explained, diverse groups experimented and borrowed ideas from each other in order to respond to the practical needs of rounding up and maintaining cattle. Over time, this trading resulted in the American-style rodeo: "These events then, the some nine or ten events of the so-called chariada [sic], the Mexican form of what we would call in English a rodeo, are all skills that have developed over the last 250 years in America; they are American equestrian skills."[43] Nava also provided photographs, flyers, event programs, and other materials documenting the presence of charros in the U.S. from as early as the 1930s.[44] Another speaker during the hearing, a San Pedro stevedore named Ignacio Arriola, who also served as the FMCH's executive assistant for charrería in the United States, spoke of attending thirty charreadas a year since he had immigrated to the U.S. from Mexico in 1945. But he also noted in his testimony that charreada had been performed in the U.S. "since 1894," referencing the inclusion of Mexican charro Vicente Oropeza in Buffalo Bill's Wild West Show of that year. In this way, both Nava and Arriola reminded Schwartz and others present at the hearing that charros had been active contributors to the making of ranching and rodeo cultures, both historically and in American popular culture, for a very long time.[45]

Yet for all of this testimony, the charros themselves acknowledged that it was difficult to locate extensive documentation about the history of charrería in California. They pointed out that most early charreadas were put on informally, often at the last minute, by groups of friends who did not have the time, money, or inclination to create formal publicity and instead relied on word-of-mouth. John Gándara, one of the first members of the East L.A. Sheriff's Posse and the Charros de Los Angeles, noted during his testimony that "they weren't really formal due to the fact that it was quite a hardship to get together. We used to have to chip in to rent the stock, and so forth, so we didn't keep any records of any kind on account of that. We'd just get together one afternoon and call it a fiesta day, you might say."[46] Similarly, Dan Robles recalled that when he was a child picking crops in California's Central Valley, "on weekends the family would go into the hills there where they would have cattle, and they'd do rodeo events, not formally in arenas but out in the open." He explained that all the people working the harvest came to watch, and people sold beer and soft drinks.[47] Other witnesses noted that California charreadas had become better publicized in recent years, but only on Spanish-language radio, not in written form and not in English. Haro Basilio testified that although he personally had not attended charreadas, he had heard many announcements for the events on the radio. Mr. Rush asked for clarification: "Was that over a Spanish-speaking radio?" Basilio replied, "Well, that's what I always got my program on, Spanish, so that's what I heard them on, you know." Rush replied, "So unless somebody was really fluent in Spanish, they could possibly miss them?" Basilio said: "Yes. Yes."[48]

The city attorney's second requirement demanded evidence that the manganas and the cola were no more dangerous to animals than comparable events in American-style rodeo. To this end, Nava collected score sheets from charreadas held throughout the Southwest, including events in Marysville, Fresno, and Tucson. His handwritten notes in the margins point out participants' low scores in the colas, demonstrating both the difficulty of the event and, by implication, the low likelihood of an animal being injured.[49] Ignacio Arriola, representing the FMCH in the United States, also presented evidence from the national championships held in Mexico in 1973, 1974, and 1975. In each of those years, he showed, only two or three bulls (out of five hundred each year), and no horses (out of 150 each year), were injured.[50]

The Charros Emiliano Zapata then called upon two veterinarians and stock contractors who had experience with both Mexican charreadas and American rodeos. Both witnesses were Anglo-American men who, like reporter Tony Kiss, professed their support and admiration for Mexican histories of ranching and riding. Their inclusion as supportive witnesses suggested that all the work the Charros Emiliano Zapata had done to build multiracial alliances might pay off, as it had for charros in other southwestern cities like San Antonio and Pueblo. Veterinarian Reginald Stocking testified that he had never seen an animal greatly injured in his observation of three charreadas, but he had seen several animals that had to be destroyed in calf roping and bulldogging competitions at American-style rodeos.[51] Rush asked if Stocking had ever served as the attending veterinarian at events sponsored by the Charros Emiliano Zapata; Stocking confirmed that he had. When Rush asked Stocking if he had been paid to do so, Stocking replied:

> I was definitely not paid. They wanted to pay me and I says, no, because those people need all the help they can get out there. They don't have that kind of money . . . I'm trying to help them because these people need help. In other words, they're a family group. They have children that sing and put on their little, well, say, dances and activities . . . I'm glad to help them, because—well, it's keeping . . . them off the street and keeping these young people in there and keeping them all interested . . . In other words, there is no crime there whatsoever.[52]

Though aimed at proving the safety of animals in charreadas, Stocking's testimony also highlighted the reputability of ethnic Mexican families and the good behavior of their children, complementing the charros' work along these lines in other contexts.

Similarly, Buzz Carson, a stock contractor who had provided livestock to both American-style rodeos and Mexican charreadas, testified that none of the horses he had leased to the Charros Emiliano Zapata had ever returned with an injury. He stated that he considered American-style bulldogging to be more dangerous to animals than the colas or the manganas. But he then noted that, even if he felt there was an equal risk at the charreada events, he would still lease his animals to the charros. Schwartz asked, "Is that because you have seen that there is really not much that's ever happened to them?" Carson replied, "Well, yes, that's right. And I have a great love for the Mexican people. I think what they have is the most beautiful show there is. Take that show with Tony [Antonio] Aguilar; it's absolutely out of this world. I have seen it a hundred times and I still go to see it."[53]

The case for the deep historical roots of ethnic Mexican landowners and ranchers in California and the U.S. Southwest, and the relative safety of animals in charrería, was a strong one. The Department of Animal Regulation's witnesses, by comparison, provided very weak testimony. The official who had issued the restrictive permit admitted that he had only observed two charreadas in his life and had no formal training in the dynamics of animal injury. The department's other two witnesses had even less experience: neither had ever attended a charreada and could only speculate that the cola and the manganas would be more dangerous than comparable American-style rodeo events because the animals' bones were positioned slightly differently. Given the unevenness of these testimonies, the Department of Animal Regulation granted the Charros Emiliano Zapata permission to continue staging charreadas in a one-year pilot program.[54]

However, it had become apparent to all involved that the lack of regulations governing the practice of charrería in the United States was a real problem. The Charros Emiliano Zapata and their supporters hoped to establish a regulatory framework for charrería in the United States that would respect the sport's Mexican traditions while recognizing the authority of American laws and municipal codes. Nava had begun working toward this goal even before the hearing. A few months prior, while the Charros Emiliano Zapata were preparing for the hearing, Nava had written to the American Humane Association (AHA), headquartered in Denver. He requested the latest rules governing rodeos and asked for the AHA's support in developing regulations for charrería in the U.S., both of which were provided.[55] After the hearing, the Los Angeles Department of Animal Regulation and the Charros Emiliano Zapata then worked together to develop a revision to the city's municipal code that would regulate charrería. They pored through the official regulations of the FMCH, the AHA, and the American Quarter Horse Association. The new regulatory framework they developed was a hybridization of Mexican and American histories of ranching and the sporting cultures of both nations, now codified in municipal law.[56] As Nava later reflected, the new municipal code constituted "the most complete rules that would assure equal protection for animals in charro competition as provided for in cowboy competition."[57]

With these new protections in place, the Charros Emiliano Zapata continued to sponsor charreadas and other events in the northeast San Fernando Valley for the next several years. However, the time, energy, and resources they devoted to bureaucratic and policy efforts caused serious strain upon the organization. While the matter was under legal consideration, and as they worked with the city to institute regulations, the Charros Emiliano Zapata could not host charreadas. They lost revenue and fell behind in their loan payments on the bleachers. Then, in June 1976, their corporate status was revoked due to nonpayment of corporate taxes.[58] After paying $812 to revive the corporation, the Charros Emiliano Zapata hired an accountant to help them keep better financial records. Still, they struggled to break even, partly because they now had to pay for veterinarian services, permits, and accounting services. Financial ledgers from charreadas held in January and February 1977 show very small profits, ranging from just $150 to $1,091.[59] Nonetheless, much like their counterparts in Colorado, the Charros Emiliano Zapata devoted virtually all of their profits to college scholarships for graduates from San Fernando High School.[60]

Then, in 1980, the Charros Emiliano Zapata were unexpectedly forced to shut down. Members were notified that their sublease, which was expiring, could not be renewed because of concerns that horse urine might pollute the groundwater.[61] They were not allowed to appeal the decision. In that year, Nava—the association's only professional member—became the U.S. ambassador to Mexico, and when he left, no other member had the necessary political leverage to navigate city bureaucracy. In his autobiography, Nava recalled:

> While we [he and his wife] were living in Mexico City, the Los Angeles city officials ordered the lienzo shut down. Our friends dismantled the entire installation and returned it to its natural conditions. We had aspired to building a cultural center connected with Mexican horsemanship but lost a chance to do something significant in the City of Los Angeles, which our ancestors had founded.[62]

Nava's narrative underscores that he and the Charros Emiliano Zapata understood the suburban practice of charrería as a return to the work of their ancestors—a reterritorialization of the Mexican ranching past and the Spanish-Mexican colonization of California more broadly. They also clearly interpreted the city's expulsion of charrería from the suburbs as a reactionary response to that effort. He wrote: "As Mexican Americans made some progress, discrimination seemed to increase in order to keep us in a subordinate place."[63] Nava interpreted the urine pollution argument as an excuse for cultural bias against Mexicans, which he thought had been the most important factor in the association's demise; after all, horse-keeping and rural landscapes in surrounding Anglo-American neighborhoods had been recently protected by new zoning codes and community plans. Apparently, in their view, only the urine of *Mexicans'* horses posed a threat to groundwater supplies, and only charreadas posed risk of harm to the animals involved, despite expert testimony and evidence to the contrary.

The hypocrisy of the city's decision to expel the suburban charros was evident in the fact that the space was soon turned into a large commercial stable with lots of horses and, presumably, lots of horse urine. The more recent history of equestrian facilities in Hansen Dam will be examined in pages to come. But in 1980, the damage to the suburban practice of charrería in the northeast San Fernando Valley was done. In Nava's elegiac phrase, "Today, only some large sycamore trees mark the location of our beautiful failure."[64]

Across metropolitan Los Angeles, the Charros la Alteña were having a markedly different experience, shaped in large part by the local contours of the
city's racial geography. Most importantly for our purposes, the suburban San
Gabriel Valley to the east of the city was a more fully and persistently Mexican
space than the San Fernando Valley to the north. After Mexican independence and feeble efforts at secularization of the missions, elite Mexicans had
owned numerous ranches, some of them quite large, around the ex-mission
San Gabriel and across eastern Los Angeles County. After U.S. conquest, as
those elite hacendados were uprooted from the land and most Mexicans
joined the urban proletariat, dozens of agricultural colonias clustered in this
part of Los Angeles County.[65] In the postwar period, outward migration
from the colonias and East L.A. transformed the entire region into an interconnected web of Mexican communities stretching from Central Los Angeles
all the way east to the county line at Pomona. The result was the transformation of the San Gabriel Valley into what Victor Valle and Rodolfo Torres have
termed the "Greater Eastside"—a sprawling suburban region inhabited by
diverse ethnic Mexicans who maintain vibrant and dynamic links to Mexico,
as well as East L.A. and other Chicano barrios across the U.S. Southwest,
through the cultural and spatial practices of everyday life.[66]

Increasingly, they took the reins of local government to do so. Mass sub-
urbanization of ethnic Mexicans and other Latinos across the Greater
Eastside during the 1950s and '60s produced significant shifts in local,
regional, and statewide political representation. Ethnic Mexicans in the San
Gabriel Valley became a formidable presence in local suburban politics in a
way that was largely impossible for their contemporaries in the San Fernando
Valley. Their empowerment was facilitated by the fact that the Greater
Eastside was part of Los Angeles *County,* not the City of Los Angeles, and
thus eligible for municipal incorporation. In the postwar period, dozens of
Eastside communities incorporated as independent suburban cities, moti-
vated by the promise of political autonomy generally and Latino political
autonomy more specifically. Much of this activity was led by the Mexican
American Political Association (MAPA), which focused on electing Mexican
Americans to local and state office from new suburban cities and political
districts.[67] Once incorporated, the Latino suburb could become the site of

ethnically and racially defined political power, creating abundant new cultural opportunities for ethnic Mexicans, including charros.

The small city of Pico Rivera is an excellent example. Throughout the 1950s and '60s, Pico Rivera was a favored destination for upwardly mobile suburban homeowners migrating from the East L.A. barrio and nearby agricultural colonias. In 1960, Spanish-surnamed individuals made up 23 percent of the city's population, but by 1970, they constituted 65 percent.[68] Even before they became a demographic majority, ethnic Mexicans exerted an important influence on city politics. In 1958, when a slim majority of residents voted to incorporate, Louis Díaz, a popular and influential aide to beloved L.A. city councilman Ed Roybal, was elected to Pico Rivera's new city council. Mexican Americans were thus represented in Pico Rivera's municipal politics from their inception.[69] When Díaz resigned in 1962, Frank Terrazas, the U.S.-born son of Mexican immigrants who had fled the Mexican Revolution in the early twentieth century, was elected as his successor. Historian Jerry González writes, "Elected on the strength of the middle class Mexican American vote in Pico Rivera, Terrazas was meant to broker ethnic Mexican needs with city policy."[70] Indeed, Terrazas and others on the Pico Rivera City Council angled to situate suburban Pico Rivera at the center of transnational Mexican culture. Charros, charrería, and associated practices of rural Mexican ranch life were integral to this vision, as were the city's own Charros La Alteña.

The Charros La Alteña formed around 1967 as an offshoot of the Charros de Los Angeles. As in the San Fernando Valley, its members were blue-collar laborers who owned modest homes in the sprawling, Latino-emergent suburbs of the Greater Eastside. One of the association's founders, Tom Cruz, who, as noted, was interviewed in the film *Cinco Vidas,* was a landscape gardener who owned a home in Los Nietos. Joe Sotomayor, a member of the Charros La Alteña in the early 1980s, lived in the suburban community of Hacienda Heights and worked as a roofer. Others worked in similarly blue-collar trades, doing the skilled work of building, maintaining, and landscaping suburban homes across the metropolitan region. The Charros La Alteña grew rapidly throughout the 1970s, drawing crowds to a three-hundred-spectator arena at the intersection of Beverly and Rosemead Boulevards in Pico Rivera.[71] By the early 1970s, that facility was regularly becoming overcrowded. The Charros La Alteña were eager to find a larger facility, and the City of Pico Rivera was eager to deliver it.

Members of the Charros La Alteña outside of Los Angeles's Mission San Gabriel, 1970. Shades of L.A. Photo Collection, Los Angeles Public Library.

Their shared vision rested on appropriating part of the Whittier Narrows Dam and Recreation Area, a 1,500-acre federal flood control project and recreational facility that spans several suburban communities in the San Gabriel Valley. Like Hansen Dam in the San Fernando Valley, Whittier Narrows was built by the U.S. Army Corps of Engineers in the mid-1950s; unlike Hansen Dam, it was leased and managed by Los Angeles County, not the City of Los Angeles. By the 1960s and '70s, Whittier Narrows was becoming a vital public recreational space for suburban Eastside communities, especially Latinos.[72] In March 1975, the City of Pico Rivera signed a fifty-year lease agreement with the U.S. Army Corps of Engineers for a forty-acre parcel of the Narrows, where they proposed to build campgrounds and tennis and handball courts, as well as landscaping, access roads, and security lighting. Under the terms of the agreement, the two jurisdictions would split the costs, with each jurisdiction contributing $750,000. But the City of Pico Rivera would also contribute an additional $632,000 specifically for the construction of a lienzo charro—later dubbed the Pico Rivera Sports Arena—complete with stadium seating, stables for two hundred horses, and parking for 935 vehicles. The total bill for the City of Pico Rivera was estimated at nearly $1.4 million, with the city bearing all costs specifically associated with constructing and maintaining the lienzo charro. Despite the city's outlay, all sales taxes and admissions taxes would accrue to Los Angeles County, which managed the site, and any other profits were to be reinvested only in facility maintenance and improvement.[73]

Like the Charros Emiliano Zapata in the San Fernando Valley, the emerging majority-Latino city of Pico Rivera voluntarily took on a tremendous amount of legal and fiscal risk. Yet in 1975, city officials did not seem concerned about the arrangement. City councilmen repeatedly noted the tremendous growth of interest and participation in "Latin" events. They believed that the Pico Rivera Sports Arena could become a major focal point for ethnic Mexican cultural events spanning the region. Indeed, many Pico Rivera city councilmen and other municipal officials, both white ethnics and Mexican Americans, were deeply invested in increasing Pico Rivera's status as a middle-class ethnic Mexican suburb known across Southern California and Mexico. Charrería would be a major key to this vision.

Toward that end, city officials in Pico Rivera crafted transnational relationships with Mexican officials that were remarkably similar to the networks forged by their counterparts in San Antonio, Denver, and Pueblo. Early in 1977, for example, representatives of the FMCH invited Pico Rivera city councilman Frank Terrazas and city manager Howard Shroyer to Mexico City to observe the world-renowned charreadas there. During the visit, the Mexican charros announced their plans to send a delegation to opening celebrations of the Pico Rivera Sports Arena.[74] At roughly the same time, the Pico Rivera City Council was establishing a sister-city relationship with the Mexican city of San Luis Potosí, much like the sister-city relationship with Puebla that had proved so important for the Pueblo charros' bicentennial celebrations in Colorado a few years earlier. One of the first gifts that representatives from San Luis Potosí gave to Pico Rivera in 1978 was a tooled and engraved saddle, now prominently displayed in the Pico Rivera Historical Museum. These relationships consolidated the development of the Greater Eastside as a transnational Mexican space, anchored in shared narratives and practices of Mexico's ranching past that were being reterritorialized by charros and their supporters in the suburban present.

To be sure, white homeowners in Pico Rivera and the San Gabriel Valley did not passively accept the city's ambitions to create a transnational Mexican suburb. Shortly after the city made its announcement, a group called the Committee to Save Horsemen's Park obtained a preliminary injunction requiring the City of Pico Rivera to adopt an amendment to its general plan and conduct an environmental impact report before it could proceed. The group protested what it perceived to be the "urbanized" nature of the proposed charreada facilities and expressed concern that animal waste could contaminate local water supplies. This was the same argument that unnamed activists in the San Fernando Valley would successfully wield against the Charros Emiliano Zapata a few years later. The group also claimed that the proposed expenditures of nearly $1.4 million had not been allocated in the city's general plan. But most of the group's members were not from Pico Rivera; the group's petition, which was signed by more than 2,100 people, included just sixty-five signatures from Pico Rivera residents.[75] Construction of a lienzo charro in the Greater Eastside seems to have drawn many white homeowners from across the region, not just the local community, into public debates about how the suburbs of Los Angeles were changing.

Yet city officials' enthusiasm for the Pico Rivera Sports Arena appeared irrepressible. The Greater Eastside, always a more Mexican space than other parts of the city, was rapidly transforming into a regional and transnational space for ethnic Mexican culture. A reporter covering the meeting where the Committee to Save Horsemen's Park presented its objections painted a scene where "speakers often shouted into microphones to be heard over the voices of orators, Mariachi music and the click of dancers' heels as a Mexican Independence Day program began on the steps of City Hall."[76] Even the group's spokesperson admitted that they had little hope of stopping the project altogether; they merely wanted to slow it down. Defying their efforts, the city council moved quickly. Less than one week after the Committee to Save Horsemen's Park lodged its protests, the Pico Rivera City Council unanimously adopted an environmental impact report and an amendment to the city's general plan. The project was cleared to proceed.[77]

Despite the grand visions and ambitions of the project's promoters, execution of the Pico Rivera Sports Arena was slapdash. By April 1977, the project was behind schedule and construction costs had increased by more than $300,000. However, the Pico Rivera City Council approved additional funding without much debate and with only one dissenting vote. The dissenter, Councilman William Loehr, objected to what he perceived as the almost exclusive use of the facility for charro events to the exclusion of the "general public." He also protested the fact that the city was investing so much in a project that fell outside city limits, on land leased from federal and county agencies, not owned by the city itself. Yet other members of the Pico Rivera City Council were undaunted. They continued to see the arena as a way to situate Pico Rivera at the center of transnational Mexican cultural space, which they believed could be highly profitable for the city. To justify spending more from the city's general fund to complete the project, Terrazas claimed that the Pico Rivera facility would be the largest of its kind in the nation; another city official maintained that the arena would "put Pico Rivera on the map."[78]

Still, even the project's most enthusiastic supporters began to temper their rhetoric. As the arena moved from conception to the design and building phases, its unstable fiscal arrangements became more apparent. In local political meetings and in the press, members of the Pico Rivera City Council began to refer to the Pico Rivera Sports Arena as a "multipurpose arena" rather than a facility designed expressly for charreadas. Their primary concern seems to have been the financial feasibility of the facility—and rightly so, given the uneven distribution of costs and risks between city, county, and federal governments.[79]

In the late summer of 1977, with construction already under way, the Pico Rivera City Council hired consultants to advise them how the sports arena could be made most profitable. In their report, released in October of that year, the consultants recommended that the city hire an arena manager immediately to begin scheduling and coordinating events. They also recommended upgrading the arena's sound and lighting equipment, widening nearby freeway exits, installing better signage, providing additional parking and security, and adding storage, telephones, office space, and box office facilities. None of these provisions had been included in the project's initial designs.[80] However, the city and its construction teams were slow to adopt these recommendations and in some cases ignored them entirely. After all, the project was already behind schedule and over budget, and commitments to the project were becoming shaky.

These snafus were partially responsible for delays in the arena's opening. By March 1978, no management or concessionaire contracts had been awarded, and few of the recommended modifications to the arena's physical structure and facilities had been made. Instead, the problems highlighted by the consultants were tackled in impromptu and temporary ways, such as by acquiring access to an adjoining dirt lot to accommodate overflow parking.[81] At the same time, the city explored the possibility of annexing the county land on which the Pico Rivera Sports Arena sat. As then-city manager John Donlevy explained, "If we spent close to $4 million [building the arena], it should become part of the city."[82] However, after meeting with the neighboring suburban city of Montebello, which also had interests in Whittier

Narrows, Pico Rivera chose not to pursue annexation. The sports arena, stables, and Bicentennial Park remained on unincorporated county and federal land, subject to a highly unfavorable lease agreement that expires in 2034.[83]

Because of ongoing problems with the sports arena's design, construction, and management, city officials at first relied heavily on Eastside charros to launch the arena and make it a success. In April 1978, just a few months before the opening of the arena, the City of Pico Rivera signed a contract with the Charros La Alteña allowing them primary use of the new facility. According to the terms of the contract, the Charros La Alteña would host a minimum of thirty charreadas and ten other events each year. In addition, the city approved a separate agreement allowing the charro association to use the stables at nearby Bicentennial Park. In addition to paying monthly rent, the charros agreed to provide feed and cleanup work.[84] Assuming significant responsibility for the success of the facility, the charros agreed to shoulder some of the risks imposed on the City of Pico Rivera through its leases and subleases with federal and county governments.

The opening ceremonies for the Pico Rivera Sports Arena were finally held from July 1 to 3, 1978, intentionally coinciding with celebrations of U.S. Independence Day, just as the Pueblo charros had done two years before with their bicentennial charreada. The California State Charreada Championships were the headline event. As promised, a delegation from the FMCH attended, but the top three winning teams were all from Los Angeles—and all were suburban. La Asociación de la Norteña, from Montebello, took first place; the Charros de Emiliano Zapata from the San Fernando Valley came in second; and La Asociación de los Compadres, also from Montebello, was third.[85]

On the one hand, the opening of the Pico Rivera Sports Arena with the California State Charreada Championships signaled the changing racial, class, and national meanings of suburbia. In particular, it highlighted what Victor Valle and Rodolfo Torres have called the "Latinization of park culture" in the Greater Eastside, especially through pastoral practices that express the rural origins and longings of displaced Mexican migrants and their co-ethnics.[86] On the other hand, the public spaces devoted to these cultural practices rest on highly unstable fiscal and legal arrangements, harbingers of economic restructuring and neoliberalism in Los Angeles. These structural changes, which persist to this day, have constrained but not eliminated ethnic Mexicans' abilities to claim suburban public space and exercise cultural citizenship.

The structures of municipal risk that undergird the Pico Rivera Sports Arena are emblematic of the broad dilemmas that structured life in majority-Latino suburbs by the end of the twentieth century. The deindustrialization of the Los Angeles area throughout the 1980s, coupled with economic recession, meant that the growing cohort of Latino city officials struggled to pay for basic municipal services once funded by corporate and industrial taxes. For majority-Latino suburbs, which tended to emerge in areas hard hit by deindustrialization, this was made much, much worse by the passage in 1978 of California's Proposition 13. Property taxes were slashed, and funding for libraries, parks, recreation centers, and other public facilities was severely cut statewide.[87]

Like their counterparts of all ethnic backgrounds in other U.S. cities, municipal officials in majority-Latino suburbs turned to neoliberal policy solutions that rested on extractive industries and subcontracting. Planning scholar William Fulton refers to these suburban communities as "suburbs of extraction"—places where Latino officials have attained political power but in a time of economic scarcity, such that they struggle to find sufficient resources to address constituents' needs and finance public services. City leaders in this position have found themselves nearly empty-handed, with few strategies available beyond luring businesses such as casinos, pawn shops, and scrap metal recycling yards—all of which ultimately serve only to extract any remaining wealth from already-disinvested sources.[88]

Into this void has stepped a new entity: the "Latin" entertainment company. Often founded by entrepreneurial Mexican and Latino suburbanites and perennially unstable and debt ridden, these small businesses have absorbed the costs of generating Latino cultural citizenship in public space.[89] Among these spaces were, and are, the suburban lienzos established as part of the broad movement of ethnic Mexicans and other Latinos to Los Angeles's suburbs in the 1970s and '80s. While, as described above, these public spaces always rested on precarious legal and fiscal structures, their risky nature grew even more so as Los Angeles weathered the worst of its economic restructuring in the late twentieth century.

In the San Fernando Valley, these processes unfolded at two public spaces that had been prime sites for the negotiation of suburban racial geographies a generation before: Hansen Dam and Orcas Park. The same area the Charros Emiliano Zapata once occupied in the Hansen Dam Recreation Area, before being evicted in 1980, did indeed become the "giant cowboy riding center" that Julian Nava described. In 1997, after years of disinvestment, the U.S. Army Corps of Engineers signed a sublease with Eddie Milligan, a former jockey turned real estate developer who promised to renovate the site. Describing his vision of the renovated Hansen Dam Equestrian Center as the "horse capital of California," Milligan built six lighted riding arenas, three hundred boarding stalls, a riding academy, a veterinary clinic, and facilities for public picnics and hayrides—repairs and improvements that cost more than $3 million. Among these improvements was a lienzo charro, located on a far corner of the property, which Milligan began renting to suburban charros on a case-by-case basis.[90]

At the same time, the City of Los Angeles was renovating Orcas Park, the small city park that had been so important for the cultivation of white suburban identity during the 1960s and '70s. By the 1980s, as neighborhoods in the northeast San Fernando Valley were becoming more integrated, their public spaces were too; however, Proposition 13's fiscal constraints limited the city's ability to provide sufficient maintenance, services, and security. Orcas Park frequently become overcrowded on weekends, and problems with public intoxication, violence, and gang-related activity arose—problems that nearby white homeowners blamed on Latino users, when in fact they were the result of decimated city services. In 1992, citing fiscal insecurity, the city closed Orcas Park, but began to reimagine the space as a public equestrian center.[91] The new facility, christened Gabrieleno Equestrian Park after the Native peoples who historically lived at Mission San Gabriel, opened in October 1999. Though formally renamed, the site continues to be known among many in the surrounding Latino communities as Orcas Park.[92]

The renovated Orcas Park and the lienzo charro at the Hansen Dam Equestrian Center next door possess distinct relationships to city and federal governments and private lessees like Milligan, yet visitors experience them as a single, seamless space. Colloquially referred to as Lienzo Charro El Orcas, it is the San Fernando Valley's signal space for charrería and associated practices of Mexican ranch life. But it is also a site of racialized economic precarity. Events there are currently organized and promoted by Bronco Entertainment, a small "Latin"-themed entertainment company run by owner José de los Santos from his San Fernando home since 2009.[93] Renting space from Milligan, Bronco Entertainment occasionally hosts full-fledged charreadas, but far more often it hosts jaripeos (bull riding events) as well as concerts featuring locally and sometimes nationally known groups playing banda, mariachi, and tamborazo music. As of November 2015, Bronco Entertainment had a legal liability of more than $11,000, faced two collections on its account, and was classified as "medium risk."[94] Like earlier ethnic Mexican suburbanites, de los Santos and his company now absorb the risks associated with creating recreational and cultural opportunities for Latinos in suburban space.

Pico Rivera's Sports Arena remains haunted by similarly complex fiscal, legal, and political structures that constrain Latinos' use of suburban public space and their access to municipal services. As we saw earlier, the facility's very financial structure nearly guaranteed it would not be profitable. Sure enough, after the sports arena's first year of operation under city management, the facility suffered an $80,000 deficit. Thus, in 1980—just two years after the arena's opening—the city signed a five-year sublease agreement with Hacendado Productions, an entertainment company based in the nearby Eastside suburb of Montebello. Led by local suburbanite Carlos Castuera, the company innovated the idea of combining charreadas with concerts by local Mexican singers. These events attracted thousands of participants and spectators every week. Still, every year that the sports arena was under Hacendado's management, it either lost money or barely broke even.[95]

When the lease agreement with Hacendado expired in 1985, the Pico Rivera City Council awarded the sublease to another Latin-themed entertainment company, Ventura Productions. Ventura was founded by two former Hacendado employees, Ralph Hauser Sr. and Ralph Hauser Jr., who had parked cars at the sports arena for years. Residents of the suburban Eastside communities of Pico Rivera and Whittier, the Hausers built on Castuera's concept of pairing charreadas with ambitious entertainment by recruiting "big-name" Mexican entertainers such as Amalia Mendoza and Vicente Fernández.[96] Other renowned Mexican singers and performers made multiple appearances there over the years, turning the Pico Rivera Sports Arena into a Latino entertainment mecca known across metropolitan Los Angeles and throughout Mexico. Ralph Hauser Jr. would go on to become an enormously influential promoter for the U.S. Latin market, building a multi-million-dollar empire representing iconic entertainers such as Vicente Fernández, Joan Sebastian, and Juan Gabriel. Even as Hauser moved on to larger and more central entertainment venues, however, he attributed his success to the business model and personal relationships he had developed at the Pico Rivera Sports Arena.[97]

Still, that model was not enough to shore up the Pico Rivera Sports Arena and its adjacent stables, so the city turned to the neoliberal strategy of using independent contractors to provide public services. In the summer of 1989, the city announced that it was negotiating a new deal with James Gándara, the manager of the stables at nearby Bicentennial Park (where the Charros La Alteña still kept their horses), in an effort to reduce the city's ongoing budget woes. Gándara, a city employee, had managed the stables since their opening more than a decade before. Under the proposal offered him by the city, he would quit his municipal job, which paid $44,000 annually with full benefits, and then immediately take over management of the complex as a private contractor with no benefits. The city was simultaneously negotiating similar neoliberal agreements with independent contractors for other municipal services, from tree trimming to janitorial services. The stables' employees and clients expressed grave concerns about the proposal. Horse owners complained that Gándara would raise stall fees, reduce staffing and services, and cut back the quality of horse food in order to make a profit, while the twelve full-time employees worried that even if they weren't fired, they would lose their benefits as municipal employees. Gándara himself acknowledged that these changes were fully possible: while he guaranteed the same quality of service, management, and food, he said these would all be "contingent on financial feasibility."[98] Despite the city's and Gándara's promises of reduced costs and greater efficiency, the stables at Bicentennial Park struggled to stay afloat. The stables finally closed in the early 2000s amid persistent financial difficulties.[99]

The Pico Rivera Sports Arena likewise continued to struggle. After Ventura Productions (later Hauser Entertainment) moved on, the Pico Rivera City Council continued to contract with private entertainment companies to coordinate charreadas, concerts, swap meets, and quinceañeras (fifteenth-birthday parties for young women). Though popular, these events failed to bring the sports arena into the black. In 2004, the City of Pico Rivera contracted with LEBA Inc., a local business operated by Leonardo López and his son Fernando López, who ran a popular chain of Mexican restaurants and night clubs.[100] The Lópezes were also longtime members of Charros La Noria, a charro association that federated with the FMCH in 1987 and has since become one of the most prominent charro associations in the United States.[101] Given the Lópezes' reputation and business success, the city was hopeful that their stature and connections could stabilize the arena, and to some extent they have. In 2009, the City of Pico Rivera renewed LEBA's concessionaire contract for twenty years more, but reduced LEBA's annual fees in recognition of both the poor state of the overall economy and increased competition for Latino entertainment from the Gibson Amphitheater in Universal City and the Home Depot Center in Carson—two private, corporate event centers operating in other Los Angeles suburbs with substantial municipal financing.[102]

As of this writing, LEBA Inc. holds the concession and the responsibility for promoting events at the Pico Rivera Sports Arena, which the city touts as the "largest Mexican rodeo ring in the country" and "a popular recreation spot for the Los Angeles area Hispanic community."[103] The Charros La Alteña, Charros La Noria, and other charro associations from both the U.S. and Mexico continue to participate in charreadas, concerts, and other events at the Pico Rivera Sports Arena to this day. It appears that the facility is stable, at least for now. Still, as we have seen, the facility rests on a shaky foundation of financial risk—precarity borne not only by the majority-Latino city of Pico Rivera, but also by Latino small businessmen and the charros themselves.

Suburban public spaces devoted to cultivation of the Mexican ranching tradition such as Hansen Dam, Orcas Park, and the Pico Rivera Sports Arena thus embody a duality. They are, on the one hand, vitally important community places where diverse ethnic Mexicans come together to remember, romanticize, and perform charrería, jaripeo, and associated cultural practices. As they do, they exercise their cultural citizenship, contest prevailing representations of Los Angeles's history and geography, and reterritorialize a Mexican tradition of landownership and ranching in the suburban present. In all of these ways, the suburban public spaces devoted to charrería have allowed ethnic Mexicans to contest the contours of Los Angeles's racial geography. But these are also fiscally and legally precarious spaces, constantly at risk of closure or demolition, and their managers and lessees—now overwhelmingly Latino—bear the risks and stresses of rising debt and bankruptcy in ways that highlight the new racial contours of the contemporary regional economy. Thus, the suburban communities where ethnic Mexicans have used charrería to claim public space are not so different from the historic barrios in which ethnic Mexicans were confined after Anglo-American conquest. Though now located (again) in the suburbs, they remain simultaneously spaces of cultural pride, political empowerment, and racialized economic precarity.

FIVE

Shaping Animal Welfare Laws and Becoming Formal Political Subjects

IN THE SUBURBS OF LOS ANGELES AT THE TURN of the twenty-first century, U.S. charros were moderately successful in claiming public space and reterritorializing a Mexican presence in Southern California via the practice of charrería, even as they absorbed new forms of financial risk. But at other scales, displacement and migration among ethnic Mexicans accelerated and took new forms. Throughout the 1980s and '90s, Mexico's economy suffered a series of shocks as national leaders devalued the peso, privatized public assets to finance national debt, and passed neoliberal trade pacts, notably the North American Free Trade Agreement (NAFTA), to spur investment by and trade with U.S. and Canadian firms. Mexico's rural laboring classes were pushed off the land and into poorly paid wage labor at unprecedented rates.[1] As in decades past, many made their way to the United States, settling not only in the border states but also in places in the deindustrializing Midwest, Northeast, and South, where firms sought new sources of cheap labor.[2] A record number of these migrants were and are undocumented. Since 1965, U.S. immigration law has severely restricted opportunities for legal migration by people from the Western Hemisphere, yet U.S. employers continue to recruit and hire them. These conditions mark Mexicans and other Latinos as what historian Mae Ngai calls "impossible subjects"—people for whom inclusion in the nation is a social reality but a legal impossibility. As subjects without rights and excluded from citizenship, they face new forms of social exclusion connected to their racialization as "illegals."[3]

The "illegal" has a long history in the United States, dating at least to the 1920s, when the newly formed U.S. Border Patrol, working closely with Texas ranchers, adopted the practice of apprehending the "Mexican Brown."[4] However, public obsession with "the illegal" has expanded dramatically since the early 1990s, a response to economic recession, the financially constrained public sector, and the increase in the number of migrants, both documented and undocumented, living and laboring in the United States. Yet rising concern about "illegals" is not strictly or even primarily connected to migrants' legal status. Rather, it registers racial anxieties, especially among whites, about the changes that Latinos are thought to pose to American culture. As such, charges of "illegality" and cultural threat target U.S. citizens of Latino heritage and legal permanent residents as much as undocumented migrants.[5]

Discursive constructions of "the illegal," circulated widely in the media, guide political behavior to powerful effect. They block Latinos' claims on U.S. society by generating support for "policies and laws that govern [migrant] behavior, limit their social integration, and obstruct their economic mobility," according to anthropologist Leo Chávez.[6] At the federal level, in 1996 legislators dramatically expanded the conditions under which undocumented migrants can be immediately deported. Since 2003, deportations are carried out by the Department of Homeland Security rather than the Departments of Justice or Labor, transforming undocumented migration from a civil and labor issue to a criminal one, bound up with anxieties about terrorism and the security of the nation-state.[7] These anxieties took more violent form under President Donald Trump, who pushed for the construction of an expanded border wall, termination of the Deferred Action for Childhood Arrivals (DACA) program, and separation of migrant children from their parents to deter further migration. The number of state and local laws related to migration, and especially to immigrant exclusion, has also skyrocketed since the 1990s. Most of these local laws and ordinances focus on social reproduction: they make it difficult or impossible for migrants to find appropriate housing, access health care, send their children to school, use public space, and more— even while migrant labor remains in high demand.[8]

In the face of this anti-immigrant onslaught, Mexican migrants, their children, and their co-ethnics have turned once again to cultural forms and practices associated with Mexican ranch life. Norteña and banda music, quebradita dancing, and mariachi festivals have all flourished since the 1990s.[9] So, too, has charrería. Ethnic Mexicans established dozens of new charro associations in this period, not only in the border states of Texas, Arizona, and California but also areas of relatively new Mexican settlement such as Nebraska, Iowa, and Kansas. As in earlier eras, charrería and other ranchero cultural forms operate as a salve for the low wages, isolation, alienation, and "illegalization" that ethnic Mexicans face. They also cohere Mexican migrants with Mexican Americans and other Latinos across differences of generation, place of origin, and citizenship status. As they pay homage to the rural villages, economic practices, and kin networks left behind, ranchero cultural practices continue to generate a shared racial identity in the face of ongoing displacement and racial subjugation.[10]

The growing popularity and visibility of charrería, especially in new locations, has focused attention on a new issue: the welfare of animals. As we saw in the previous chapter, concerns about animal welfare in the charreada first emerged in the 1970s, when officials from the Los Angeles Department of Animal Regulation protested the Charros Emiliano Zapata's events. Since then, concerns about the charreada have accelerated, corresponding with the maturation of the animal welfare movement, the growth of the Mexican migrant population in the United States, and renewed interest among ethnic Mexicans in ranchero cultural forms.[11] Animal activists have focused on the so-called "horse-tripping" events of the charreada: the manganas a pie and manganas a caballo, which involve roping the front legs of a galloping mare while on foot or on horseback, respectively, to bring her to the ground in a shoulder roll, and the piales, which involve roping a running mare by the hind legs to bring her to a slow stop. Since 1994, animal activists have successfully pushed more than a dozen U.S. states to ban the manganas and/or the piales. Other states and counties have also banned the *cola,* or tailing of the steer.[12]

These animal welfare laws have forced a complicated reckoning between charros, animal activists, and elected officials as they confront each other in the U.S. legislative system. On the one hand, the laws against the manganas, piales, and colas—though almost always originating among progressives— threaten to exacerbate racialized constructions of migrant "illegality." Directly corresponding with the surges in anti-immigrant sentiment that erupted in the mid-1990s and again in the 2010s, the "horse-tripping" laws have often been passed by the very same state legislatures that adopted anti-immigrant laws. The animal welfare laws also have many of the same effects: they discursively construct charros and those who participate in their events as criminal, barbarian, and threatening subjects, and they exclude charros from many public spaces and cultural institutions where they had previously secured a toehold. The laws against "horse-tripping" thus extend a long history in which conflicts over animal practices bolster power inequalities during times of rapid social and demographic transition.[13]

On the other hand, the animal welfare laws register a real and growing critique of the structures of domination that lie at the core of charrería, especially the ways that cattle and horses are made to risk injury or even death in the name of cultural heritage protection. These critiques are also directed at other animal practices such as American-style rodeo, factory farming, and live-food markets, though protests against them have been less effective given the political power of these industries. Moreover, critiques of the manganas, piales, and colas are not strictly racialized; they also emanate from Mexican American animal activists, organizations working for civil rights and immigrant rights, and Latino legislators. Some of these critics draw connections between charros' domination of animals and the patriarchy and homophobia they see within Mexican cultural nationalism. These critiques and tensions have propelled the evolution of other ranchero cultural forms, like mariachi music, and they are also eliciting adaptive responses from U.S. charros.[14]

The debates over "horse-tripping" are thus complicated and multifaceted, but one thing is certain: as charros have responded to concerns about animal welfare in the legislative arena, they have emerged as formal political subjects for the first time in U.S. history. This chapter documents this process, exploring the laws against "horse-tripping" and their effects on charros' political formation since the 1990s. In the same way that the passage of anti-immigrant laws has propelled Mexicans and other Latinos to become naturalized citizens, register to vote, and turn out for elections, so too have the animal welfare debates spurred charros to mobilize politically.[15] Charros have become frequent presences at city council meetings and in state legislative chambers, where they assert the contributions of charros and vaqueros to the making of historic ranch cultures in both the United States and Mexico. They have also developed tactics for working with professional rodeo and ranching organizations dominated by Anglo-Americans, with whom charros now position themselves as a shared interest group. More to the point: it is in and through the legislative disputes over "horse-tripping" that U.S. charros have proactively claimed their status as "original cowboys." In doing so, they lay claim to a core facet of American identity while resisting the constructions of illegality and cultural threat that frame the racialization of ethnic Mexicans in the United States.

While attentive to regional differences between the border states where "horse-tripping" laws first emerged and more recent disputes in the interior and middle West, this chapter necessarily scales up to the national level, mirroring charros' own emergence as national political subjects. Previous chapters examined how charros worked locally, intervening in urban and regional economies, cultural institutions, and social networks when and where they could. But the animal welfare debates, which usually began at the local level and then moved to state legislatures, required U.S. charros to organize themselves differently. As they strategized around how to respond to the animal welfare critiques, U.S. charros traveled from state to state, sharing information with each other and developing new policies and guidelines meant to regulate charrería across the United States. In the process, they, too, began to think and act both regionally and nationally. They also formed new regional and national governance structures that not only regulate charro competitions but also act as conduits for continued and proactive political action. U.S. charros have thus become formal political subjects working at the national scale: they are an organized political bloc working to redefine American identity through their engagement with core narratives of American history, culture, and geography.

"HORSE-TRIPPING" AND ILLEGALITY
IN THE BORDER STATES: CALIFORNIA
AND TEXAS, 1994–1995

Concerns about animal welfare in the charreada emerged first in the border states of California, Texas, and New Mexico during the mid-1990s. At the time, these states were gripped by debate about the impact of expanded Mexican migration on public services and American culture. While many elected officials, especially Latinos, lobbied for expanded social programs to aid migrants and their children, nativist groups such as Save Our State and the Minuteman Project organized white voters to participate in direct actions aimed at defending "American" (white, English-speaking) culture and restricting migrants' access to public services. The first animal welfare laws targeting events in the charreada emerged within this volatile context.

California was the first state to ban "horse-tripping," in 1994. At the time, the state was gripped by debates surrounding Proposition 187, which sought to deny medical care, public education, and other social services to undocumented immigrants and their children. In the context of deep economic recession and growing anxiety among white voters about the state's emerging Latino majority, Proposition 187 passed by nearly 60 percent of the state's voters, with higher percentages among whites. Support was also building for an English-only law, enacted a few years later in the form of Proposition 227, which severely restricted state funds for bilingual education in public schools.

Both laws were later declared unconstitutional, but their passage and the public debates around them succeeded in presenting undocumented migrants in California as illegitimate subjects—valuable for their labor, but unworthy of political participation or social membership, and threatening to American identity.[16]

By contrast, the source of California's "horse-tripping" bill—which was considered in the same historical moment—was unquestionably progressive. Since the mid-1980s, an Oakland-based organization called Action for Animals had worked to pass laws prohibiting animal injuries, taking aim at practices ranging from American-style rodeo to live-food markets.[17] Its director, Eric Mills, is a gay man who was involved in the environmental movement before turning to animal welfare. He articulates a "universalist philosophy—that the abuse of animals is deeply linked with the same domineering mindset that has subjugated women, ethnic minorities, and gay people throughout history."[18]

In 1993, Mills approached state assemblyman Joe Baca, a Latino Democrat representing a working-class, majority-Latino district in San Bernardino County, to sponsor a "horse-tripping" ban. Later that year, Baca introduced Assembly Bill 1809, which would make it a misdemeanor to intentionally trip or fell an equine by the legs for entertainment or sport. The state's charro associations immediately registered their opposition, as did the Professional Rodeo Cowboys Association (PRCA), which feared the bill would allow animal rights groups to target calf roping, a popular event in U.S.-style rodeo.[19] Responding to their concerns, the California State Legislature's agriculture committee, of which Baca was a member, adopted amendments to regulate the manganas rather than prohibit them outright. Disappointed with the amendments, Mills asked Baca to drop the bill.[20] Mills then took his proposal to the county level. In both Alameda and Contra Costa Counties, both located in the San Francisco Bay area, he worked with local officials to ban the manganas and the colas; he also helped pass an ordinance that required veterinarians to be physically present at all charreadas.[21]

The following year, Mills returned to the state legislature, seeking a bill following the blueprint of the county ordinances. This time, he arranged for the California Equine Council to sponsor the bill through Assemblyman John Burton, a white Democrat from the San Francisco Bay area. The new bill proposed to amend an existing section of the California penal code that already banned horse "poling" (using a pole fitted with sharp objects to make a horse jump higher) to also prohibit "horse-tripping." A violation would be punished by up to six months in jail and a fine of up to $1,000. Exceptions were made for medical and identification purposes.[22] Though the bill specified that it should not "be construed as condemning or limiting any cultural or historical activities, except those prohibited therein," it clearly targeted an event with cultural and historical significance to many ethnic Mexicans.[23] Despite its progressive origins, the bill could not help but invoke the contentious issues of race, culture, and nation circulating in California.

Media coverage played a key role in activating racialized anxieties about the charreada and linking them with concerns about immigration, race, and national identity, transforming ethical concerns for animal welfare into a reactionary force. While the "horse-tripping" bill was before the California State Legislature, a television special titled "Pity the Horses" aired on ABC's *20/20* program. Veterinarians, animal rights activists, and a Chicana activist testified to the danger and cruelty of the charreada. The one representative of the charros simply defended charreada in the name of tradition. Ramping up the sense of danger and secrecy, the reporter claimed that she "needed to blend in to attend" because "armed guards are present and conduct full body searches for weapons and cameras." As anthropologist Olga Nájera-Ramírez observes, the segment hinted that charrería is un-American through pointed references to charrería as Mexico's national sport; it offered no recognition of charrería's roots in the southwestern borderlands or its influences on American-style rodeo. By failing to mention that activists similarly oppose American-style rodeos, the segment isolated charros as the unitary threat, thus racializing the debate in a way that did not necessarily reflect animal activists' goal to target *all* rodeos.[24] Despite these biases and blind spots, the *20/20* program was included as the main piece of evidence in the legislative analysis prepared for Burton's bill, demonstrating the power of media spectacles to influence law.

The matter of committee assignment proved a subtle but significant factor in shaping the California bill's fate. The previous year's bill had been read and discussed by the state assembly's agricultural committee, but the 1994 version was taken up by the public safety committee, repositioning the manganas as a criminal matter. Likewise, during the committee hearing, animal welfare activists refuted the idea that the events in question were necessary or legitimate parts of the Mexican ranching tradition—at least not when practiced in the context of urban sporting culture—and argued that they must be considered as criminal matters. In its testimony, for example, the San Francisco Society for the Prevention of Cruelty to Animals submitted:

"Although practiced at certain rodeo shows, 'horse tripping' has no legitimate ranching or agricultural application. It is solely in the name of 'entertainment' that horses running at full gallop have their legs lassoed and yanked out from under them." Similarly, the Fund for Animals denied the possibility that charros could be qualified caregivers of horses if they engaged in such practices: "No [true] horseperson would subject his or her horse to such treatment."[25] Notably, while the Professional Rodeo Cowboys Association had opposed the prior year's legislation, in this case the PRCA remained neutral, claiming that the organization felt no kinship with charros and saw no reason to protect charrería.[26]

Defenders of the manganas, who were overwhelmingly Latino, rejected the implication that charreada events were illegitimate, even criminal, and argued that the bill would contribute to the climate of anti-immigrant sentiment and anti-Mexican racism in the state. Former state assemblyman and then–Los Angeles City Councilman Richard Alatorre said he supported charrería because it is part of Mexican American culture and a traditional form of family entertainment. He rejected the characterization of charros as abusers who do not care about animal welfare, saying: "I think [the ban] . . . was prompted not by what is the norm, but by some renegade groups that made it seem like charros are unsympathetic to the welfare of animals, which could not be further from the truth." Opponents argued that the bill unfairly singled out ethnic Mexican cultural events because it proposed to punish "horse-tripping" but did not outlaw similar activities associated with Anglo-American rodeo, such as calf roping. As Pedro Vaca, then-president of the Charros de Los Angeles, told a reporter: "This is a Mexican sport, and I think that has something to do with this. If they take this away from us, what happens next? That's what many of us Latinos are saying." Manuel Escobedo, an organizer of charreadas at the Pico Rivera Sports Arena, believed there were undertones of racism in the bill: "The Americans are trying to take away one of the greatest Mexican traditions . . . Plenty of horses die [at racetracks] but no one has complained about that like this."[27]

However, the debate about "horse-tripping" in California was not clearly defined along racial or ethnic lines. Influential groups representing Mexican Americans—including some that had been closely involved with charros in the past—also registered their opposition to the manganas and piales. The Mexican American Political Association, the Mexican American Chamber of Commerce, the United Farm Workers (UFW), and the International

Longshore Workers Union all supported the California bill to ban "horse-tripping." The Mexican American Chamber of Commerce, for example, said:

> The tripping of horses serves no useful or beneficial purpose and is neither an art nor a sport nor can it be defended on the grounds of cultural diversity or national tradition . . . You don't have to know how to trip horses to be considered a good Mexican or Californian charro . . . No true horseman would consider, much less allow, his/her horse to be tripped.[28]

Mills also submitted as evidence a letter that César Chávez, founder of the UFW, had written to him in 1990, which says:

> There is great need for legislation to ensure the humane treatment of animals employed in rodeos, and I would certainly support any such bills . . . Racism, economic deprival, dog fighting, and cock fighting, bullfighting and rodeos are cut from the same fabric: violence. Only when we have become nonviolent towards all life will we have learned to live well ourselves.[29]

While Chávez referred to *all* rodeos, not just charreadas, Mills also submitted a 1993 letter he had received from Arturo Rodríguez, then-president of the UFW, which was more specific: "The legislation concerning charreadas and the banning of the most dangerous and harmful of the events that you [Action for Animals] are currently trying to put through is worthwhile and much needed . . . I support your efforts on behalf of animals."[30]

Given its cross-section of supporters, including organizations representing ethnic Mexicans, passage was swift. After moving through the public safety committee, the bill passed the State Assembly 64 to 2, and then passed the Senate in what journalists called a "stunning 117–3 floor vote."[31] On September 19, 1994, Governor Pete Wilson—a figure widely known for campaigning on the basis of anti-immigrant sentiment—signed the bill into law. Section 597g was added to the California Penal Code, making the practice of "horse-tripping" a state misdemeanor.

Responses to the new law among California's charros reflect the wider vulnerability, economic dislocation, and political marginalization that ethnic Mexicans and Latinos experienced during the 1990s. Ramiro Rodríguez, national press secretary of the American Charro Association and operator of Lienzo Charro Los Alazanes in El Monte (a suburban city in Los Angeles's San Gabriel Valley), blamed the bill for the demise of his business, as the de facto criminalization of his charreada caused weekly attendance to drop from 1,800 people to 200 or 300. He told a reporter: "They almost made it seem like going to a charreada was illegal, like going to a cockfight or dog-fight." In Rodríguez's telling, a broader impact on the community and economy was already visible:

> The arenas in Escondido, Coachella, Bakersfield, they went away. People went from training horses to working as truck drivers. A lot of people that were liv-ing well went from being on top to being on the bottom ... Mr. Mills shoots that gun up in the air and doesn't see where the bullet falls, how many lives it destroys.[32]

To be sure, there were other structural forces contributing to these changes. Deindustrialization had led to Latinos being overrepresented among the urban poor, and urbanization of the American population had made char-readas and rodeos less familiar to voters. Alcohol-induced violence was also an emerging problem at some charreadas, jaripeos, and coleaderos, especially those lacking official sanction.[33] But charros interpreted these processes as linked phenomena—a cumulative attack on their livelihoods and cultures. Marcos Franco, national director of the FMCH in the United States and a charro from California's East Bay, described the vulnerability and exaspera-tion that charros felt:

> From what I know of Mills, he's trying to do a noble thing ... [but] we're like the 99-cent store for the animal activists. Eric Mills and these animal activ-ists, that's all they do, they're at the state capitol eight hours a day, but I lost time at work and money going back and forth to the state capitol to lobby.

He recalled that when the charros went to Sacramento to protest the bill, their president spoke no English and needed a translator; because of their outfits, "the senators thought the guys were mariachis." For Franco, the charros had been delegitimized as political subjects: "They really decimated us, and at that time we weren't prepared. We didn't know why everything was happening."[34]

For the California charros, these experiences were a wake-up call. They invited representatives from all U.S.-based charro associations to a meeting in California, where they decided to proactively modify the practice of man-ganas across the United States. As the result of that meeting, since 1994, U.S. charros may rope the horse's legs in the manganas and piales by using a "breakaway rope," but they are prohibited from bringing the horse to the ground; strict punishments are imposed on those who do. Américo García, then-president of the San Antonio Charro Association, who attended the California meeting, relayed the general sentiment among participants:

[We] came to the conclusion that tripping the mare was not necessary to preserve what we know as the sport. That was needed 200 years ago, when we didn't have corrals ... Now we don't need to stop the horse completely. All we preserve is the *act* of roping the horse. We'll rope the hind legs, but we'll let the rope go.[35]

While it responded to critiques about animal welfare emanating from California, this voluntary change also evened the playing field among U.S. charros nationally, given that California charros would otherwise be at a disadvantage when competing with charros from other states. U.S. charros also began working with the FMCH to develop a revised qualification system that permits U.S. charros to compete at the national championships in Mexico despite having lower point totals in qualifying charreadas in the U.S. according to traditional scoring methods.[36] These modifications signaled U.S. charros' recognition of their need to be more politically organized as a cohesive body in the United States. They also contributed to the ongoing evolution of charrería, both in the United States and transnationally.

Despite the charros' modifications, charrería remained a target for animal welfare activists throughout the mid-1990s. During this period, Texas, New Mexico, Illinois, and Oklahoma joined California in passing amendments to their state penal codes that banned and punished "horse-tripping."[37] With the exception of Oklahoma, where the law made it illegal to promote or profit from "horse-tripping" but did not outlaw its performance, these were all places where the impacts of Mexican migrants and their co-ethnics on public services and American culture were inflamed political topics. In this context, animal welfare laws banning the manganas and the piales inevitably compounded debates about race, migration, and national identity. Once passed, the laws also had the effect of marginalizing ethnic Mexicans from cultural and political institutions where they had made significant inroads in previous decades.

This was certainly the case in Texas, where concerns about "horse-tripping" first bubbled up in San Antonio among activists whose goal was to remove the charros from Fiesta. By the 1990s, San Antonio had become an indisputably Mexican city in terms of its demographics, politics, and image. Mexican Americans, who represented more than 50 percent of the city's population, had achieved significant political power, notably through the election in 1981 of Henry Cisneros, the city's first Latino mayor since the 1840s. Racialized poverty and processes of urban displacement certainly persisted, as did the popularity of the Alamo and its narrative of Anglo conquest of Mexicans. Even so, the city's political culture and tourist industry were becoming increasingly rooted in a metropolitan and transnational Mexican identity—a fact that was perceived as threatening to some, especially at the regional and statewide level.[38] During the 1980s and '90s, and much like California, the state of Texas considered several high-profile lawsuits and pieces of legislation related to race-based affirmative action and English-only laws. Activists' efforts to remove the charros from Fiesta occurred at this scalar disjuncture, between the ethnically defined power that charros enjoyed at the local level in San Antonio and the defense of Anglo-American culture rippling statewide.

In San Antonio, the campaign against the charreada was led by VOICE for Animals, a local nonprofit organization with a national membership. Capitalizing upon the 1994 airing of the *Hard Copy* and *20/20* programs as well as the legislation brewing in California, VOICE launched a "Charreada Blitzkrieg" that called for the removal of the San Antonio Charro Association's charreada from Fiesta. Unlike animal activists in other places, VOICE did not just target the manganas or the piales, but rather the entire charreada, which it deemed irremediably cruel and violent. In addition to staging rallies and protests at the Battle of Flowers—the oldest Fiesta event—and holding a candlelight vigil for injured animals, VOICE coordinated a phone- and letter-writing campaign asking the Fiesta San Antonio Commission (FSAC) to stop sponsoring the San Antonio Charro Association's charreada. Between April 1 and May 2, 1994, approximately twenty people called the commission to lodge their complaints. Another forty people sent letters. A few letters and calls came from individuals with Spanish surnames, but the majority appears to have come from Anglos.[39]

Most of these letters followed a standardized format. In virtually all of the letters, the writer first claimed to have viewed the *Hard Copy* and *20/20* programs, which showed horses being "badly injured, beaten and abused" in the charreadas. Because this same language was used in virtually all of the letters, it is hard to know whether each writer had actually seen the television programs, or if they simply relied upon a template provided by VOICE. Second, the writer asked the Fiesta commission to stop sponsoring the charreada. Lastly, the writer stated that he or she would not visit San Antonio for vacation if the city allowed charreadas to continue. Most included the phrase, "I will *not* visit a city that condones animal abuse!" The writers' call for excluding the charros directly targeted San Antonio's heavy reliance upon tourism—much of which was now based on the city's Mexican identity.

A handful of letters came from California-based members of VOICE, who spoke with authority about the legislative process to ban the manganas then under way in their state. One couple, the Knopoffs, wrote:

> The people of California were outraged to learn that this brutality was taking place in their midst. A bill was presented in our legislature that would ban the intentional tripping of horses for any reason. This horse-tripping ban has already passed in our Assembly and will soon go before the State Senate. It is important to note that the Charreada itself was not the object of a legislative ban—only the cruel practice of horse-tripping.[40]

Significantly, this couple was the only one to distinguish between the manganas and the charreada as a whole. Other writers failed to make this distinction and called for the wholesale exclusion of charros and charrería from Fiesta. Another set of Californians, the Browns, wrote: "We have charradas [sic] in California but not in Sacramento. We did not know how obscene they are until we saw it on 20/20 and Hard Copy. They are against California's anti-cruelty laws and will be banned here."[41] In fact, the Browns were wrong: the California law did not target the charreadas as a whole, only the manganas. The Browns' statement suggests the power of media spectacles to shape public opinion in ways that can exacerbate racialized constructions of illegality: they had never seen a charreada before viewing one on television and knew nothing about its internal structure or meaning to participants, but after viewing the media spectacle, they acted politically in ways that targeted a cultural practice of deep significance to many ethnic Mexicans.

As in California, however, VOICE activists were careful to deflect potential charges of anti-Mexican racism. They were, for instance, quick to cite the growing heterogeneity of thought among ethnic Mexicans about charrería. Sandra James, a San Antonio resident and accountant, noted that not all of the ethnic Mexican community supported the charreadas: "Certainly the event reflects badly upon the Charro Association, and it doesn't reflect the spirit of some of the greatest Hispanic leaders, including Cesar Chávez, who spoke out strongly for the need for kindness and compassion toward all living things."[42] San Antonio residents George and Louise Taylor took a more personal approach: "People who know us could tell you we are as far as we could be from being racists. We appreciate Mexican culture. But culture is no excuse for barbarism. It is high time to discourage cruelty and real-life violence against humans and non-humans alike."[43]

Though they disavowed racism, the VOICE letter writers drew upon discourses of crime that were increasingly racialized and associated with immigrants, especially Mexicans, during the 1990s. Writers to the San Antonio Fiesta Commission suggested that crime and violence were increasing in the United States and implied that those who participated in charrería were at least partially responsible. Greta Bunting of St. Petersburg, Florida, linked the charreada directly to crime:

> How do you expect crime to ever be reduced in our crime-ridden country if you cater to the basest instincts of human beings? Cruelty to animals is a premise for cruelty to humans, and your Commission should be ashamed of catering to it. You are also contributing to violence in society. There is too much of it already. If you think carefully about what I have said, your choice must be to do away with "charreadas" forever.[44]

Similarly, VOICE member Nanette Bradley scoffed at the idea that the charreada constituted a tradition worth preserving. She asked: "Drive-by shootings have become a tradition . . . will you consider that for a Fiesta Event?"[45]

Outraged as the letter writers may have been, the leadership of the Fiesta San Antonio Commission continued to depend on charros to provide a strong cultural identity for the city's tourism industry. As we have seen, the San Antonio charros were also well connected with the city's power brokers. These facts provided the San Antonio charros with some political leverage in shaping the outcome of the dispute. After receiving complaints from VOICE members, Marleen Pedroza, the vice president of the Fiesta San Antonio Commission, met with charro association members to work out a solution. Afterward, she sent letters to each of the animal welfare activists who had written her office. Pedroza's letter explained that the charros loved their animals and didn't want the charreadas to be perceived as a venue for animal cruelty. She affirmed that the San Antonio charros would work with the commission and VOICE to modify their events. Specifically, the charros agreed that the manganas would be changed: "The pageantry and athleticism of the event will remain but the actual tripping of the animal will not take place."[46] This concession did not occur in a vacuum: the San Antonio charros were well aware of what was happening in California and knew they would soon need to modify the events on a national level. Indeed, shortly after their meeting with Pedroza, the San Antonio charros attended the California meeting described above, where charros agreed that horses would no longer be brought to the ground in the manganas or piales anywhere in the United States. Since 1995, the San Antonio

Charro Association has continued to participate in Fiesta by staging a char-reada, which remains an officially sanctioned Fiesta event and is always coupled with "A Day in Old Mexico." However, they now perform only six of the nine traditional suertes; they no longer perform the manganas or the piales.

The power that charros exercised in San Antonio did not translate so easily to state politics, however, revealing the scalar politics of race in Texas (and other states where the issue was considered, as we shall see later in the chapter). A few months later, animal activists lobbied the Texas State Legislature to consider a statewide "horse-tripping" ban. As in California, committee assignment was crucial: the bill bypassed the agricultural or ranching committee and instead was handled by the legislature's criminal justice committee and the state attor-ney general, shoring up the sense of a linkage between charrería and crime. John Whitmire, chair of the criminal justice committee, requested that the state attorney general, Dan Morales, issue an opinion. Morales—who would later extend the statewide ban on affirmative action in university admissions, decided in *Hopwood v. Texas* (1996), to *all* internal university functions—argued that "horse-tripping" was sufficiently cruel and sadistic that a jury could reasonably conclude that it constitutes "torture." However, he noted that "since 'torture' is no longer defined in Texas law ... we believe that a jury would be obliged to construe the term in accordance with its commonly understood meaning."[47] Recognizing the ambiguity within the law, he recommended an amendment to the existing animal cruelty laws. That amendment, which was approved by the Texas State Legislature in September 1995, banned the intentional tripping of horses under the animal cruelty section of the state penal code.[48]

Several years later, members of the San Antonio Charro Association explained how these campaigns had shifted their sense of belonging in the city. Like the California charros, they experienced the laws and campaigns as an attack on their personal integrity, ethnic identity, and culture, even if they conceded the need for greater animal protection. San Antonio charro Raul Gaona told a reporter that he generally agreed the modifications had been a good thing, adding: "But I want to say this: The charreada practices are not designed to hurt the animals. After all, the rancher wanted to sell his bulls and steers and he certainly didn't want them hurt. The same with horses. They were needed and valued. The rules of the sport protect both horseman and animal."[49] The San Antonio charros also believed that prejudice and anti-Mexican racism had been at play. Jerry Díaz, an internationally renowned charro who had been involved with the San Antonio Charro Association for decades, suggested that the charreadas were targeted not because they were any more harmful or cruel to animals than American-style rodeos, but because they were poorly funded and less politically powerful. He explained, "The only difference I see is that the charreada is not funded like the American rodeo, which is a professional sport. There could be a big controversy because who's to say what's more cruel than the other. Really, there is no right or wrong. It's just different traditions and cultures."[50]

Yet, by the mid-1990s, defenses of charrería that invoked its importance for Mexican tradition or culture were not only ineffective, but politically damaging. Given widespread anxieties about migration and changing racial demographics, charros made themselves vulnerable to charges of criminality, barbarism, and cultural threat when they claimed to represent Mexican tradition. Charros thus recognized the need to change strategies. Amid the darkening national mood, they scaled up to the national level, organizing themselves more deliberately as political subjects and making more direct claims to American cultural identity.

SCALING UP: FORGING NEW POLITICAL GEOGRAPHIES AND SUBJECTIVITIES

The 1994 meeting in California, during which charros agreed to change their practice of manganas and piales in the United States, represented a major turning point in the political organization of U.S. charros. That meeting signaled growing recognition that they could no longer work primarily at the local level, nor could they rely solely on ethnically defined networks. Instead, they would need to begin organizing nationally and forging new coalitions. Over the course of the late 1990s and early 2000s, charros in the United States developed innovative organizations, tactics, and alliances that facilitated their emergence as national political subjects.

New organizations were key to scaling up their activities. For decades, the Mexico City–based Federación Mexicana de Charrería (FMCH) had regulated the practice of charrería in the United States from abroad by appointing special executive assistants to represent the federation at U.S. charreadas and other events. In 1991, the FMCH changed course, creating an organizing body specifically for U.S.-based charros: the FMCH-USA. The establishment of the FMCH-USA formalized the governance of charrería as a transnational practice and recognized the significance of US-based charros as full participants in the ongoing evolution of charro culture. As of this writing, the FMCH-USA provides administrative support to more than one hundred officially federated charro associations and thirty escaramuza teams in the United States. It also sanctions more than four hundred charreadas each year. In turn, the national FMCH-USA is organized into eleven state-level associations. Some of these represent charros in border states with long histories of Mexican migration: Arizona, California, Colorado, New Mexico, and Texas, as well as Illinois (principally Chicago). Others help organize charros in interior locations, farther from the U.S.-Mexico border, where Mexicans are newer but growing populations: Idaho, Kansas, Nebraska, Oregon, and Washington.[51] Other charro organizations that claim national membership but are rooted in specific borderlands localities, such as the American Charro Association in Texas and the Charros Federation USA in California, were also established in the 1990s and early 2000s.

These organizations have played a major role in enabling the emergence of charros as formal political subjects. Beyond sanctioning and regulating charreadas, they have organized charros and their supporters to participate in letter-writing campaigns, attend political hearings, and speak authoritatively to journalists. They have also provided a vehicle through which U.S. charros have intervened in arts, history, and cultural spheres. Since 2000, for example, U.S. charro organizations have co-curated exhibits at museums both regional and national, such as the Autry Museum of Western Heritage (now the Autry National Center) in Griffith Park, California; the Haggin Museum in Stockton, California; and the Smithsonian Museum of American History in Washington, D.C.[52] The national charro organizations have also coordinated their own animal welfare initiatives, such as the FMCH-USA's CUIDA program—Charros and Cowboys United Institution Defending Animals and Culture. The acronym "cuida" translates from Spanish to English as "care," and the program educates participants about best practices in animal care, feeding, and handling.[53] Significantly, it also positions Mexican charros and U.S. cowboys as united in their defense of their respective sports.

Indeed, perhaps the most important of the charros' new interventions is their work to solidify strategic alliances with Anglo-dominated U.S. rodeo and ranching industries. Charros recognize that American-style rodeo and ranching interests have significant political and economic power that they lack, given that U.S.-style rodeo is seen as a valuable form of American heritage in a way that charrería is not—at least, not yet. Across the U.S. West, American-style rodeo as well as ranching and agriculture retain influential political lobbyists, whose institutional power charros hope to share. This relationship between charros and cowboys may be uneven, but it is not one-sided. American-style rodeo has also been targeted by animal welfare activists in recent years, and it faces many of the social and cultural changes that have made ranching and rodeo less familiar and less appealing to urban audiences.[54] As Marcos Franco Águilar explained in the early 2000s: "As Vice President [of the FMCH-USA], I've had to speak with various institutions, especially ones involved with rodeos, for mutual support. As a result, they are starting to have a better understanding of our sport and they recognize that we are a strong sector with organizational power that, in the long run, can attract a lot of sponsors."[55]

Professional American rodeo and the charros first collaborated officially in 2002, when the U.S. charros asked the Professional Rodeo Cowboys Association (PRCA) to help them oppose a California ban on coleaderos spearheaded by Eric Mills. The PRCA referred the charros to Bob Fox, California lobbyist for the PRCA, whom the charros then hired as a consultant. At a meeting in Las Vegas, Fox and PRCA officials advised the charros to lobby the legislature's Latino Caucus to get the bill moved to the agricultural committee, which Mills had characterized as a "death bed for animals." Acting on this advice, the charros succeeded in moving the bill to the agricultural committee and pushing the vote back by two weeks. Following a massive letter-writing campaign to the bill's sponsor, state senator Liz Figueroa of Fremont, Figueroa stated that she did not have enough votes, and withdrew the bill. Steer-tailing remains legal in California charreadas, except in those counties (Alameda and Contra Costa) that had previously outlawed it via local ordinance, owing in part to the legal advice given the charros by lobbyists and consultants associated with American-style professional rodeo.[56]

Since the early 2000s, with lessons learned from corporate American rodeo, the U.S. charros have developed a toolkit of strategic alliances and tactical interventions in the legislative arena. One of these, as just described, is to ensure that any "horse-tripping" bill is read and heard by a legislature's agricultural, livestock, or ranching committee. If a bill is assigned elsewhere, such as a criminal justice committee, the charros lobby to have it moved. This tactic of committee assignment has helped to ensure that any bill directed at charros and their sport is heard by a more sympathetic audience—one that is invested in representing the interests and histories of ranchers and agriculturalists, not adjudicating criminal matters. For this same reason, charros are also better able to call upon America-style rodeo and ranching interests for support in opposing a bill, while resisting the criminalization of charros and the ethnic Mexican community more broadly.

U.S. charros have also remained consistent in seeking a respectable, moderate politics. Charros are careful to register themselves as modern, rational political subjects, rather than ethnic radicals or political extremists. They are eager to negotiate and develop compromise bills. When a bill seems likely to pass despite their efforts, charros negotiate amendments that reward both Mexican and American rodeo interests for implementing high-quality animal welfare provisions. For example, charros have supported some laws that target charrería when they allow counties to give permits for events on a case-by-case basis, following the county's review of planned veterinary and logistical procedures. Charros signal that they would prefer to consider changes and amendments like these rather than having their events eliminated altogether. In doing so, they show that they are active agents in the making of a modern, transnational cultural practice, not premodern relics of a static cultural tradition. Given widespread public debate about the racial and cultural change that migrant traditions portend for American culture, this is a significant and strategic move.

Finally, through their participation in the U.S. legislative process, charros assert their centrality to American history and culture. In testimonies at hearings and in their written opposition, charros explain the similarities between U.S. and Mexican versions of rodeo events. They also insist on the use of terms such as "forefooting" and "wrangling" to describe the contested events, rather than the inflammatory phrase "horse-tripping." Essentially, they position the contested events within Mexican rodeo as akin to their counterparts in American rodeo, emanating as they did from a shared historical borderlands. In some cases, the U.S. charros directly claim their status as "original cowboys"—not criminal threats or animal abusers—whose practice should be protected on the basis of its historical and enduring contribution to American culture. Through these techniques of historical interpretation and linguistic framing, charros have narrated a multicultural and transnational history of ranching that resists the racial and nationalist constructions of that history in both the United States and Mexico.

When the second wave of "horse-tripping" bills hit in the 2000s and 2010s, alongside a renewed onslaught of anti-immigrant laws, charros and their supporters mobilized all of these tactics flexibly in their engagements with city, county, and state governments. While scaling up to the national level, they also encountered significant regional differences in political cultures and racial climates, especially between the border states and those of the interior and middle West.

Concerns about animal welfare in the charreada continued to percolate through border states with large numbers of Mexican migrants and Mexican Americans in the 2000s. In 2009, the Arizona State Legislature overwhelmingly passed House Bill 2282, which banned the manganas even while it explicitly protected "jumping or steeplechase events, racing, training, branding, show events, calf or steer roping events, bulldogging or steer wrestling events or any other traditional western rodeo events, including barrel racing, bareback or saddled bronc riding or other similar activities or events."[57] The Arizona bill originated with two progressives, Phoenix city councilperson Thelda Williams and state representative Kyrsten Sinema, who were concerned with the ethical issues at stake in the charreada and their links to other problems facing ethnic Mexican communities. But it became a maelstrom for debates about race, citizenship, and culture in Arizona, signified by the legislature's passage the following year of Senate Bill 1070, which authorized police to engage in racial profiling for the purposes of apprehending undocumented migrants. Through the exemptions made for white "western" equine sports, the racialized nature of Arizona's "horse-tripping" law was made similarly clear.

However, the intertwined nature of concerns about the charreadas and Mexican migrant culture did not translate so easily to states in the interior and middle West, which also considered a series of laws against the manganas and piales in the 2000s and '10s. In these places, Mexican migrants were proving themselves vital contributors to the restructuring of animal industries such as rodeo, ranching, dairying, and factory farming, all of which retained significant power in political and popular culture. Given the growing importance of Mexican laborers to economic revitalization, the charros' political efforts have been significantly more effective in these regions, both in shaping the laws that govern their cultural practice and in allowing them to claim status as the "original cowboys"—that is, as legitimate American subjects.

Nevada is an interesting case of this phenomenon given the demographic split between its large cities and rural areas, which roughly mirrors the political differences between border states and those in the interior West. Mexicans and other Latinos had a long-established presence in Nevada, but until the 2000s they were concentrated in just two urban counties: Clark County, which houses the city of Las Vegas, and Washoe County, which includes the city of Reno.[58] These counties adopted local ordinances prohibiting the manganas in the mid-1990s, alongside the border states of California, Texas, and New Mexico. However, a statewide ban was a nonstarter given the political power of ranching and rodeo interests across Nevada, much of which remains rural. When Senator Dina Titus, a Democrat from Las Vegas, introduced a bill banning "horse-tripping" to the state legislature in 1995, it was referred to the natural resources committee, where it died after rancher and committee chairman Dean Rhodes, a Republican from the northern Nevada town of Tuscarora, refused to grant the measure a hearing.[59]

It was only in the 2000s and '10s, when Latinos began migrating beyond their established population centers in Las Vegas and Reno to small towns across Nevada, that a statewide measure prohibiting "horse-tripping" gained traction. In 2011, Senator Allison Copening, who represents Las Vegas and Clark County, introduced a new bill to ban "horse-tripping" statewide, with the American Society for the Prevention of Cruelty to Animals (ASPCA) listed as the bill's official sponsor. The impetus was an upcoming charreada to be held in Winnemucca, a small city in northern Nevada that had become one-third Hispanic/Latino in the previous decade.[60] Copening's bill, which took language directly from the Clark County ordinance established nearly two decades before, proposed to "prohibit a person from engaging in horse tripping for enjoyment, entertainment, competition, or practice" as well as "organizing, sponsoring, promotion, overseeing, or receiving money for the admission of a person to a horse tripping event." Punishment would range from a jail sentence of up to six months and a fine of $1,000 for a first offense to a felony conviction, punishable by imprisonment and a fine of up to $10,000, for a third offense. As in other state and local ordinances, exemptions were made for medical purposes—though not, as in Arizona, for "traditional western events" associated with Anglo-Americans.[61] Indeed, it was the law's failure to exempt American-style rodeo that initially stalled its passage.

Copening's bill was again referred to the natural resources committee, now chaired by Mark Manendo, which heard testimony in the state capitol, Carson City, in April 2011. Beverlee McGrath, who identified herself as a member of the ASPCA, Best Friends Animal Society, and Action for Animals, spoke first in support of the bill. McGrath requested an amendment to the language of the bill to include the words "or lassoing or roping the legs," in addition to the existing language making it illegal to intentionally engage in "horse-tripping." Eric Mills, the key figure behind the passage of the 1994 California legislation, spoke next and asked the committee members to "forgive this plea from out-of-state, but animal abuse knows no boundaries." He supported McGrath's amendment and explained the reasons why, from his perspective, it was necessary: "Presently, the charros claim that they no longer fell the horses, but let the rope go slack. But horses can still become entangled in the ropes and fall. A total ban is the only viable solution." Mills then provided the letters of support from César Chávez and Arturo Rodríguez, past presidents of the United Farm Workers, that he had submitted in numerous other legislative debates, as well as video footage of a charreada held in Winnemucca fifteen years before.[62]

Representatives of Nevada's charro associations immediately objected to the dated nature of Mills's sources, as well as the essentialist and unchanging picture they gave of charro culture. Alejandro Galindo, president of the Las Vegas Charros Association, reminded the legislators and the public that "horse-tripping" had not occurred in Nevada or the entire U.S. for nearly twenty years, since the charros' voluntary agreement in 1994. Galindo described the legislative process as "a constant attack from state to state" in which charros were repeatedly asked to respond to dated and biased sources, despite the fact that no data on animal injury had ever been provided. He noted that similar legislation had recently been considered in Oregon and Colorado, but those bills died because there was no evidence that animals were being harmed (the Oregon bill would later pass, in 2013, but the Colorado bill stalled in committee).[63]

Stretching the scale of the issue beyond the city of Las Vegas, which he represented, to encompass state and regional history, Galindo reframed the manganas as an essential part of western history in which ethnic Mexicans had played—and continued to play—prominent roles. He made the important point that "horse-tripping" had become naturalized language in the legislative process, even though it was mistranslated and decontextualized. He stated: "Someone has erroneously translated manganas to mean horse tripping. Manganas is not horse tripping, manganas is the act of horse wrangling. Wrangling is part of the West." Elmer Pacheco, representing the Charro Association of Northern Nevada (which includes Winnemucca), expressed a similar perspective. Pacheco noted the slippage between the idea of "horse-tripping" as understood by animal welfare activists and the manganas as understood and practiced by charros: "We never have horse tripping, we have a manganas." For Pacheco, these were distinct things. Chairman

Manendo replied by asking, "When you get together with your family, do you do horse tripping?" Pacheco responded, "We do not do horse tripping . . . Manganas is not a horse-tripping event. The law since 1995 eliminates horse tripping from charreadas. We do manganas without tripping the horse."[64]

However, the decisive opposition came not from the charros, but rather Nevada's enormously influential corporate rodeo and ranching industries, which retained a firm group on the state's political culture. At the hearing, those advocates argued that the "horse-tripping" bill could be interpreted to eliminate their own events and rangeland practices. There would be major repercussions, they warned, for Nevada's economy—and not just the state's rural areas, but also its cities, where ranching traditions took the form of a highly profitable urban sports culture. Senators John Lee and Tom Collins both worried aloud that the legislation might affect the National Finals Rodeo held annually in Las Vegas. Phillip Hacker, an intern to Senator Lee, testified that the National Finals Rodeo and the Reno Rodeo had a combined annual economic impact of over $85 million, before warning:

> Passing this will send a message to the rodeo community that Nevada does not stand with them. Mind you this is a community which brings hundreds of thousands of visitors and contributes millions of dollars to the economies of communities throughout the state . . . we can ill afford to burn bridges with people who reliably contribute to the state's economy.[65]

Although Copening clarified that corporate rodeo and ranching would not be affected, the natural resources committee was not convinced, and a motion to pass the bill failed for lack of a second.[66] The strength of Nevada's ranching and rodeo industries, which had become increasingly dependent on Mexican labor, thus prevented a "horse-tripping" ban from being passed in 2011.

Several weeks later, the Winnemucca charreada proceeded as planned, and participants described it as a peaceful event in which no people or animals were seriously injured. Shortly thereafter, however, a Reno television station aired a video created by an activist who had attended. Though filmed with a mobile phone and of very poor quality, the video claimed to provide evidence that horses had indeed been "tripped"—a claim refuted by participating charros as well as other spectators (in my own viewing of the video, whether or not the horse was "tripped" is not clear). Nonetheless, members of the natural resources committee were furious, believing they had been lied to. Committee chairman Mark Manendo spearheaded a new bill to ban the

Bus stop advertisement in Las Vegas, Nevada, for the World Series of Charrería prior to the event's cancellation in the wake of a new animal rights law. Photo by Alonso Reyes for Graphic Illusion Design Studio, used with permission.

manganas and the piales. The new bill passed both houses in a special session, and in June 2013—after twenty years of lobbying by the state's animal welfare agencies—Governor Brian Sandoval signed Nevada's "horse-tripping" bill into law.[67] The law's passage signified a major scalar shift: while Latinos' cultural practice had once been seen as a local issue, confined to Nevada's biggest cities, it was now a matter of statewide concern.

Even so, the scalar tension between Nevada's large cities and rural towns persisted in the structure of the law. The new law allowed local governments to issue conditional permits for events with "horse roping"—where the horse would be caught but not downed—a loophole meant partially to ensure that events associated with the corporate rodeo and ranching industries could proceed at the discretion of municipal governments. That loophole created a quandary for the World Series of Charrería, scheduled for September 2013 at Las Vegas's South Point Hotel Resort and Casino. The event's planned location at South Point, which hosts some of the country's most prestigious equestrian events, was a milestone for U.S.-based charros. The commissioners of Clark County had to decide whether to use the loophole to allow the World Series of Charrería to proceed with all nine events, three in modified form. After several hours of "impassioned debate," commissioners voted 6–1 against such a proposal. The Nevada charros explored other options, including holding the event without the manganas and piales or relocating it to another state, but ultimately the entire event was scrapped.[68]

After the event's cancellation, Alejandro Galindo, president of the Las Vegas Charros Association, asserted that twenty thousand visitors, primarily Latinos, had been anticipated to attend the World Series of Charrería. He argued that through Clark County's failure to grant an available exemption, Latinos had been told they were not welcome in one of the city's premiere recreational spaces. Finally, Galindo remarked upon the nativist and exclusionary history embedded in the law: "The only thing American about American rodeo is 'American' in front of it because *rodeo* is Spanish for 'roundup' . . . One culture is able to rodeo but yet the other one can't."[69] Ultimately, in Nevada, charros' access to recreational space was curtailed, while their claims to be considered similar to American-style rodeo were deflected. Still, these outcomes were variegated by place and scale. Nevada charros in cities with large Latino populations, like Las Vegas, experienced the law as an attack on their culture and identity. But the impact of the law in rural areas, where Latinos are aiding the revitalization of animal industries, remains to be seen.

A similar scalar dynamic emerged in both Nebraska and Utah, where city councils and state legislatures took up the issue of "horse-tripping" amid the growth of ethnic Mexican populations who have been lauded by industry leaders for their contributions to economic restructuring. Mexicans had begun migrating to Nebraska in the early twentieth century, fleeing the violence of the Mexican Revolution and attracted by jobs in the state's meatpacking, railroad, and sugar beet industries. Their share of the Nebraska population remained small, however, until the 1980s, when the Mexican peso crisis, coupled with the relocation of meatpacking to rural parts of the state, propelled a dramatic expansion of Mexican migrant labor. By 1990, Mexicans in Nebraska numbered more than sixty-three thousand—an increase of more than 700 percent since 1970. By taking low-paying, non-unionized jobs in meatpacking and dairying, Mexican migrant workers enabled the survival of Nebraska's cattle industry during a crucial period of economic restructuring.[70] The state's political leaders were wary of creating a law that would be read as racially discriminatory or that would alienate Mexican labor, including a potential ban on the manganas or other charreada events.

As in other places, disputes about "horse-tripping" in Nebraska emerged first at the local level in Omaha, the state's largest city, and then scaled up. By the mid-2000s, there were approximately two hundred charros in Nebraska, including twenty men in Omaha who competed together as Charros La Amistad. The Charros La Amistad put on four or five events a year, not only in Omaha but across Nebraska and neighboring Iowa and Kansas. In July 2007, Nebraska Humane Society investigators found five malnourished horses with extensive scars on their legs at the ranch of Omaha charro Armando Pliego, who, along with eight other men, was cited for animal cruelty and fined $900. Later that year, the Nebraska Humane Society lobbied the Omaha City Council to ban the manganas, the piales, and the coleadero, charging that those events were more painful and dangerous to animals than American rodeo events, which it did not oppose.[71]

Significantly, though, in Omaha, elected officials, veterinarians, and the media were sympathetic to charros and charrería, which they did not see as fundamentally different from, or more dangerous than, American-style cowboys and rodeo. The white American veterinarians and equestrian leaders who were called to provide expertise refused to condemn the practices in question. A local university professor of equine surgery argued that injury in the manganas or colas was certainly possible, but said it was highly unlikely a horse would break a leg or that a steer's tail would even become sore. Local media coverage also spoke favorably of charros. Reporters made a point of highlighting the similarities between the Mexican and American versions of rodeo. One article in the *Omaha World Herald* opened as follows:

> Steer tailing is a traditional Mexican rodeo event in which a cowboy on horseback grabs a running steer's tail, wraps it around his leg or stirrup, and pulls the steer to the ground.
>
> Calf roping is a traditional American rodeo event in which a cowboy lassos a running calf around the neck, pulls it down and then ties three of the animal's legs together as quickly as possible.
>
> Is one inherently more dangerous than the other when it comes to the safety and welfare of the animals involved?
>
> No, say some cowboys—known as charros—who participate in the Mexican rodeos called charreadas.[72]

Not only did the reporters deliberately compare Mexican and American rodeo events, but they explicitly named charros as "some cowboys"—not as aberrations, whether racially or nationally, but as members of a multicultural ranching tradition that remained important to Nebraska's history, economy, and identity. Similarly, in their discussion of the issue at a city council meeting, city council members said they failed to see any substantial difference between American and Mexican rodeo, and observed a clear ethnic bias within the proposed ordinance. As Councilman Jim Suttle stated, "If we're going to do something like this, we better be prepared to do it for white, Caucasian rodeos."[73]

In their testimonies, Omaha charros registered their willingness to amend the events, rather than ban them entirely. Pliego, who spoke against the bill at the Omaha City Council meeting where it was first debated, reported that his association would happily work with the Nebraska Humane Society to make the contested events safer. He suggested that charros could put leg protection on the horses used in the manganas and the piales, and they could end the steer tailing before the animal was propelled to the ground.[74] Ultimately, the Omaha City Council adopted an ordinance with these modifications. As Toby de la Torre, a California-based charro who runs Charros Federation USA, later recalled, he and other charros allowed this bill to pass because they thought it was a good compromise that protected the interests of all involved. In their view, the Omaha ordinance also created a national model that might be adopted in other states.[75]

After the Omaha City Council decision, some members of the Nebraska State Legislature worried that even the modified manganas, piales, and colea-deros created unnecessary risk for the animals involved. Republican state senator Deb Fischer introduced Legislative Bill 865, the Livestock Animal Welfare Act, to the Nebraska Senate in January 2010. The bill classified intentional "horse-tripping" for sport or entertainment as a misdemeanor. It also included a statement that the tripping of horses "shall not be considered a commonly accepted practice occurring in conjunction with sanctioned rodeos, animal racing, or pulling contests." State senator Abbie Cornett, who cosponsored the bill, observed that the law was necessary despite charros' modified way of doing the manganas because horses could still get tangled up in the ropes and fall. She also suggested that while charros associated with the FMCH might have changed their practices, unsanctioned "backyard" charreadas were still occurring across the state. The bill's expansive nature—it provided criminal penalties for a range of animal practices, including neglect and sexual "indecency" (bestiality)—ensured its passage by the state legislature. In July 2010, Nebraska governor Dave Heineman signed a statewide "horse-tripping" bill into law.[76] Even so, the process of getting a statewide ban passed in Nebraska was not easy, and animal activists had to engage in extensive lobbying to secure its passage. As Kristie Biodrowski, chief investigator for the Nebraska Humane Society, later recalled, "We had to convince people that we weren't going after agricultural practices" or unfairly targeting one ethnic group over another.[77]

In Utah, charros benefited even more substantially from the emerging labor and political power of ethnic Mexicans as they worked to shape a "horse-tripping" law there in 2015. Mexican migrants and other Latinos had begun moving to Utah during World War II in search of industrial and agricultural employment, especially in mining and sugar beets. Though their numbers remained small, they soon became the state's largest minority group and founded chapters of the GI Forum and other organizations to protect their civil rights.[78] As in rural Nevada and Nebraska, the number of Latinos in Utah accelerated rapidly in the early twenty-first century, as migrants accepted jobs in restructuring meatpacking, dairying, and shepherding industries. While some migrated directly from Mexico, others moved to Utah from elsewhere in the United States, especially California, where housing costs had become unaffordable. In just a five-year period, between 2010 and 2015, Utah's Latino population grew by nearly fifty-three thousand people, topping more than four hundred thousand total and making them 13.7 percent of the state population. Most of that population growth represented births of U.S. citizens, the children of immigrants, who spoke English as their first language and constituted a substantial minority in the state's public schools.[79]

In Utah, state legislators initially considered a complete ban on "horse-tripping," but pulled back after a hearing before its committee on natural resources, agricultural, and environmental quality, where representatives from rodeo and farm industries protested that the bill could easily lead to banning their events and practices. Charros and rodeo advocates also questioned whether the bill was even necessary, given the lack of data about rates of animal and human injury. In response, the bill's sponsor, Ken Ivory, submitted a revised version of the bill, which passed the state legislature in 2015. The Utah law strongly discourages event promoters from holding "horse-tripping" events, but does not ban them outright. Instead, it requires organizers to register their events with the Utah Department of Agriculture and Food (UDAF), and to submit a full report within thirty days after the event's conclusion with data about the number of animals used, whether a veterinarian was called, and the number of injuries, if any. Failure to report incurs a fine of $500 per violation.[80]

The Utah law also required the state agricultural department to embark on an educational campaign about "horse-tripping" and to make regular reports to the state legislature. The campaign consisted of a letter and brochure, first sent to equestrian facilities in Utah in 2015, that outlined the new procedures. It warned facility managers to think carefully about sponsoring the contested events, even if they were not legally banned, because "the over-all public perception of these events is generally negative" and because wide-spread use of smart phones and social media "makes it very likely that some-body will put your event in the news." The brochure and accompanying letter also noted that the primary purpose of the law might well be transitional, stating that the UDAF "want[s] to better understand the impacts these events are having on horses," and that the information gathered would allow the department and the state's agriculture advisory board to make recom-mendations about the need for additional restrictions or regulations on "horse-tripping."[81] Essentially, the Utah agricultural officials hope to use education, public pressure, and the power of social media to phase the con-tested practices out of existence. This process does not criminalize charros; instead, it has allowed them a central role in shaping the evolution of char-rería and the future directions of state law.

THE ONGOING EVOLUTION OF CHARROS AND CHARRERÍA

As of this writing, the Utah law is the most recent instance of a statewide law to ban "horse-tripping," although animal welfare groups across the United States continue to petition city councils, county governments, and state leg-islatures to ban the contested events. The outcomes of recent disputes are diverse, but their general arc points to the increasing capacity and sophistica-tion of U.S. charros as political actors. Moreover, the charros continue to refine their tactical toolkit in ways that further contribute to the evolution of charrería in both the United States and Mexico.

One recent strategy has been to petition the United Farm Workers to with-draw the letters that César Chávez and Arturo Rodríguez wrote in the early 1990s, which Eric Mills and other animal activists continue to circulate despite significant changes to the practice of manganas, piales, and colas in the United States. The letters from Chávez and Rodríguez registered real debate within the ethnic Mexican community in the 1980s and '90s about the ethics of char-reada and their relation to other forms of domination. By the 2010s, however, these statements no longer accurately reflected the way U.S. charreadas were organized, misleading elected officials. U.S. charros lobbied the UFW to withdraw the letters, arguing that protection of rodeo and ranching was on par with issues of immigration reform, labor, voting, and education that are of major concern to Latino voters, and that the animal welfare laws had too often contributed to the criminalization of Latinos. In 2013, the UFW formally withdrew the letters that Chávez and Rodríguez had written two decades before.[82]

U.S. charros have also become more active in using social media to publish their own statistics and visual information. Texas charros have recently published results from 1,035 charreadas on Wikipedia, two-thirds of which were held in Mexico and one-third in the United States. They reported a handful of minor animal injuries and only one animal death.[83] The San Antonio charros also began recording many charro events and posting video compilations to YouTube. As of 2011, they had posted more than three hundred videos of traditional manganas (from Mexico) and piales (in U.S. states where they were still allowed), in which no animals suffered a major injury.[84] To be sure, these are not unbiased, peer-reviewed, or comparative studies; they reflect charros' vested interest in portraying their events as regulated and safe. However, they do provide data and visual evidence that the charros control; in this respect, they are important sources through which charros resist the power of media spectacles that otherwise racialize charros and Latinos as criminal and "illegal" subjects.

U.S. charros also continue to promote awareness of their sport and culture through joint programming with influential art, history, and cultural institutions, especially those that celebrate regional traditions of ranching and horsemanship. In 2009–10, they collaborated in the production of a traveling exhibit titled "Arte en la Charrería: The Artisanship of the Mexican Equestrian Culture," which debuted at the National Cowboy and Western Heritage Museum in Oklahoma City and then went on to shows at history museums in Kentucky, Oregon, Indiana, and Texas.[85] More recently, in 2017, the American Quarter Horse Hall of Fame and Museum in Amarillo, Texas, launched an exhibit titled "Nacidos Charros: Born Charro," with a focus on charros' horses, equipment, clothing, and music.[86] U.S. charros have also been active in other kinds of public history programming. In 2013, the FMCH-USA began to participate in California's "Ag Day," an annual event sponsored by the California Department of Food and Agriculture. According to Alejandro Galindo, then-president of the FMCH-USA and a charro from Las Vegas who led the planning, the goal was to take "a proactive approach in securing the future of our Western Heritage" and to "teach what charrería is and how it contributes immensely to American agriculture and Western Heritage culture." The FMCH-USA paid all costs associated with the event from a special outreach and legal fund, financed by annual membership dues, that was established to "raise community awareness and build strong government relations."[87] As with earlier initiatives led by U.S. charros, these programs reorient public understanding of ranching and rodeo in ways that recognize their multicultural and transnational dimensions, both past and present, as well as the historical and ongoing contributions of charros to American culture.

Finally, U.S. charros have created new organizations, beyond the charro associations themselves, that are dedicated specifically to lobbying and advocacy. In 2014, charros affiliated with the FMCH-USA established the Hispanic Western Heritage PAC. The purpose of the PAC is "to educate political campaigns, candidates, and office holders who make decisions that affect laws and regulation impacting true Hispanic grassroots and the Western Heritage Culture." The PAC focuses on building relationships with supportive public officials and like-minded organizations, and increasing voter registration and turnout. It is a nonpartisan organization that bases its decisions "on the record of support on Hispanic values and the Western Heritage Culture."[88] Hispanic Western Heritage maintains a sporadic blog in which it reports on the status of legislation related to rodeo and charrería, including the many "horse-tripping" bills winding their way through city councils and state legislatures. It has also sponsored events to increase public awareness of charrería, such as a 2014 fund-raiser for City of Hope and a 2016 trail ride in honor of Rafael Rivera, the Mexican scout who historically "discovered" Las Vegas.[89] Hispanic Western Heritage has also joined forces with the FMCH-USA to award an annual $1,000 college scholarship to young people from within the charro community who have been accepted to veterinary school. José Covarrubias, the sports secretary of the FMCH-USA, reported that charro associations "are hurting together with other rodeo organizations when it comes to large animal veterinarians that have the knowledge of what [their] heritage is about, where it comes from, and what it has provided for this great country." To remediate that gap, Covarrubias explained that they were "seeking dedicated veterinary professionals to provide and advocate for the health and welfare of the livestock at FMCH-USA events."[90]

In all of these ways, charros in the United States have become formal political actors of growing sophistication. Newly organized at the regional and national levels, they operate with a keen sense of how to work effectively within the U.S. legislative and policy context. By lobbying elected officials, forging alliances with like-minded constituencies, fund-raising, and controlling media messaging, they demonstrate their capacity as activated political subjects. To be sure, charros have adopted these measures and tactics, sometimes begrudgingly, in the face of animal welfare concerns raised mostly by outsiders. But their willingness to respond in an organized, collaborative, and progressive way has spurred the evolution of charrería and charro culture, both in the United States and Mexico. Charrería has indisputably emerged from these disputes as a modern, transnational, and increasingly humane cultural practice, rather than a static representation of Mexican nationalist tradition, as its adherents were previously wont to claim.

The impacts of the U.S. charros' work in the legislative arena go well beyond matters of animal welfare, however. They also involve a fundamental remapping of core narratives of American history and geography. Through their discursive and narrative work to explain and defend charrería, U.S. charros recuperate a multicultural, transnational history of cowboys, rodeo, and ranching in which Mexicans played central roles. As they scale up to the national level, their petitions transcend the border states where charros have historically worked and are now reshaping the very "heartland" of American identity. By asserting charros' status as the "original cowboys," U.S. charros make claims to belonging in ways that resist the contemporary racialization of ethnic Mexicans and other Latinos as "illegals" who threaten American cultural identity. Quite the contrary: they show how American cultural identity is, and has always been, indebted to the labor, skill, and creativity of ethnic Mexicans and other diverse peoples of the Americas.

Conclusion

HOVER OVER VIRTUALLY ANY CITY in the U.S. West using the satellite view of a web mapping service, and you will almost certainly spot the distinctive keyhole shape of at least one lienzo charro. Over the past half-century, ethnic Mexicans have built these physical spaces across the U.S. West and, increasingly, beyond. In some cases, these are individual projects: middle-class and wealthy ethnic Mexican men purchase large properties on the metropolitan fringe, where they construct arenas, stables and corrals, outbuildings, and large ranch homes—complexes that, in many ways, resemble the historic haciendas and ranchos of the Mexican North before and just after U.S. conquest. In other cases, the production of lienzo space is a collective endeavor, in which charro associations negotiate leasing or purchase agreements with private landowners or local governments. In all cases, the existence of these spaces testifies to charros' acuity in negotiation, persuasion, and maintaining relationships across ethnic lines, as well as their design and construction skills and their abilities to secure finance capital. To be sure, some of these lienzos, as we have seen, rest on highly unstable fiscal and legal arrangements, while others face suspicion or hostility from their neighbors, making them vulnerable to closure. Still, for whatever time they exist—whether a few years, as in the case of the Charros Emiliano Zapata or the Pueblo Charro Association, or decades, as for the San Antonio Charro Association or the Pico Rivera Sports Arena—the lienzos offer an important space for cultural affirmation and transnational connectivity, while facilitating ethnic Mexicans' collective response to their racial subjugation in the United States.

Descend from satellite view and enter the lienzo, and these processes will be on full display. For its diverse participants, charrería offers a sense of belonging—to a community, to a history, and to the land. As charros and escaramuzas practice privately or perform for a public audience, they recuperate a sense of skill and dignity, as well as connection with each other and with animals and collective pride in their Mexican cultural heritage. Moreover, these qualities are not limited to those who compete in charreadas; they also extend to spectators. Charreadas have long cohered ethnic Mexicans across differences of class, citizenship status, and place of origin in their invocation of a shared rural Mexican ranching past left behind, whether voluntarily or by force. This sense of connection is especially important in contexts of migration structured by inequality and violence. In the face of economic subjugation, charges of "illegality," and exclusionary policy outside the lienzo, many ethnic Mexicans find sustenance, shared values, and a sense of kinship and belonging within it.

These sensibilities have repeatedly transcended the physical spaces of the lienzos to inform ethnic Mexicans' collective action for social change in the broader society. As we have seen throughout this book, the members of the U.S. charro associations and their interlocutors have labored for nearly a century to transform American institutions—such as local law enforcement, the regional economy, education, public history, film, public art, and legislative and municipal politics, to name just a few—in ways that make them more responsive to the needs and concerns of ethnic Mexicans in the United States. Charros and their interlocutors have also transformed the vernacular spaces of American life through their place-making efforts—from the streets and boulevards where they ride in parades, to the public parks and recreational facilities where they host cultural events, to the universities where they appear in support of Latino student groups, to the civic centers and historic districts where they erect charro statues, to the stores where they sell Mexican-style cowboy boots, hats, and belts. Where there is an ethnic Mexican community of virtually any size, there will be ranchero landscapes, and the charro and lo ranchero will operate as forces for the transformation of everyday life.

Of course, the sense of culture, community, and political potential that charrería enables is not universally shared or embraced, resting as the sport does on a series of interlocking hierarchies and tensions. Some of these tensions, as we have seen, relate to the complicated interactions between human and nonhuman participants. Domination of animals is a central part of charrería, especially in those competitive events in which charros violently bring steers or horses to the ground. But in other respects, which occur more often outside the public eye, charrería may inculcate respect, compassion, and interconnectedness between humans and animals. This is especially true of the relationships that charros and escaramuzas nurture with their highly trained, sensitive, and skilled personal horses. Certainly, for some migrants who came from rural subsistence economies, in which animals were both members of the household and vital economic resources, these sensibilities coexist without tension. Moreover, animal attitudes and practices are continuing to evolve, both among U.S. charros and their counterparts in Mexico, in response to both internal conversations and outside pressures.

Hierarchies of class, gender, region, and race also structure charrería and inform its political mobilization. As we have seen repeatedly throughout this book, the projects pursued by charros and their associations reflect the perspectives and goals of the ethnic Mexican middle class, as well as aspirational members of the working class and some members of the Mexican American elite. Through their use of the charro and many other ranchero cultural forms, these actors have pursued opportunity in American institutions in ways that recall histories of Spanish and Mexican colonialism and associated aspirations to whiteness and modernity, while reproducing aspects of those historic social relations in the present. Yet, it is this same sensibility and class politics that has enabled the charro to transform areas to which working-class actors and militant activists have had less consistent access, such as business, law enforcement, and legislative politics. As we have also seen, the use of the charro is not limited to middle-class or influential men. Women, too, have used the charro to create more inclusive institutions, for example, in public education, public art, and public history. Despite the apparent fixity of its nationalist construction, then, in practice charrería is a flexible cultural formation that has been—and will continue to be—broadly useful to a wide range of subjects.

Though this book has focused on charrería, it is important to note that the spaces and practices of lo ranchero—as well as its symbolic, cultural, and political potential—are not limited to the charro associations or the lienzos where they practice and compete. A more temporary, but no less important, phenomenon occurs through the staging of one-off jaripeos and coleadores (bull-riding and steer-tailing events, respectively) at vacant dirt lots in many urban areas. Usually sponsored by "Latin" entertainment companies run by middle-class migrants, these events are held in makeshift arenas built of pipe corrals, surrounded by bleachers or folding chairs, using steers rented from a stock contractor and trailered in for the afternoon. Unlike the full-fledged charreadas, which require a charro to own or have access to a well-trained horse and multiple trajes de charro, the temporary jaripeos and coleaderos are far more accessible to the working class, who can pay as little as $10 to ride a thousand-pound steer for a few seconds or to bring a running steer to the ground in a tail-spin. While these events are rife with danger, they offer ethnic Mexicans—mostly men, but also some women—a chance to show off their skill, strength, and bravery.[1] They also allow migrants and their children to socialize, flirt, dance, and simply be together while dressed in cowboy boots and hats, in homage to lo ranchero. Events like these are not limited to the U.S. Southwest or even the locations in the interior and Midwest that I examined in chapter 5. They are also occurring in cities and towns far from the U.S.-Mexico border and with small Mexican populations. For example, in New Haven, Connecticut, where I live, a Bronx-based company called Rodeo Tierra Caliente stages occasional jaripeos on an abandoned postindustrial lot near the Long Island Sound, as part of a traveling circuit that moves seasonally between New York, New Jersey, Connecticut, Maryland, Rhode Island, Massachusetts, and Ohio. In these parts of the United States especially, jaripeos and coleaderos attract a wide range of Latino participants, not just ethnic Mexicans.[2]

As ethnic Mexicans negotiate these fluid landscapes across the United States, they participate in the simultaneous evolution of local, regional, national, and transnational cultures. On the one hand, they shape the nationalist content of Mexican culture from abroad. For decades, individual charros and charro associations have sustained vibrant transnational networks with Mexican people and organizations that serve cultural, business, and political purposes simultaneously. In more recent years, they have lobbied for changes to scoring and qualification guidelines such that U.S. charros can continue to compete in Mexican events, even after implementing animal welfare modifications in the United States. U.S.-based charros have also sponsored the financing and construction of arenas for both charreadas and jaripeos in their Mexican villages of origin, often drawing on American ideas about architecture and materiality in their designs.[3] All of these practices have fostered an evolution of Mexican culture that is distinctly shaped by the perspectives, needs, and experiences of migrants and their co-ethnics in diaspora.

Simultaneously, as we have seen, ethnic Mexicans, including large numbers of migrants, have used charrería and lo ranchero to claim belonging and membership in U.S. society. Asserting the historic presence of ethnic Mexican ranchers and vaqueros as the "original cowboys" in the region that became the U.S. Southwest, they have transformed core narratives of American identity centered on the cowboy, ranching, and the rodeo. In doing so, they have claimed membership and rights in American institutions while creating more inclusive and equitable conditions.

Charros and charrería enable ethnic Mexicans in the United States to engage in all of these practices simultaneously and without contradiction. Whether they are migrants who have been in the U.S. for just a few months or eighth-generation Hispanos whose families still own land in rural New Mexico, the charro, the vaquero, and lo ranchero offer powerful means for ethnic Mexicans to simultaneously nurture their Mexican cultural heritage, maintain transnational connections with Mexican culture and people, and assert their rights to resources and a sense of belonging in the United States.

NOTES

INTRODUCTION

1. In addition to his performances on *America's Got Talent*, where judges Howard Stern, Sharon Osbourne, and Howie Mandel applauded his talents in "mainstreaming mariachi," de la Cruz performed at regional venues such as the Mandalay Bay Casino in Las Vegas, elementary schools throughout Texas, several other San Antonio Spurs games, and the retirement gala for the space shuttle *Endeavour.* Sebastien El Charro de Oro's Facebook page, www.facebook.com /teamsebastien/info (accessed October 29, 2013).

2. "A Mexican American Boy Sang the National Anthem, and Racist NBA Fans Can't Handle It," *Daily Dot,* June 12, 2013, www.dailydot.com/news/sebastian-de-la-cruz-spurs-heat-national-anthem/ (accessed October 29, 2013).

3. Public Shaming, "Racist Basketball Fans Pissed a Mexican-American Boy Dared to Sing Their National Anthem," http://publicshaming.tumblr.com /post/52763976629/racist-basketball-fans-pissed-a-mexican-american-boy (accessed October 29, 2013).

4. Donald Henriques, "Performing Nationalism: Mariachi, Media, and the Transformation of a Tradition (1920–1942)," PhD diss., University of Texas at Austin, 2006; Gary Moreno, "Charro: The Transnational History of a Cultural Icon," PhD diss., University of Oklahoma, 2014; Deborah Vargas, "Rita's Pants: The *Charro Traje* and Trans-Sensuality," *Women and Performance: A Journal of Feminist Theory* 20, no. 1 (2010): 3–14.

5. Olga Nájera-Ramírez, "Engendering Nationalism: Identity, Discourse, and the Mexican Charro," *Anthropological Quarterly* 67 (1994): 1–14; Cristina Palomar, "El papel de la charrería como fenómeno cultural en la construcción del Occidente de México," *Revista Europea de Estudios Latinoamericanos y del Caribe* 76 (2004): 83–98; Kathleen Sands, *Charrería Mexicana: A Mexican Folk Tradition* (Tucson: University of Arizona Press, 1993).

6. Public Shaming, "Racist Basketball Fans."

7. "Spurs' 11-Year-Old Anthem Singer Won't Let Racist Comments Bring Him Down," *Fox News Latino,* June 12, 2013, http://latino.foxnews.com/latino/news/2013/06/12/spurs-11-year-old-anthem-singer-wont-let-racist-comments-bring-him-down/ (accessed June 2, 2015).

8. Sean Esco, "President Obama and Celebrities Support Sebastien de la Cruz after Racist Bashing!" *Red Alert Live,* June 14, 2013, http://redalertlive.com/2013/06/14/president-obama-celebrities-support-sebastien-de-la-cruz-racist-bashing-video/ (accessed October 29, 2013); see also Colby Itkowitz, "He Endured Racist Attacks after Singing at NBA Game: Now He's the Opener for Democratic Debate," *Washington Post,* March 9, 2016, www.washingtonpost.com/news/inspired-life/wp/2016/03/09/he-endured-racist-attacks-after-singing-at-nba-game-now-hes-the-opener-for-democratic-debate/ (accessed October 10, 2016); *Go, Sebastien, Go!* (film), produced by Eva Longoria, www.espn.com/video/clip?id = 12832072 (accessed October 10, 2016).

9. Nájera-Ramírez, "Engendering Nationalism"; Sands, *Charrería Mexicana.*

10. Elleke Boehmer, *Stories of Women: Gender and Narrative in the Postcolonial Nation* (Manchester, U.K.: Manchester University Press, 2005), 6.

11. Esteban Barragán López, *Con un pie en el estribo: Formación y deslizamientos de las sociedades rancheras en la construcción del México moderno* (Zamora, Michoacán: El Colegio de Michoacán, 1997), 30–33; see also Nájera-Ramírez, "Engendering Nationalism."

12. Sands, *Charrería Mexicana,* 36–37.

13. Nájera-Ramírez, "Engendering Nationalism"; Palomar, "El papel de la charrería"; Sands, *Charrería Mexicana.*

14. Nájera-Ramírez, "Engendering Nationalism," 3.

15. Nájera-Ramírez, "Engendering Nationalism," 3.

16. Cattle, horses, sheep, and other livestock were brought along on the earliest Spanish expeditions to expand empire through livestock production and ranching. Horses were quickly incorporated into American Indian societies across the Mexican North and Great Plains, and by the eighteenth century, the Spanish missions in Texas and California ran many hundreds of thousands of cattle. The missions at first banned Indians from riding or working horses, but soon lifted the restrictions out of sheer necessity for labor power; mission Indian vaqueros became expert horsemen. Sands, *Charrería Mexicana,* 30; Andrew Isenberg, "Between Mexico and the United States: From *Indios* to Vaqueros in the Pastoral Borderlands," in *Mexico and Mexicans in the Making of the United States,* ed. John Tutino (Austin: University of Texas Press, 2012), 83–109; Peter Iverson, *When Indians Became Cowboys: Native Peoples and Cattle Ranching in the American West* (Norman: University of Oklahoma Press, 1994), 3–14.

17. Barragán López, *Con un pie,* 123–24.

18. For example, Manuel Gonzales, *The Hispanic Elite of the Southwest* (El Paso: Texas Western Press/University of Texas at El Paso, 1989); David Weber, *The Mexican Frontier, 1821–1846* (Albuquerque: University of New Mexico Press, 1982).

19. D. Weber, *Mexican Frontier,* 207–41.

20. Albert Camarillo, *Chicanos in a Changing Society: From Mexican Pueblos to American Barrios in Santa Barbara and Southern California, 1848–1930* (Cambridge: Harvard University Press, 1979); Lisbeth Haas, *Conquests and Historical Identities in California, 1769–1936* (Berkeley: University of California Press, 1995); David Montejano, *Anglos and Mexicans in the Making of Texas, 1836–1986* (Austin: University of Texas Press, 1987); Leonard Pitt, *Decline of the Californios: A Social History of the Spanish-Speaking Californians, 1846–1890* (Berkeley: University of California Press, 1999); David Torres-Rouff, *Before L.A.: Race, Space, and Municipal Power in Los Angeles, 1781–1894* (New Haven: Yale University Press, 2013).

21. Mary Lou LeCompte, "The Hispanic Influence on the History of Rodeo, 1823–1922," *Journal of Sport History* 12, no. 1 (1985): 28; Américo Paredes, "The Problem of Identity in a Changing Culture: Popular Expressions of Culture Conflict along the Lower Rio Grande Border," in *Views across the Border: The United States and Mexico,* ed. Stanley Ross (Albuquerque: University of New Mexico Press, 1978), 68–94.

22. For example, Camarillo, *Chicanos in a Changing Society;* Haas, *Conquests and Historical Identities;* Jacqueline Moore, *Cow Boys and Cattle Men: Class and Masculinities on the Texas Frontier, 1865–1900* (New York: New York University Press, 2009).

23. Kelly Lytle Hernández, *City of Inmates: Conquest, Rebellion, and the Rise of Human Caging in Los Angeles, 1771–1965* (Chapel Hill: University of North Carolina Press, 2017), chap. 1; Michael Magliari, "Free Soil, Unfree Labor: Cave Johnson Couts and the Binding of Indian Workers in California, 1850–1867," *Pacific Historical Review* 73, no. 3 (2004): 349–90.

24. Moore, *Cow Boys and Cattle Men,* 40–41.

25. For example, Tomás Almaguer, *Racial Fault Lines: The Historical Origins of White Supremacy in California* (Berkeley: University of California Press, 1994); Camarillo, *Chicanos in a Changing Society;* Arnoldo de León, *They Called Them Greasers: Anglo Attitudes toward Mexicans in Texas, 1821–1900* (Austin: University of Texas Press, 1983); Sarah Deutsch, *No Separate Refuge: Culture, Class, and Gender on an Anglo-Hispanic Frontier in the American Southwest, 1880–1940* (New York: Oxford University Press, 1987); William Deverell, *Whitewashed Adobe: The Rise of Los Angeles and the Remaking of Its Mexican Past* (Berkeley: University of California Press, 2004); Haas, *Conquests and Historical Identities;* Montejano, *Anglos and Mexicans;* Torres-Rouff, *Before L.A.*

26. Robin D.G. Kelley, "Notes on Deconstructing 'The Folk,'" *American Historical Review* 97, no. 5 (1992): 1400–1408.

27. Monica Rico, *Nature's Noblemen: Transatlantic Masculinities and the Nineteenth-Century American West* (New Haven: Yale University Press, 2013).

28. David Anthony Tyeeme Clark and Joanne Nagel, "White Men, Red Masks: Appropriations of 'Indian' Manhood in Imagined Wests," in *Across the Great Divide: Cultures of Manhood in the American West,* ed. Matthew Basso, Laura McCall, and Dee Garceau (New York: Routledge, 2001), 109–30.

29. Melissa Bingmann, *Prep School Cowboys: Ranch Schools in the American West* (Albuquerque: University of New Mexico Press, 2015).

30. Le Compte, "Hispanic Origins," 30–32.

31. Peter La Chapelle, *Proud to Be an Okie: Cultural Politics, Country Music, and Migration to Southern California* (Berkeley: University of California Press, 2007).

32. Jeremy Agnew, *The Creation of the Cowboy Hero: Fiction, Film, and Fact* (Jefferson, NC: McFarland, 2015); Stanley Corkin, *Cowboys as Cold Warriors: The Western and U.S. History* (Philadelphia: Temple University Press, 2004); LeCompte, "Hispanic Influence."

33. For example, the Professional Bull Riders Association, founded in 1993 and headquartered in Pueblo, Colorado, operates in five countries: the United States, Australia, Canada, Brazil, and Mexico.

34. Sands, *Charrería Mexicana.*

35. Tania Carreño King, *El charro: La construcción de un estereotipo nacional, 1920–1940* (Mexico City: Instituto Nacional de Estudios Históricos de la Revolución Mexicana, 2000); Nájera-Ramírez, "Engendering Nationalism"; Olga Nájera-Ramírez, "Unruly Passions: Poetics, Performance, and Gender in the Ranchera Song," in *Chicana Feminisms: A Critical Reader,* ed. Gabriela Arredondo and Aída Hurtado (Durham, NC: Duke University Press, 2003), 184–210.

36. Carreño King, *El charro;* Nájera-Ramírez, "Engendering Nationalism"; José Murià, "En defensa de la originalidad," *Orígenes de la charrería y de su nombre* (Mexico City: Miguel Ángel Porrúa, 2010), 87–96; and Palomar, "El papel de la charrería."

37. The definitive text, authored by the most esteemed charro of this period, is Carlos Rincón Gallardo, *El charro mexicano* (Mexico City: Miguel Ángel Porrúa, 1939); see also J. Álvarez del Villar, *Orígenes del charro mexicano* (Mexico City: Librería A. Pola, 1968); José Ramón Ballesteros, *Origen y evolución del charro mexicano* (Mexico City: Manuel Porrúa, 1972).

38. Quoted in David Luis-Brown, *Waves of Decolonization: Discourses of Race and Hemispheric Citizenship in Cuba, Mexico, and the United States* (Durham: Duke University Press, 2008), 186; see also Nájera-Ramírez, "Engendering Nationalism."

39. Sands, *Charrería Mexicana,* 19.

40. For example, Linda Basch, Nina Glick Schiller, and Cristina Szanton Blanc, *Nations Unbound: Transnational Projects, Postcolonial Predicaments and Deterritorialized Nation-States* (New York: Routledge, 1993); Albert Sergio Laguna, *Diversión: Play and Popular Culture in Cuban America* (New York: New York University Press, 2017); Dixa Ramírez, *Colonial Phantoms: Belonging and Refusal in the Dominican Americas, from the 19th Century to the Present* (New York: New York University Press, 2018).

41. Literary scholar Vincent Pérez argues that the hacienda and its associated cast of characters—especially those who exercised power and agency, such as the charro/hacendado—offered an important way for elite Mexican American writers such as María Amparo Ruíz de Burton, Jovita González, and Leo Carrillo to negotiate the erosion of Spanish and Mexican agrarian societies caused by U.S. conquest and industrial capitalism. Their texts, like others produced by Mexican nationalist interests, tended to ignore or minimize the ways in which hacienda society and the

world of the charro depended on indigenous dispossession, captive labor and debt peonage, and gender and sexual inequality. Vincent Pérez, *Remembering the Hacienda: History and Memory in the Mexican American Southwest* (College Station: Texas A&M University Press, 2006). For a discussion of this tendency among the elite of transnational societies more broadly, see Basch, Glick Schiller, and Szanton Blanc, *Nations Unbound.*

42. The Mexican consuls, for example, often tried to mediate labor disputes among Mexican workers in the United States. Frequently, they called striking Mexican workers back to the fields and factories by reminding them of the need to represent Mexico well in the United States. For example, George Sánchez, *Becoming Mexican American: Ethnicity, Culture, and Identity in Chicano Los Angeles, 1900–1945* (New York: Oxford University Press, 1993), esp. 108–25; for a more general discussion of how Mexican elites cultivated loyalty among the working classes, see Richard García, "The Exiled Ricos," in *Rise of the Mexican American Middle Class: San Antonio, 1929–1941* (College Station: Texas A&M University Press, 1991), 221–52.

43. For example, in 1944, Carlos Rincón Gallardo, an esteemed charro from an influential Mexican family who was then president of the FMCH, as well as the author of numerous Spanish-language books about charrería, visited Los Angeles at the request of the California Trails Conference. The *Los Angeles Times,* after commenting on Gallardo's "perfect English," reported that Gallardo "indisputably is Mexico's most distinguished horseman" and expressed gratitude for his visit. "Horse Is Here to Stay, Spatted Charro Hopes," *Los Angeles Times,* June 17, 1944, C1.

44. LeCompte, "Hispanic Influence."

45. Rogelio Agrasánchez, *Mexican Movies in the United States: A History of the Films, Theaters, and Audiences, 1920–1960* (Jefferson, NC: McFarland, 2006); Miguel Flores, *El Charro en U.S.A.* (Glendora, CA: Associated Publications, 1998); Desirée Garcia, "'Not a Musical in any Sense of the Word': *Allá en el Rancho Grande* Crosses the Border," in *The Migration of Musical Film: From Ethnic Margins to American Mainstream* (New Brunswick: Rutgers University Press, 2014); Colin Gunckel, *Mexico on Main Street: Transnational Film Culture in Los Angeles before World War II* (New Brunswick: Rutgers University Press, 2015).

46. Carey McWilliams, "The Fantasy Heritage," in *North from Mexico: The Spanish-Speaking People of the United States* (Philadelphia: J. B. Lippincott, 1949).

47. Matthew Bokovoy, *The San Diego World's Fairs and Southwestern Memory, 1880–1940* (Albuquerque: University of New Mexico Press, 2005); Dydia DeLyser, *Ramona Memories: Tourism and the Shaping of Southern California* (Minneapolis: University of Minnesota Press, 2005); Laura Hernández-Ehrisman, *Inventing the Fiesta City: Heritage and Carnival in San Antonio* (Albuquerque: University of New Mexico Press, 2008); Phoebe Kropp, *California Vieja: Culture and Memory in a Modern American Place* (Berkeley: University of California Press, 2006); Charles Montgomery, *The Spanish Redemption: Heritage, Power, and Loss on New Mexico's Upper Rio Grande* (Berkeley: University of California Press, 2002); Chris Wilson, *The Myth of Santa Fe: Creating a Modern Regional Tradition* (Albuquerque: University of New Mexico Press, 1997).

48. Film historian Desirée García has argued that comedias rancheras like *Allá en el Rancho Grande* (1936), for example, appealed to Mexican migrant audiences because of their "ability to attenuate the harsh effects of migration and the pressures of a transnational existence" by featuring "timeless rural settings and communities that shared in the collective expression of folk song and dance." D. García, "Not a Musical," 73.

49. Wendy Wolford, *This Land Is Ours Now: Social Mobilization and the Meanings of Land in Brazil* (Durham: Duke University Press, 2010), 409–10.

50. For example, Geraldo Cadava, *Standing on Common Ground: The Making of a Sunbelt Borderland* (Cambridge: Harvard University Press, 2013); Mario García, *Mexican Americans: Leadership, Ideology, and Identity, 1930–1960* (New Haven: Yale University Press, 1989); R. García, *Rise of the Mexican American Middle Class*.

51. Juan Javier Pescador, "*Los Heroes del Domingo:* Soccer, Borders, and Social Spaces in Great Lakes Mexican Communities, 1940–1970," in *Mexican Americans and Sport*, ed. Jorge Iber and Samuel Regalado (College Station: Texas A&M University Press, 2007), 74.

52. Nicole Guidotti-Hernández, *Unspeakable Violence: Remapping U.S. and Mexican National Imaginaries* (Durham: Duke University Press, 2011); David Lloyd and Laura Pulido, "In the Long Shadow of the Settler: On Israeli and U.S. Colonialisms," *American Quarterly* 62, no. 4 (2010): 795–809; Laura Pulido, "Geographies of Race and Ethnicity III: Settler Colonialism and Nonnative People of Color," *Progress in Human Geography* 42, no. 2 (2018): 309–18; Rosaura Sánchez and Beatrice Pita, "Rethinking Settler Colonialism," *American Quarterly* 66, no. 4 (2014): 1039–55.

53. For example, Matthew Gutmann, *The Meanings of Macho: Being a Man in Mexico City* (Berkeley: University of California Press, 2006); Aída Hurtado and Mrinal Sinha, "More than Men: Latino Feminist Masculinities and Intersectionality," *Sex Roles* 59, no. 5–6 (2008): 337–49; Cathy McIlwaine, "Migrant Machismos: Exploring Gender Ideologies and Practices among Latin American Migrants in London from a Multi-Scalar Perspective," *Gender, Place, and Culture: A Journal of Feminist Geography* 17, no. 3 (2010): 281–300; Alfredo Mirandé, *Hombres y Machos: Masculinity and Latino Culture* (Boulder: Westview Press, 1997); Pedro Saez, Adonaid Casao, and Jay Wade, "Factors Influencing Masculinity Ideology among Latino Men," *Journal of Men's Studies* 17, no. 2 (2009): 116–28.

54. Guillermo Miguel Arciniega, Thomas Anderson, Zoila Tovar-Blank, and Terence Tracey, "Toward a Fuller Conception of Machismo: Development of a Traditional Machismo and Caballerismo Scale," *Journal of Counseling Psychology* 55, no. 1 (2008): 19–33.

55. The image of stoop labor is especially resonant in two industries where Mexican and Central American labor has become essential: agriculture and the horse industry. These are highly exploitative industries; for example, horse-racing workers frequently compare their subjugation as laborers to the commodification of the horses for whom they care. Yet, as Gabriela Núñez has argued, their exploitation is disguised by the "Latino pastoral narrative," which characterizes Latino migrants as naturally attuned to land and animals, excusing their poor treatment

and low pay. Gabriela Núñez, "The Latino Pastoral Narrative: Backstretch Workers in Kentucky," *Latino Studies* 10, no. 1–2 (2012): 107–27.

56. Jorge Iber, Samuel Regalado, and José Alamillo, *Latinos in U.S Sport: A History of Isolation, Cultural Identity, and Acceptance* (Champaign: Human Kinetics, 2011); Jorge Iber and Samuel Regalado, *Mexican Americans and Sport* (College Station: Texas A&M University Press, 2007); Pescador, "Los Heroes del Domingo."

57. José Alamillo, *Making Lemonade out of Lemons: Mexican American Labor and Leisure in a California Town, 1880–1960* (Urbana: University of Illinois Press, 2006); Michael Messner, *Taking the Field: Women, Men, and Sports* (Minneapolis: University of Minnesota Press, 2002).

58. For example, Melissa Repko, "A Deadly Ride," *Dallas Morning News,* March 3, 2016, http://interactives.dallasnews.com/2016/unregulated-rodeos/ (accessed January 3, 2018).

59. Boehmer, *Stories of Women;* Olga Nájera-Ramírez, "Mounting Traditions: The Origin and Evolution of La Escaramuza Charra," in *Chicana Traditions: Continuity and Change,* ed. Norma Cantú and Olga Nájera-Ramírez (Urbana: University of Illinois Press, 2002), Rosa Linda Fregoso, "The Chicano Familia Romance," in *MeXicana Encounters: The Making of Social Identities on the Borderlands* (Berkeley: University of California Press, 2003).

60. Claire Jean Kim, *Dangerous Crossings: Race, Species, and Nature in a Multicultural Age* (New York: Cambridge University Press, 2015); Olga Nájera-Ramírez, "The Racialization of a Debate: Charreada as Tradition or Torture," *American Anthropologist* 98, no. 3 (1996): 505–11.

61. Ana C. Ramírez, "Escaramuzas Charras: Paradoxes of Performance in a Mexican Women's Equestrian Sport," in *The Meaning of Horses: Biosocial Encounters,* ed. Dona Lee Davis and Anita Maurstad (New York: Routledge, 2016), 164–76; Nájera-Ramírez, "Mounting Traditions"; Robin Rosenthal and Bill Yahraus, *Escaramuza: Riding from the Heart* (documentary film, 2012).

62. Lyanne Alfaro, "How an All-Woman Mariachi Band Is Owning the Genre," *NBC News* online, May 23, 2016, www.nbcnews.com/news/latino/how-all-woman-mariachi-band-owning-genre-n577731 (accessed February 14, 2017); Abel Salas, "L.A.'s Only All-Gay Mariachi Band," *L.A. Weekly,* December 8, 2014, www.laweekly.com/arts/las-only-all-gay-mariachi-band-5226910 (accessed February 14, 2017).

CHAPTER ONE. CLAIMING STATE POWER
IN MID-TWENTIETH-CENTURY LOS ANGELES

1. Miguel Flores, *El Charro en U.S.A.* (Glendora, CA: Associated Publications, 1998).

2. Miroslava Chávez-García, *Negotiating Conquest: Gender and Power in California, 1770s to 1880s* (Tucson: University of Arizona Press, 2004), esp. 3–24; Lisbeth Haas, *Conquests and Historical Identities in California, 1769–1936* (Berkeley: University of California Press, 1995); Steven Hackel, *Children of Coyote, Missionaries of*

Saint Francis: Indian-Spanish Relations in Colonial California, 1769–1850 (Chapel Hill: University of North Carolina Press, 2005); Kelly Lytle Hernández, *City of Inmates: Conquest, Rebellion, and the Rise of Human Caging in Los Angeles, 1771–1965* (Chapel Hill: University of North Carolina Press, 2017), chap. 1; Albert Hurtado, *Intimate Frontiers: Sex, Gender, and Culture in Old California* (Albuquerque: University of New Mexico Press, 1999), 1–20; David Torres-Rouff, *Before L.A.: Race, Space, and Municipal Power in Los Angeles, 1781–1894* (New Haven: Yale University Press, 2013), chap. 1.

3. The Mexican call for independence included republican government, formal citizenship among men, and, in the far north, the secularization of mission lands, which were to be distributed among former mission Indians. However, these commitments did not translate into practice. After 1833, the Mexican governors in Alta California awarded 270 private grants in the Los Angeles area. The vast majority of the land, including the largest grants and most of the ex-mission land, was distributed among just fifty elite Mexican families. At approximately the same time, Anglo-American and European men were settling in Alta California, forging business partnerships with Mexican men, and marrying into Mexican families, securing a strong foothold in California's system of land tenure and further displacing the region's indigenous peoples from the centers of political and economic control. Albert Hurtado, "Customs of the Country: Mixed Marriage in Mexican California," in *Intimate Frontiers;* Torres-Rouff, *Before L.A.,* esp. 55–132; David Weber, *The Mexican Frontier, 1821–1846* (Albuquerque: University of New Mexico Press, 1982), 179–206.

4. William Deverell, "The Unending Mexican War," in *Whitewashed Adobe: The Rise of Los Angeles and the Remaking of Its Mexican Past* (Berkeley: University of California Press, 2004), 11–48. David Torres-Rouff elaborates on how elite Mexican men and elite Anglo men jointly participated in the violence. For example, in 1836, Jonathan Temple and thirteen other Anglo immigrants joined a mob of sixty-seven Californian Mexicans to lynch an adulterous Spanish-speaking couple after the ayuntamiento (town council) failed to act in ways they thought appropriate. Later, during the Mexican-American War, elite Anglo and Mexican men (including many who held seats on the ayuntamiento) again joined forces to destroy an Indian ranchería where Indians, Mexican Californians, and U.S. soldiers had gathered for drinking, gambling, and sex. In 1852, the newly established and demographically mixed common council empowered a group of leading local citizens, many of whom had previously cycled in and out of political office, to run an informal "jury trial" that ultimately convicted three Mexican men accused of horse thievery; two of the three were publicly hanged. A few years later, in January 1855, two men—one Mexican (Felipe Alvitre) and one Anglo (Dave Brown)—were to be lynched on the same day; while Alvitre was executed as scheduled, Brown's execution was stayed due to appeal by the California Supreme Court. In response, many locals took the law into their own hands and lynched him. One of the locals who participated in this lynch mob was the city's mayor, who resigned specifically for this purpose, then was reelected two weeks later. Torres-Rouff, *Before L.A.,* 94–132; see also John Mack Faragher, *Eternity Street: Violence and Justice in Frontier Los Angeles* (New

York: W. W. Norton, 2015); and Ken Gonzales-Day, *Lynching in the West: 1850–1935* (Durham: Duke University Press, 2006).

5. See Deverell, "The Unending Mexican War"; Edward Escobar, "Beginnings: 1900–1920," in *Race, Police, and the Making of a Political Identity: Mexican Americans and the Los Angeles Police Department, 1900–1945* (Berkeley: University of California Press, 1999), 18–36.

6. A pueblo of just 1,610 people in 1850, Los Angeles had grown to a small city with more than 11,000 residents by 1880. The growth occurred almost entirely as a result of migration by white American settlers, which knocked the city's racial demography upside down. In 1850, Californio-Mexicans made up 75 percent of the city's population, whereas Euro-Americans were only 25 percent. By 1880, just thirty years later, the Euro-American population had swelled to 81 percent of L.A.'s population, while Californio-Mexicans had declined to just 19 percent. With such a small share of the population, Mexicans lost virtually all meaningful political power. After 1872, no Mexican person would be elected to political office in Los Angeles for decades. Chávez-García, *Negotiating Conquest*, 142–43; Robert Fogelson, *Fragmented Metropolis: Los Angeles, 1850–1930* (Berkeley: University of California Press, 1993), 21.

7. The California Land Act of 1851 required Spanish and Mexican landowners to prove their titles before a U.S. land court. Most Californio claims were actually successful even though they often lacked paperwork to prove their ownership and had sometimes deviated from the requirements of their deeds. Nonetheless, the adjudication process took many years—seventeen on average—and during this time many Californio landowners fell victim to high-interest loans, taxes, depressed cattle prices, and droughts and floods that killed livestock and ruined crops. Because Californio landowners had operated within a subsistence economy, they often lacked cash to pay their debts. Many sold their land, usually to Anglo investors, while they waited for title proceedings to be completed. Then, in 1853, the California State Legislature passed a preemption act that opened all land whose title had not been verified by the land commission to the public domain. This act effectively sanctioned squatting on lands whose cases were still pending in court. Through these processes, the Californios, like their elite counterparts across the U.S. Southwest, were widely dispossessed. In 1850, 61 percent of Mexican heads of families in Los Angeles owned land, but by 1870 only 21 percent did, and the median value of their holdings was cut in half, from $2,105 to $1,072. Only 10 percent of the Mexicans who had owned land in 1850 still did so in 1860. Steven Bender, "Born in East LA: The Legacy of Loss and Exclusion in Southern California," in *Tierra y Libertad: Land, Liberty, and Latino Housing* (New York: New York University Press, 2010), 98. Without land, Mexicans were forced into the proletariat, working as wage laborers in the city's burgeoning industrial and agricultural economies. By 1900, 57 percent of Los Angeles's Mexican population worked in unskilled jobs. By 1920, that figure had risen to 71.5 percent (compared with just 6 percent of Anglos), and only 9.5 percent of Mexicans held white-collar jobs (compared with 47 percent of Anglos). Escobar, *Race, Police*, 29–30. For a broader discussion of Mexicans' displacement, barroization, and proletarization in California during this period, see Albert Camarillo,

Chicanos in a Changing Society: From Mexican Pueblos to American Barrios in Santa Barbara and Southern California, 1848–1930 (Cambridge: Harvard University Press, 1979); Chávez-García, *Negotiating Conquest,* 123–50; Haas, *Conquests and Historical Identities,* 56–68; Douglas Monroy, *Rebirth: Mexican Los Angeles from the Great Migration to the Great Depression* (Berkeley: University of California Press, 1999).

8. Bender, "Born in East LA"; Monroy, *Rebirth;* Ricardo Romo, *East Los Angeles: History of a Barrio* (Austin: University of Texas Press, 1983); George Sánchez, *Becoming Mexican American: Ethnicity, Culture, and Identity in Chicano Los Angeles, 1900–1945* (New York: Oxford University Press, 1993); Torres-Rouff, *Before L.A.,* 204–53.

9. The commanding officer of the LAPD's Red Squad kept his office in the Chamber of Commerce building rather than LAPD headquarters, and local employers paid Red Squad members special bonuses and provided them with tear gas guns and projectiles. Officers were hired or fired, promoted or demoted, based on whether or not they helped rig elections, allowed "friendly" vice to continue, or harassed groups and organizations that the political machine saw as enemies. Mike Davis, "Sunshine and the Open Shop," in *Metropolis in the Making: Los Angeles in the 1920s,* ed. Tom Sitton and William Deverell (Berkeley: University of California Press, 2001), 96–122. On the agricultural and industrial development of Los Angeles in this period, see Deverell, *Whitewashed Adobe;* Laura Barraclough, *Making the San Fernando Valley: Rural Landscapes, Urban Development, and White Privilege* (Athens: University of Georgia Press, 2011); Matt García, *A World of Its Own: Race, Labor, and Citrus in the Making of Greater Los Angeles, 1900–1970* (Chapel Hill: University of North Carolina Press, 2001); Becky Nicolaides, *My Blue Heaven: Life and Politics in the Working-Class Suburbs of Los Angeles, 1920–1965* (Chicago: University of Chicago Press, 2002); Douglas Sackman, *Orange Empire: California and the Fruits of Eden* (Berkeley: University of California Press, 2005).

10. Approximately 1.5 million Mexican nationals—one-tenth of Mexico's population—moved north to the United States between 1900 and 1930. Sánchez, *Becoming Mexican American,* 18. With its wealth of industrial and agricultural opportunities, Los Angeles was a choice destination. In just two decades, the city's Mexican-origin population increased nearly twentyfold, from about 5,000 people in 1910 to 30,000 in 1920 and at least 90,000 in 1930. Mark Wild, *Street Meeting: Multiethnic Neighborhoods in Early Twentieth-Century Los Angeles* (Berkeley: University of California Press, 2005), 30n63.

11. During the Mexican Revolution, many migrants in Los Angeles supported anarchist and socialist movements, notably the Partido Liberal Mexicano, which was organized from Los Angeles by exiles and brothers Ricardo and Enrique Flores Magón. They clustered daily in the plaza by the hundreds or even thousands to hear speeches about social, political, and economic issues. Their leaders, such as the Magón brothers, were routinely harassed, arrested, and imprisoned. Ward S. Albro, *Always a Rebel: Ricardo Flores Magón and the Mexican Revolution* (Fort Worth: Texas Christian University Press, 1992); Hernández, *City of Inmates,* 92–130; Wild, *Street Meeting,* 148–99.

12. Escobar, *Race, Police,* 18–36.

13. Escobar, *Race, Police,* 17.

14. Luis Álvarez, *The Power of the Zoot: Youth Culture and Resistance during World War II* (Berkeley: University of California Press, 2009); Elizabeth Escobedo, *From Coveralls to Zoot Suits: The Lives of Mexican American Women on the World War II Home Front* (Chapel Hill: University of North Carolina Press, 2013); Gerardo Licón, "Pachucas, Pachucos, and Their Culture: Mexican American Youth Culture of the Southwest, 1910–1955" (PhD diss., University of Southern California, 2009); Anthony Macías, *Mexican American Mojo: Popular Music, Dance, and Urban Culture in Los Angeles, 1935–1968* (Durham: Duke University Press, 2008); Eduardo Obregón Pagán, *Murder at the Sleepy Lagoon: Zoot Suits, Race, and Riot in Wartime L.A.* (Chapel Hill: University of North Carolina Press, 2006); Catherine Ramírez, *The Woman in the Zoot Suit: Gender, Nationalism, and the Cultural Politics of Memory* (Durham: Duke University Press, 2009).

15. Kenneth Burt, *The Search for a Civic Voice: California Latino Politics* (Claremont, CA: Regina Books, 2007); Escobar, *Race, Police.*

16. For example, Steve Herbert, *Policing Space: Territoriality and the Los Angeles Police Department* (Minneapolis: University of Minnesota Press, 1997); Darnell Hunt, *Screening the Los Angeles "Riots": Race, Seeing, and Resistance* (Cambridge, U.K.: Cambridge University Press, 1997).

17. Lindley Bynum and Idwal Jones, *Biscailuz: Sheriff of the New West* (New York: William Morrow, 1950).

18. Bynum and Jones, *Biscailuz.*

19. Bynum and Jones, *Biscailuz,* 10.

20. Bynum and Jones, *Biscailuz,* 7, 8–9.

21. Bynum and Jones *Biscailuz,* 10.

22. Cecilia Rasmussen, "Long Arm of This Lawman Bridged a City's History," *Los Angeles Times,* October 21, 2007.

23. In 1935, the Mexican Chambers of Commerce of Los Angeles and Belvedere jointly sponsored a banquet in Biscailuz's honor at the Paris Café in East Los Angeles. Hundreds of Mexican American business owners and their families attended. *Banquet in Honor of Sheriff Eugene Biscailuz* (photograph with caption), University of Southern California Special Collections, Eugene Biscailuz Scrapbooks, Scrapbook 4, n.p. Biscailuz remained an advocate for Mexican American business owners throughout his tenure as sheriff.

24. Bynum and Jones, *Biscailuz,* 120.

25. Bynum and Jones, *Biscailuz,* 127.

26. Bynum and Jones, *Biscailuz,* 192.

27. Bynum and Jones, *Biscailuz,* 127.

28. John Nichols, *St. Francis Dam Disaster* (Charleston, SC: Arcadia, 2002).

29. Bynum and Jones, *Biscailuz,* 136.

30. See, for example, "92,115 Cheer Sheriff's Rodeo In Coliseum," *Los Angeles Examiner,* August 28, 1950, 247; "Posse to Ride in Sheriff's Rodeo Aug 27," *Citizen,* July 28, 1950, 248.

31. William Estrada, "Los Angeles' Old Plaza and Olvera Street: Imagined and Contested Space," *Western Folklore* 58, no. 2 (1999), 124.

32. Bynum and Jones, *Biscailuz,* 122–23.

33. Bynum and Jones, *Biscailuz,* 152.

34. Sánchez, *Becoming Mexican American,* 209–26.

35. Álvarez, *Power of the Zoot;* Pagán, *Murder at the Sleepy Lagoon;* C. Ramírez, *Woman in the Zoot Suit.*

36. Pagán, *Murder at the Sleepy Lagoon,* 73.

37. Pagán, *Murder at the Sleepy Lagoon,* 162.

38. Carlos Larralde, "Josefina Fierro and the Sleepy Lagoon Crusade, 1942–1945," *Southern California Quarterly* 92, no. 2 (2010): 117–60.

39. Stuart Cosgrove, "The Zoot-Suit and Style Warfare," *History Workshop Journal* 18, no. 1 (1984): 77–91.

40. Álvarez, *Power of the Zoot,* 155–99.

41. Rasmussen, "Long Arm."

42. Los Angeles County Sheriff's Department, "1940–1949," http://shq.lasdnews.net/content/uoa/SHM/1940%20-%201949.pdf (accessed July 6, 2017).

43. "Mexican Horsemen Fly into Town for Rodeo," *Los Angeles Times,* August 24, 1946, A8.

44. A 1957 photograph shows Biscailuz with José Castillo-Lepe, representing a charro association from Guadalajara, standing before Biscailuz's desk at the LASD headquarters in downtown Los Angeles, looking over that year's program for the Sheriff's Rodeo. University of Southern California Special Collections, Eugene Biscailuz Scrapbooks, Scrapbook 5.

45. "Long Parade Marks Mexican Anniversary," *Los Angeles Times,* September 17, 1957, 2.

46. Bynum and Jones, *Biscailuz,* 207.

47. Bynum and Jones, *Biscailuz,* 207.

48. "Mounted Posse Still on Job," *Los Angeles Herald-Express,* February 14, 1955, 62.

49. U.S. Department of Commerce, Bureau of the Census, *Sixteenth Census of the United States: 1940, Population Schedule,* Los Angeles City, California, Sheet 11-A.

50. M. Flores, *El Charro en U.S.A.,* 12.

51. M. Flores, *El Charro en U.S.A.,* 12.

52. U.S. Department of Commerce, Bureau of the Census, *Sixteenth Census of the United States: 1940, Population Schedule,* Pasadena, California, Sheet 18-B.

53. M. Flores, *El Charro en U.S.A.,* 15–17.

54. U.S. Department of Commerce, Bureau of the Census, *Sixteenth Census of the United States: 1940, Population Schedule,* Enumeration District 60–703, Sheet 8-B; *Hearing re: Advisability and Legality of Charro Rodeos,* Los Angeles Department of Animal Regulation, January 29, 1976, p. 92, California State University, Northridge, Special Collections and Archives, Julian Nava Papers, Box 20, Folder 4.

55. *Hearing re: Advisability,* 92.

56. "Mounted Posse Still on Job."

57. "Belvedere to Mark Cinco de Mayo," *Los Angeles Times,* May 4, 1947, A2.

58. "Homage Paid Heroes of Mexican Freedom," *Los Angeles Times,* September 17, 1947, 6.

59. Cholly Angeleno, "Posse's Party Gay Fete," *Los Angeles Times,* December 1955, 80, UCLA Special Collections, Eugene Biscailuz Scrapbooks, Box 66.

60. See M. Flores, *El Charro en U.S.A.*

61. M. Flores, *El Charro en U.S.A.,* 18.

62. *The Young Land,* directed by Ted Tetzlaff (Columbia Pictures, 1959).

63. Valerie J. Nelson, "Roberto de la Madrid Dies at 88: U.S.-Born Governor of a Mexican State," *Los Angeles Times,* April 14, 2010, http://articles.latimes.com/2010 /apr/14/local/la-me-roberto-delamadrid14–2010apr14 (accessed May 7, 2014).

64. Laura Barraclough, "Rural Urbanism: Producing Western Heritage and the Racial Geography of Postwar Los Angeles," *Western Historical Quarterly* 39 (2008): 177–202.

65. M. Flores, *El Charro en U.S.A.,* 17–19; Julian Nava, *My Mexican-American Journey* (Houston: Arte Público Press, 2002).

66. "Cityside with Gene Sherman," *Los Angeles Times,* November 9, 1953, 2.

67. "1,000 Honor Biscailuz for Long Service," *Los Angeles Times,* May 18, 1954, A2.

68. University of Southern California Special Collections, Eugene Biscailuz Scrapbooks, Scrapbook 5.

69. "Cityside with Gene Sherman," *Los Angeles Times,* November 9, 1953, 2; Lieutenant C. D. Fountaine to Sheriff Eugene Biscailuz, "Memorandum," January 23, 1958, UCLA Special Collections, Eugene Biscailuz Scrapbooks, Box 32.

70. The Los Angeles Police Department had already made initial efforts at professionalization after a 1938 police recall election and the subsequent dismissal of the corrupt chief of police. Police Chief William Parker, who embraced military might and described the LAPD as the "thin blue line" standing between civilization and chaos, had fully implemented most of these initiatives by the mid-1950s. Escobar, *Race, Police,* 13.

71. Myrna Oliver, "Peter Pitchess, Sheriff Who Modernized Agency, Dies," *Los Angeles Times,* April 5, 1999.

72. Oliver, "Peter Pitchess."

73. M. Flores, *El Charro en U.S.A.,* 19.

74. M. Flores, *El Charro en U.S.A.,* 18. After leaving the posse, Arteaga continued to work on several Westerns in Los Angeles, including *High Plains Drifter* (1973), *Bite the Bullet* (1975), and *The Master Gunfighter* (1975). See "Mario Arteaga," IMDB, www.imdb.com/name/nm0037642/ (accessed September 10, 2015).

75. "Cinco de Mayo Fiesta to Open in Old Plaza," *Los Angeles Times,* May 4, 1964, B10; *Charros from Various Groups at Lion's Parade down Hollywood Boulevard, 1965* (photograph), Los Angeles Public Library, Shades of L.A. Collection; "Blessing of Animals Set," *Los Angeles Times,* April 9, 1966, D6.

76. M. Flores, *El Charro en U.S.A.,* 19.

77. In 1964, the Charros de Los Angeles wrote to Eduardo Quevedo asking Quevedo to publicize their upcoming Gran Baile Ranchero, the proceeds of which would be used to build a new lienzo, on KMEX, a Spanish-language television station that had begun broadcasting in Los Angeles the year before. R. S. Bateman to Eduardo Quevedo, July 14, 1964, Stanford Special Collections, Eduardo Quevedo Papers, Box 2, Folder 11.

78. A post with a historic photo on the Charros de Los Angeles's Facebook page shows members of the group alongside Águilar during Águilar's performance at the Pico Rivera Sports Arena in Los Angeles, soon after the facility's opening in 1978. Charros de Los Angeles Facebook page, August 9, 2015, www.facebook.com /CharrosdeLosAngeles/ (accessed August 23, 2015).

79. Pepe Arciga, "Aguilar to Star in Latin Rodeo," *Los Angeles Times,* August 4, 1967, D9.

80. "'Viva Mexico' Celebration at Disneyland," *Los Angeles Times,* May 3, 1969, OC9; "Tito Guizar, Mexican Singer, Actor for 70 Years, Dies at 91," *Los Angeles Times,* December 27, 1999.

81. "Latin Fiesta Slated at Universal City," *Los Angeles Times,* June 23, 1969, C17.

82. Oliver, "Peter Pitches."

83. Notable examples include the Biscailuz Training Center in Monterey Park, a suburb of Los Angeles in the San Gabriel Valley; Biscailuz Street in Castaic, in the far northern part of the county; and Biscailuz Park in Lakewood, an industrial suburb in the southern part of the county.

CHAPTER TWO. BUILDING SAN ANTONIO'S POSTWAR TOURIST ECONOMY

1. "Frontier Attire Urged for Fiesta," *San Antonio Light,* March 18, 1946, 11.

2. "City Set for Final Events," *San Antonio Light,* April 27, 1946, 2.

3. Even those Mexicans who retained title often could not afford the high taxes imposed by new state and local governments. Their land frequently fell into foreclosure and was systematically transferred to Texas's wealthiest investors, almost always Anglos, through "sheriff's sales." Still other Mexican landowners chose to sell their land while they could. Many who were displaced by these processes moved south to the Rio Grande Valley or across the newly established borderline into northern Mexico, where they had deep familial and community connections. Arnoldo de León, *They Called Them Greasers: Anglo Attitudes toward Mexicans in Texas, 1821–1900* (Austin: University of Texas Press, 1983); David Montejano, *Anglos and Mexicans in the Making of Texas, 1836–1986* (Austin: University of Texas Press, 1987).

4. Montejano, *Anglos and Mexicans,* 73.

5. During the 1830s and '40s, faced with threats of violence and intimidation from white settlers emboldened by Texas secession and U.S. military victories, many Bexareños (Tejanos from San Antonio Bexar) fled to the historic ranching communities of the Rio Grande Valley. Still others, such as San Antonio mayor Juan Seguín,

who had fought on behalf of Texas independence at the Battle of San Jacinto, had no choice but to escape across the international border to Mexico when death threats were made against him and his family. Those Tejano landowners who remained in San Antonio moved from the central plaza areas to the western side of the San Pedro Creek throughout the 1840s and '50s. In doing so, they vacated the central part of the city for Anglo-American and German business owners, who developed elite, racially exclusive businesses and social sites such as the Menger Hotel and the Vance Hotel (later renamed the Gunter Hotel). Their westward movement after U.S. conquest established the spatial foundation for the westside barrio, which would expand dramatically during the Mexican Revolution. In the early twentieth century, San Antonio was a particularly attractive destination for migrants from both South Texas and Mexico because of its longstanding administrative, economic, and cultural importance in the region and its still sizable, though segregated and disenfranchised, ethnic Mexican population. While not as economically powerful as Los Angeles, San Antonio had a small manufacturing sector as well as a merchant class that sometimes played a mediating role in lessening the worst effects of Jim Crow. From 1900 to 1930, the ethnic Mexican population of San Antonio increased from 13,722 to 82,373, catapulting ethnic Mexicans from 25 to 35 percent of the city's population. Mario García, *Mexican Americans: Leadership, Ideology, and Identity, 1930–1960* (New Haven: Yale University Press, 1989), 29; see also Montejano, *Anglos and Mexicans*. Regarding migrant workers' use of San Antonio as home base, see Neil Foley, *The White Scourge: Mexicans, Blacks, and Poor Whites in Texas Cotton Culture* (Berkeley: University of California Press, 1997), 42.

6. In the 1940s, Mexican-origin people in San Antonio occupied more than 50 percent of the city's substandard housing. Sewage systems, playgrounds, paved roads, lighted streets, and mosquito eradication programs were almost completely lacking; a 1947 study by the city health department found nearly twelve thousand homes without sewer connections, serviced almost entirely by pit toilets. The Mexican death rate from tuberculosis was almost four times that of Anglos, and the infant death rate was more than double; fully 24 percent of infant deaths were caused by diarrhea, a product of poor sanitary conditions. See M. García, *Mexican Americans;* San Antonio City Health Department, *Annual Report, 1946–47*, referenced in Frances Woods, *Mexican Ethnic Leadership in San Antonio, Texas* (Washington, DC: Catholic University of America Press, 1949).

7. The ricos had chosen San Antonio because of its cosmopolitan nature and established ethnic Mexican population, including elite descendants of Canary Islanders that the Spanish Crown had recruited to settle in San Antonio during the 1730s. Once in San Antonio, the ricos tried to critique and direct the evolution of the new Mexican government from abroad. The definitive study of the ricos is Richard García, "The Exiled Ricos," in *Rise of the Mexican American Middle Class: San Antonio, 1929–1941* (College Station: Texas A&M University Press, 1991), 221–52. On *La Prensa* and its founder Ignacio Lozano, an exile from Nuevo León, see Maggie Rivas-Rodríguez, "Ignacio E. Lozano: The Mexican Exile Publisher Who Conquered San Antonio and Los Angeles," *American Journalism* 21, no. 1

(2004): 75–89; Vicki Mayer, "From Segmented to Fragmented: Latino Media in San Antonio, Texas," *Journalism and Mass Communication Quarterly* 78, no. 2 (2001): 291–306.

8. By the mid-1960s, the middle class made up approximately 20 percent of San Antonio's ethnic Mexican population. As U.S. citizens, the members of the Mexican American Generation were more acculturated than their parents: they had been socialized in American schools, were drawn into the Democratic Party during the Great Depression, participated in World War II in large numbers, and witnessed the effects of the Cold War and deportations on ethnic Mexicans who embraced radical politics. David Montejano, *Quixote's Soldiers: A Local History of the Chicano Movement* (Austin: University of Texas Press, 2010), 24; see also M. García, *Mexican Americans;* R. García, *Rise of the Mexican American Middle Class;* John Martínez, "Leadership and Politics," in *La Raza: Forgotten Americans,* ed. Julian Samora (Notre Dame: University of Notre Dame Press, 1962), 47–62.

9. John Hart Lane, *Voluntary Associations among Mexican Americans in San Antonio, Texas: Organizational and Leadership Characteristics* (New York: Arno Press, 1976), 70–71.

10. While other Texas cities focused on securing defense manufacturing plants, San Antonio's leaders pursued military installations, a strategy that paid off handsomely in terms of increased population and investment. Between 1940 and 1950, San Antonio's population increased by 61 percent, adding roughly 150,000 new citizens, and by 1960, the city's population had reached 588,000, making San Antonio the third largest city in Texas. Robert Goldberg, "Racial Change on the Southern Periphery: The Case of San Antonio, Texas, 1960–1965," *Journal of Southern History* 49, no. 3 (1983): 349–74; see also Robert Fairbanks, *The War on Slums in the Southwest* (Philadelphia: Temple University Press, 2014). Demographic growth propelled spatial expansion: San Antonio's city limits surged from 36 square miles in 1940 to more than 450 square miles by 1999, with most of this growth concentrated in the two decades after World War II. John Hutton, "Landscape, Architecture, and the Social Matrix," in *On the Border: An Environmental History of San Antonio,* ed. Char Miller (University of Pittsburgh Press, 2007), 231.

11. For example, Betsy Beasley, "Exporting Service: Houston and the Globalization of Oil Expertise, 1945–2008" (PhD diss., Yale University, 2016).

12. At midcentury, government employees made up almost one-third of the local workforce, and nearly 40 percent of the city's economy came from federal spending, principally through defense. Fairbanks, *War on Slums;* Hutton, "Landscape, Architecture, and the Social Matrix"; John L. Kriken, "The Arts and City Livability," *Ekistics* 48, no. 288 (1981): 181–91.

13. San Antonio began using at-large, nonpartisan elections in the early 1950s, and the Good Government League (GGL) formed a slating group that controlled the nomination process. Although the GGL consistently nominated at least one Chicano and one Black candidate in each election, these candidates were likely to live outside of the city's Mexican and Black neighborhoods and to embrace pro-business positions. As a result, according to political scientist Rodolfo Rosales, the

Chicano middle class had to choose whether to pursue individual political inclusion while neglecting the problems facing the Chicano community as a whole or to challenge the pro-business terms of inclusion, but with little foreseeable success. Even so, this conundrum represented significant progress from years past. Historian David Montejano explains: "Despite segregation, San Antonio was considered a 'moderate' southern city because the GGL had included token representation from the Mexican and Black communities on its city council slates since the mid-fifties. Selected by a secret nominating committee of the Anglo business elite, these 'minority' representatives rarely lived in the Mexican or Black neighborhoods . . . [but] such token representation was a progressive step from the Jim Crow system of the 1940s, and it was emblematic of the paternalistic rule of San Antonio's Anglo business-political elite." Montejano, *Quixote's Soldiers,* quote on 15, larger discussion on 279–81; see also Rodolfo Rosales, *The Illusion of Inclusion: The Untold Political Story of San Antonio* (Austin: University of Texas Press, 2000). For similar processes elsewhere in postwar cities of the U.S. South, see Nathan D. B. Connolly, *A World More Concrete: Real Estate and the Making of Jim Crow South Florida* (University of Chicago Press, 2014); Alex Sayf Cummings, "'Brain Magnet': Research Triangle Park and the Origins of the Creative City, 1953–1965," *Journal of Urban History* 43 (2017): 470–92; Kevin Kruse, *White Flight: Atlanta and the Making of Modern Conservatism* (Princeton: Princeton University Press, 2005).

14. Daniel Arreola, "Urban Ethnic Landscape Identity," *Geographical Review* 85, no. 4 (1995), 528–31; Lewis Fisher, "Preservation of San Antonio's Built Environment," in *On the Border: An Environmental History of San Antonio,* ed. Char Miller (Pittsburgh: University of Pittsburgh Press, 2007), 199–221; Kenneth Hafertepe, "Restoration, Reconstruction or Romance? The Case of the Spanish Governor's Palace in Hispanic-Era San Antonio Texas," *Journal of the Society of Architectural Historians* 67, no. 3 (2008): 412–33; Laura Hernández-Ehrisman, *Inventing the Fiesta City: Heritage and Carnival in San Antonio* (Albuquerque: University of New Mexico Press, 2008), 94–96.

15. Richard Flores, *Remembering the Alamo: Memory, Modernity, and the Master Symbol* (Austin: University of Texas Press, 2002).

16. Char Miller, "Where the Buffalo Roamed: Ranching, Agriculture, and the Urban Marketplace," in *On the Border: An Environmental History of San Antonio,* ed. Char Miller (Pittsburgh: University of Pittsburgh Press, 2007), 79; see also San Antonio Stock Show and Rodeo, "History and Mission," www.sarodeo.com/about/history-mission (accessed July 13, 2018).

17. Anthony Knopp, Manuel Medrano, Priscilla Rodríguez, and the Brownsville Historical Association, *Charro Days in Brownsville* (Charleston, SC: Arcadia, 2009).

18. Geraldo Cadava, "Fiesta de los Vaqueros," in *Standing on Common Ground: The Making of a Sunbelt Borderland* (Cambridge: Harvard University Press, 2013).

19. Genevieve Carpio, "Multiracial Suburbs and Unrest in the California Inland Empire," paper presented at the American Association of Geographers annual meeting, San Francisco, April 2, 2016.

20. Timothy Bowman, *Blood Oranges: Colonialism and Agriculture in the South Texas Borderlands* (College Station: Texas A&M University Press, 2016); John Weber, *From South Texas to the Nation: The Exploitation of Mexican Labor in the Twentieth Century* (Chapel Hill: University of North Carolina Press, 2015).

21. Otey Scruggs, "Texas and the Bracero Program, 1942–47," *Pacific Historical Review* 32, no. 3 (1963): 251–64; Kitty Calavita, *Inside the State: The Bracero Program, Immigration, and the I.N.S.* (New York: Routledge, 1992).

22. Kelly Lytle Hernández, *Migra! A History of the U.S. Border Patrol* (Berkeley: University of California Press, 2010), esp. 155–56.

23. Al Rendón, *Charreada: Mexican Rodeo in Texas* (Denton: University of North Texas Press, 2002), 4; see also "3rd Charro Unit Planned," *San Antonio Light,* April 6, 1955, 25.

24. By the late 1960s, ethnic Mexicans in San Antonio, on average, had only 5.7 years of schooling, and only 13.2 percent had finished high school. By contrast, according to a study by John Hart Lane, 58 percent of the leaders of Mexican American organizations had completed high school; this figure appears to be even higher for members of the charro associations. See Lane, *Voluntary Associations.*

25. In addition, members of the charro associations were regularly named LULAC's "Rey Feo." See Scholarship Fund, "Royal Council of Past Kings," www.reyfeoscholarship.com/content.php?sec = consejo (accessed October 28, 2013).

26. In his late 1960s study of ethnic Mexican voluntary associations in San Antonio, John Hart Lane found that over two-thirds of the Mexican American leaders of these groups were opposed to the militant tactics then being used by Black organizations and leaders, though they were generally supportive of farmworker strikes in the Rio Grande Valley. Lane, *Voluntary Associations.*

27. Quoted in Lane, *Voluntary Associations,* 72–73.

28. 1940 Federal Census, Enumeration District 259–60, Sheet 2B; see also "Letter of Correspondence," July 15, 1950, University of Texas–San Antonio Special Collections, San Antonio Hispanic Chamber of Commerce Records, MS 126, Box 1, Folder 13.

29. "Casanova Also Falstaff Agent," *San Antonio Express,* October 6, 1953, 9.

30. This information has been compiled through searches for individual charros' names and identifying information in news articles in *La Prensa,* the *San Antonio Light,* and the *San Antonio Express,* triangulated with the 1940 United States census.

31. "Reina 1950 de la Asociación de Charros de San Antonio," *La Prensa,* February 26, 1950, 7.

32. César Serrato, "San Antonio al día," *La Prensa,* October 26, 1948, 6.

33. "Maya Fiesta Dance Scheduled," *San Antonio Light,* June 21, 1949, 5; see also "Un festival del 'Charro Riding Club' a los periodistas," *La Prensa,* December 8, 1949, 1.

34. Terry Jordan, *Trails to Texas: The Southern Roots of Western Cattle Ranching* (Lincoln: University of Nebraska Press, 1981), 127; see also D. Weber, *Mexican Frontier.*

35. "El Club de Boleritos auspiciado por la Asociación de Charros," *La Prensa,* November 19, 1950, 7; "Gran día campestre ranchero para el próximo domingo,"

La Prensa, May 6, 1951, 1; "Éxito de la función de medianoche organizada por la Asociación de Charros de San Antonio," *La Prensa,* May 13, 1951, 6; "Fiesta de los Charros en honor de los ex-prisioneros," *La Prensa,* May 10, 1953, 13; "Noticias locales," *La Prensa,* May 16, 1953, 2; "Esta noche es el gran baile a beneficio de la Clínica Stella Maris, en La Villita," *La Prensa,* July 29, 1956, 10.

36. For the Tampico flood victims event, see "Fiesta Charro-Taurina a beneficio de los jaibos," *La Prensa,* September 21, 1955, 1–2; "Corrida de toros de los locutores y lucha libre en el R. del Charro," *La Prensa,* October 2, 1955, 5; "Gran fiesta charro-taurina en el Rancho del Charro el domingo," *La Prensa,* October 4, 1955, 2; "Pedro Armendáriz en la fiesta charra," *La Prensa,* October 9, 1955, 1; "Gran fiesta de la Asociación de Charros," *La Prensa,* October 16, 1955, 11. For the benefit for the children of Monterrey, see "Celebrase hoy el gran festival de la Asociación de Charros," *La Prensa,* July 1, 1956, 6.

37. "Hoy es la lunada del Club Marizel," *La Prensa,* November 20, 1949, 7.

38. Julie Pycior, *Democratic Renewal and the Mutual Aid Legacy of U.S. Mexicans* (College Station: Texas A&M University Press, 2014).

39. Frank Jasso, "Resonante éxito fue la Fiesta de las Flores organizada por los Lulacs," *La Prensa,* May 13, 1951, 5; Porter Loring Mortuary, "Lawrence Mazer" (obituary), www.porterloring.com/memsol.cgi?user_id = 468665 (accessed October 4, 2013).

40. "Charro Assn. Head Re-elected," *San Antonio Light,* January 9, 1962, 2. For Reed's biography, see https://www.legacy.com/obituaries/sanantonio/obituary.aspx?page=lifestory&pid=124666290 (accessed November 1, 2018).

41. "Legislative Races a Political Smorgasbord," *San Antonio Light,* April 26, 1964, 2-AA.

42. Advertisement, *San Antonio Express,* October 19, 1950, 1-C.

43. "Posse Aid Charriada Set," *San Antonio Light,* May 29, 1951 [page number indecipherable].

44. "Campaña de los charros de S.A. en favor de la Marcha de Décimos," *La Prensa,* January 17, 1954, 1.

45. "Rodeo y jaripeo," *La Prensa,* September 6, 1953, 13.

46. For example, the city's charros participated in a rally sponsored by the Loyal American Democrats, a Chicano liberal caucus within the Democratic Party, to support Adlai Stevenson's campaign for U.S. president in 1952. The *San Antonio Express* described the event: "The Charros and Dorados formed a guard of honor for Stevenson at Milam Plaza and the candidate walked to the speaker's platform between a line of gayly dancing youngsters—little Charros and little Chinas Poblanas." Clarence A. LaRouche, "Stevenson Somewhat like Bullfighter as Spanish Cries, Placards Greet Him," *San Antonio Express,* October 19, 1952, quoted in Rosales, *Illusion of Inclusion,* 57.

47. "President to Get Charro Hat from Mexican Chamber," *San Antonio Express,* September 25, 1948, 2.

48. "Black and White Ball Attracts Beauties, Texas and Mexican Notables," *San Antonio Express,* December 11, 1949, 1-A.

49. "Coliseum Dedicated, Exposition Opens," *San Antonio Express,* February 18, 1950, 3; see also Miller, "Where the Buffalo Roamed."

50. "Governor to Lead Big Western Fete Friday," *San Antonio Express,* February 14, 1951, 1-C, emphasis added.

51. In San Antonio, the practice of selecting queens for civic affairs had begun in the early twentieth century, when the Battle of Flowers Association, an organization of southern white women, chose queens for its parade to the Alamo; by 1909, the Order of the Alamo, an elite white men's organization, had taken over the selection process. Hernández-Ehrisman, *Inventing the Fiesta City;* see also Holly Beachley Brear, *Inherit the Alamo: Myth and Ritual at an American Shrine* (Austin: University of Texas Press, 1995).

52. In 1954, for example, the *San Antonio Express* announced that the "beauteous Oralia Martínez-Gil," the San Antonio Charro Association's queen, had been crowned "Mexico Day Queen" at the State Fair of Texas in Dallas. Among her many prizes was a five-day trip to Mexico City. Caption, photo of Oralia Martínez-Gil, *San Antonio Express,* October 13, 1954, 1. Similarly, Norma Flores, a young woman who was elected duchess of the San Antonio Charro Association several times in the late 1950s, traveled a circuit of pageants and competitions as far north as Wisconsin. She spent her young adulthood competing to be queen of Mexican Independence Day and Pan American parades across the U.S. Southwest and Midwest, developing networks and winning occasional prizes along the way. "Miss Norma Flores Is Engaged to John Brian Clark," *San Antonio Express and News,* September 17, 1961, 5-F.

53. At the 1950 LULAC Feria de la Flores, for example, *La Prensa* reported that the fair's queen, Gloria de la Mora of San Antonio Technical High School, had designed her own china poblana costume with the help of her club associates. Evita María Gallegos, queen of the San Antonio Charro Association, was named princess and wore a Spanish colonial–style dress. Jasso, "Resonante éxito," 5. For a wider discussion of queen contests among Mexican American organizations in this period, see Lori Flores, "Mexican American Civil Rights Organizations' Queen Contests and the Pageantry of Respectability," paper presented at the Newberry Library, Borderlands and Latino History Seminar, Chicago, May 12, 2017.

54. "Los charros de San Antonio participarán en las Fiestas Patrias," *La Prensa,* September 10, 1950, 9. In subsequent years, Independence Day festivities took nearly identical forms. See, e.g., "Regias Festividades Patrias de la Asociación de Charros de San Antonio," *La Prensa,* September 11, 1955, 11.

55. "Colorful Parade Sparks Friendship Fiesta," *San Antonio Express,* September 17, 1950, 10.

56. Ésther Ruíz, "Regresaron del capital de la república los miembros de la Asociación de Charros de San Antonio," *La Prensa,* August 5, 1951, 7.

57. Oswaldo Alarcón, "Vamos a Tepa...," *La Prensa,* September 2, 1951, 11.

58. Frank Jasso, "La Asociación de Charros prepará extraordinaria fiesta para celebrar su tercera fiesta anual," *La Prensa,* August 26, 1951, 11; "Llegaron a San Antonio los charros de Tepatitlán," *La Prensa,* August 31, 1951, 5; "Será estupenda la fiesta de los charros hoy, en Pablo's Grove," *La Prensa,* September 3, 1951, 5.

59. "Nos visita un grupo de industriales de Mexico," *La Prensa,* March 11, 1952, 2.

60. "Gran fiesta el domingo 12 en el Rancho del Charro," *La Prensa,* October 5, 1952, 5; "Personajes regiomontanos han venido para apadrinar una fiesta de charros," *La Prensa,* October 12, 1952, 2.

61. "Gran jornada de los 'charros' está en preparación," *La Prensa,* August 8, 1952, 5; "Una gran fiesta charra en San Antonio," *La Prensa,* August 24, 1952, 11; "Lo que veremos en el Coliseo," *La Prensa,* August 28, 1952, 5.

62. "Oro, seda, y sol," *La Prensa,* June 26, 1955, 2; "La novillada charra fue un gran éxito," *La Prensa,* July 6, 1955, 5.

63. "S.A. Area Awards Made: History Retained," *San Antonio Light,* May 19, 1957, 20-A.

64. For example, "Cathedral Rite Joins Pair," *San Antonio Light,* September 19, 1957, 45; "Miss Norma Flores," 5-F.

65. Manuel Ruíz Ibáñez, "De la vida real," *La Prensa,* August 29, 1956, 6; see also "Entusiasto agasajo de la Asociación de Charros de S.A. a Henry B González," *La Prensa,* August 26, 1956, 2.

66. "Una novillada a beneficio de Henry B. González," *La Prensa,* October 21, 1956, 2.

67. Montejano, *Quixote's Soldiers,* 15, 20, 229–31; Rosales, *Illusion of Inclusion,* 70–73.

68. San Antonio Charro Association, "Constitution and By-Laws," p. 2, Institute of Texan Cultures, Fiesta San Antonio Commission Collection, Box 7, Folder 5.

69. San Antonio Charro Association, "Constitution and By-Laws," 3–4.

70. Marilyn Bennett, "Charreada Comes to San Antonio—1959," *It Happened in San Antonio* (Guilford, CT: Globe Pequot Press, 2006), 95.

71. Bennett, *It Happened in San Antonio,* 96.

72. S.B. Zisman, "Missions, Malls, and Monkeys," *San Antonio Light,* March 29, 1959, 1, 14; see also Miguel De Oliver, "Multicultural Consumerism and Racial Hierarchy: A Case Study of Market Culture and the Structural Harmonization of Contradictory Doctrines," *Antipode* 33, no. 2 (2001), 245.

73. Bennett, *It Happened in San Antonio,* 97.

74. "La Asociación de Charros de San Antonio adquirió terrenos para su rancho," *La Prensa,* June 28, 1959, 12-A.

75. Interview with Socrates Ramírez, August 2003, by Laura Hernández-Ehrisman, quoted in *Inventing the Fiesta City,* 154. In the late 1970s a promissory note signed by members of the charro association indicates they agreed to pay $70,000 to Westside Bank of San Antonio, at 10 percent interest, in monthly installments of $925.00, for the property and improvements. Real Estate Lien Note, San Antonio Charro Association to Westside Bank, February 15, 1979, Institute of Texas Cultures, Fiesta San Antonio Commission Records, Box 7, Folder 5.

76. For the current association's website, see www.sacharros.com

77. Fairbanks, *War on Slums,* 147. Andrew Highsmith has documented a similar process in Flint, Michigan. Andrew Highsmith, *Demolition Means Progress: Flint,*

Michigan, and the Fate of the American Metropolis (Chicago: University of Chicago Press, 2015).

78. Fairbanks, *War on Slums*, 144–47.

79. Beth Helen Bruinsma Chang, "Complicated Lives: Engendering Self-Sufficiency after Welfare Reform in San Antonio, TX" (PhD diss., University of Texas at Austin, 2007); De Oliver, "Multicultural Consumerism"; Fairbanks, *War on Slums*, 144–47; Kriken, "The Arts and City Livability."

80. Katherine Nickas, "Tourism Grows to $13B Economic Impact," *Rivard Report*, October 21, 2014, https://therivardreport.com/san-antonio-tourism-generating-13-4-billion-annually-trinity-study-shows/ (accessed April 13, 2017).

81. R. C. Jones, "San Antonio's Spatial Economic Structure, 1955–1980," in *The Politics of San Antonio: Community, Progress, and Power,* ed. David Johnson, John Booth, and Richard Harris (Lincoln: University of Nebraska Press, 1983), 48–49.

82. In 1955, *La Prensa* reported the association's pride in being selected, for the first time, to be in the front of the line in that year's mounted section of the Battle of Flowers parade. "El próximo día 5 de mayo."

83. Hernández-Ehrisman, *Inventing the Fiesta City*, 153–55.

CHAPTER THREE. CREATING MULTICULTURAL PUBLIC
INSTITUTIONS IN DENVER AND PUEBLO

1. Máximo Virgil, "Mexican American Women Excel: La Charreada," *La Luz,* November 1978, 13–15.

2. Nancy MacLean, "The Civil Rights Act and the Transformation of Mexican American Identity and Politics," *Berkeley La Raza Law Journal* 18 (2007), 124. See also Carlos K. Blanton, "George I. Sánchez, Ideology, and Whiteness in the Making of the Mexican American Civil Rights Movement, 1930–1960," *Journal of Southern History* 72, no. 3 (2006): 569–604; Neil Foley, "Becoming Hispanic: Mexican Americans and the Faustian Pact with Whiteness," in *Reflexiones: New Directions in Mexican American Studies,* ed. Neil Foley (Austin: University of Texas Press, 1998); Ariela J. Gross, "'The Caucasian Cloak': Mexican Americans and the Politics of Whiteness in the Twentieth-Century Southwest," *Georgetown Law Journal* 95, no. 2 (2007): 337–92; Danielle Olden, "Becoming Minority: Mexican Americans, Race, and the Legal Struggle for Educational Equity in Denver, Colorado," *Western Historical Quarterly* 48, no. 1 (2017): 43–66.

3. As historian Charles Montgomery has argued, in New Mexico, "even in the heyday of the Chicano movement, the belief that Spanish-speaking people were culturally Spanish, not Mexican or Indian, was never in question. The spirit of *chicanismo,* so strong in Texas and California, could not dislodge a Spanish colonial legacy in New Mexico that seemed to reach back to 1598." Charles Montgomery, *The Spanish Redemption: Heritage, Power, and Loss on New Mexico's Upper Rio Grande* (Berkeley: University of California Press, 2002), xii. See also Sarah Deutsch, *No Separate Refuge: Culture, Class, and Gender on an Anglo-Hispanic Frontier in the*

American Southwest, 1880–1940 (New York: Oxford University Press, 1987); Richard Nostrand, *The Hispano Homeland* (Norman: University of Oklahoma Press, 1992).

4. Fawn-Amber Montoya, "From Mexicans to Citizens: Colorado Fuel and Iron's Representation of Nuevo Mexicans, 1901–1919," *Journal of the West* 45, no. 4 (2006): 29–35; Deutsch, *No Separate Refuge,* 107–26.

5. Although Denver and Pueblo attracted substantial numbers of Mexican migrants during and after the Mexican Revolution, they were far fewer than those received by cities in Texas and California and always outnumbered by Hispano migrants from rural villages in New Mexico and southern Colorado. Nostrand, *Hispano Homeland,* 164.

6. In Denver, as manufacturing work increased in the buildup to World War II, Hispano and Mexican immigrant sugar beet workers who had long wintered in the city began to settle there permanently, while in Pueblo, the opening of the Army Depot in 1942 and the ramping up of production at Colorado Fuel and Iron, the city's largest employer, propelled both Hispano and Mexican urbanization. Deutsch, *No Separate Refuge;* Donald W. Meinig, *Southwest: Three Peoples in Geographic Change, 1600–1970* (New York: Oxford University Press, 1971), 55–56; David Sandoval, *Spanish/Mexican Legacy of Latinos in Pueblo County* (Pueblo, CO: Pueblo City-County Library District, 2012), 61.

7. Nostrand, *Hispano Homeland,* 208–9.

8. One study found that "Chicano" was a very weak identity among Denver's Hispanic voters in the 1970s, and that they expressed significantly more moderate, even conservative viewpoints than the city's African American population, particularly with regard to direct action tactics and violence. Nicholas P. Lovrich Jr. and Otwin Marenin, "A Comparison of Black and Mexican American Voters in Denver: Assertive versus Acquiescent Political Orientations and Voting Behavior in an Urban Electorate," *Western Political Quarterly* 29, no. 2 (1976): 284–94; see also Rodney Hero, "Hispanics in Urban Government and Politics: Some Findings, Comparisons and Implications," *Western Political Quarterly* 43, no. 2 (1990), 403–14.

9. Carl Abbott, "Suburb and City: Changing Patterns of Socioeconomic Status in Metropolitan Denver since 1940," *Social Science History* 2, no. 1 (1977): 53–71; Carl Abbott, "Plural Society in Colorado: Ethnic Relations in the Twentieth Century," *Phylon* 39, no. 3 (1978): 250–60; Vincent De Baca, ed. *La Gente: Hispano History and Life in Colorado* (Denver: Colorado Historical Society, 1998); Denver Area Welfare Council, *The Spanish-American Population of Denver: An Exploratory Survey* (Denver: Denver Area Welfare Council, 1950); Denver Unity Council, *The Spanish-Speaking Population of Denver: Housing, Employment, Health, Recreation, Employment* (Denver: Denver Unity Council, 1946).

10. In urban environments, Hispanos created public art celebrating rural life, produced music remembering the irrigation systems of their home villages, and used birth and burial practices to remain connected with their villages of origin. Interest in charros and charrería developed within this larger pattern of what geographer Jeffrey Smith has called "rural place attachment." Jeffrey Smith, "Rural Place Attachment in Hispano Urban Centers," *Geographical Review* 92, no. 3 (2002): 432–51. But

rural place attachment was more than just sentimental nostalgia; it also expressed an active political problem. Unlike other parts of what became the U.S. Southwest, most of the Spanish and Mexican land grants in New Mexico and Colorado rested on complex arrangements of communal property and usufructuary rights. After U.S. conquest, as much as 80 percent of those land grants were lost through taxation, litigation, and fraud. By the 1960s, Hispanos were struggling to reclaim and assert their rights to what was left. In 1965, a Colorado district court dealt a crushing blow by extinguishing communal land rights on the massive Beaubien and Miranda land grant in southern Colorado. Hispano villagers fought this decision through lawsuits and direct actions that lasted well into the twenty-first century (and eventually resulted in the Colorado Supreme Court's 2002 restoration of communal rights on the grant). Also in the 1960s and '70s, Reies López Tijerina was leading a grassroots effort to restore land grants in New Mexico to the descendants of the Spanish and Mexican grantees. Urban Hispanos in places like Denver and Pueblo were intimately aware of these land-based struggles, which often impacted the livelihoods and futures of their own families. In this context, many Hispanos rightly saw the charro as a figure that represented histories of land ownership and economic self-sufficiency, even if he had only a vague relation to the agrarian practices of their historic homeland. On the making of Spanish and Mexican land grants, see Harold Dunham, "Spanish and Mexican Land Grants in the Southwest," 43–63, and Charles Vigil, "Mexican Land Grants in Colorado," 65–77, both in *The Hispanic Contribution to the State of Colorado,* ed. José de Onís (Boulder: Westview Press, 1976). On the struggles by Hispanos to retain and reclaim their land, see David Correia, *Properties of Violence: Law and Land Grant Struggle in Northern New Mexico* (Athens: University of Georgia Press, 2013); Nicki M. Gonzales, "'Sin tierra, no hay libertad': The Land Rights Council and the Battle for La Sierra, San Luis, Colorado, 1863–2002" (PhD diss., University of Colorado at Boulder, 2007); María Montoya, *Translating Property: The Maxwell Land Grant and the Conflict over Land in the American West, 1840–1900* (Berkeley: University of California Press, 2002); Tom Romero II and Nicki M. Gonzales, "Colorado," in *Latino America: A State-by-State Encyclopedia,* vol. 1, ed. Stephen Pitti (Westport, CT: Greenview Press, 2008), 111; Reies López Tijerina, *They Called Me "King Tiger": My Struggle for the Land and Our Rights,* ed. José Ángel Gutiérrez (Houston: Arte Público Press, 2000).

11. Nancy Burkhart, "Mexican Culture in the Ring," *Sunday Denver Post,* April 30, 1978, 16, 18.

12. Juan Espinosa, "Spanish Empire Coming Back in Region," *Pueblo Chieftain,* March 21, 1993; Mary Jean Porter, "Lassoing Memories: Former Charro Celebrates Mexican Heritage," *Pueblo Chieftain,* May 5, 2011.

13. See Espinosa, "Spanish Empire"; Porter, "Lassoing Memories"; and "John Delgado Guerrero," *Pueblo Chieftain,* February 18, 2009, as well as the following obituaries, none of which are dated: Miguel "Torro" Torrez, www.chiefads.com/obituaries /miguel-torro-torrez/article_ce49f281-c317-5b28-9714-6d722f24daff.html; Leonel Leo Arthur Romero, www.romerofamilyfuneralhome.com/obituaries/Leonel-Leo-Romero; Francisco Manuel García, www.montgomerysteward.com/_mgxroot/obits;

José Gabino Granillo, www.chieftain.com/news/obituaries/2896434–119/granillo-family-gabby-santos#sthash.qMpCoaXS.dpuf.

14. Mary Jean Porter, "Charro Art Exhibit," *Pueblo Chieftain,* September 19, 1993.

15. Espinosa, "Spanish Empire."

16. Ryan Severance, "Calantino's Irish Pub Was Pueblo's Gathering Place," *Pueblo Chieftain,* October 4, 2015.

17. Antonio Duane López, interviewed by Henry Vélez, Denver, Colorado, August 9, 2010, University of Texas Voces Oral History Project; see also Mike McPhee, "War Vet in a Battle against Time to Make Reunion," *Denver Post,* February 10, 2010.

18. Frank Carrillo, LinkedIn profile, www.linkedin.com/in/frank-carrillo-3550b126 (accessed April 18, 2016); see also his letter to the editor of the *Denver Post,* printed online on September 25, 2007, www.denverpost.com/letters/ci_6986579.

19. Frank Moya, "Mexican Charreada a Delightful Event," *Rocky Mountain News,* November 27, 1972, 8.

20. Abbott, "Suburb and City."

21. "Asociación Charros de Denver Colorado Presents Charreada 1973" and "Asociación Charros de Denver Colorado Presents Charreada 1975," both in the Denver Charro Association Collection (MSS #1189), Stephen H. Hart Library and Research Center, History Colorado Center, Denver.

22. Lena Archuleta, "The Rodeo and Cattle Industry: Its Rich Spanish-Mexican Heritage" (Denver Public Schools, 1973), 17.

23. Archuleta, "Rodeo and Cattle Industry," 17.

24. Porter, "Lassoing Memories."

25. "Asociación de Charros (Pueblo Charro Association)," American Revolution Bicentennial Administration [hereafter ARBA] collection, folder: "Colorado Correspondence, Oct–Dec 1974," Box 1, National Archives and Records Administration (Broomfield, Colorado regional office).

26. Rubén Donato, *Mexicans and Hispanos in Colorado Schools and Communities* (Albany: State University of New York Press, 2007).

27. Denver Area Welfare Council, *Spanish-American Population,* 65; Denver Unity Council, *Spanish-Speaking Population,* 51–52; Donato, *Mexicans and Hispanos,* 70–88.

28. In the years just after World War II, a small but influential cohort of Hispano leaders graduated in spite of the odds and went on to earn bachelor's degrees, achieve middle-class status, and assume leadership positions in education, social services, and elected office. This upwardly mobile cohort formed local chapters of national organizations, such as the GI Forum and LULAC, as well as the Colorado Latin American Conference and the Latin American Education Foundation. All of these groups made education a top priority, often working with white liberals on the implementation of cultural pluralism in schools. Tom I. Romero II, "Our Selma Is Here: The Political and Legal Struggle for Educational Equality in Denver, Colorado, and Multiracial Conundrums in American Jurisprudence," *Seattle Journal for Social Justice* 3, no. 1 (2004): 72–142.

29. U.S. Commission on Civil Rights, *Mexican American Education Study, Report I* (Washington, DC, 1970); U.S. Civil Rights Commission, *Mexican American Education Study, Report VI: Toward Quality Education for Mexican Americans* (Washington, DC, 1974).

30. Christine Marín, *A Spokesman of the Mexican American Movement: Rodolfo "Corky" Gonzales and the Fight for Chicano Liberation, 1966–1972* (San Francisco: R and E Research Associates, 1977), 9–10; "History of Escuela Tlatelolco," http:// escuelatlatelolco.org/Escuela_2013/History.html (accessed July 28, 2017). Other organizations of the period, such as the Westside Coalition, also prioritized working with youth and pressuring schools for change. Richard Gould, *The Life and Times of Richard Castro: Bridging a Cultural Divide* (Denver: Colorado Historical Society, 2007).

31. Guadalupe San Miguel, *Chicana/o Struggles for Education: Activism in the Community* (College Station: Texas A&M Press, 2013), 11.

32. San Miguel, *Chicana/o Struggles for Education*, 84.

33. A. Reynaldo Contreras, "Impact of Brown on Multicultural Education of Hispanic Americans," *Journal of Negro Education* 73, no. 3 (2004): 314–27; Olden, "Becoming Minority"; Romero, "Our Selma Is Here."

34. U.S. Department of Education Office of Civil Rights, "Developing Programs for English Language Learners: Lau v. Nichols," www2.ed.gov/about/offices /list/ocr/ell/lau.html (accessed July 28, 2017).

35. "Mexican Charro Rodeo Coming to Colorado Springs over 4th Holiday," *Cragmor Newsletter* 2 (June 29, 1970), 2; "LAEF to Hold Mexican Rodeo," *Denver Post*, June 25, 1972, 26.

36. "Asociación Charros de Denver Colorado Presents Charreada 1973," 18.

37. For example, Amalia Millán and Beatrice Krone, "El Charro" (audio recording), in *Cantos de México (Folk songs of Mexico): A Supplementary Book of Songs in Spanish for Beginning Classes* (Park Ridge, IL: Neil A. Kjos Music Co., c1968); James Norman, *Charro: Mexican Horseman* (New York: Putnam, 1969); "Charro Team" (video recording), episode 102 of television program *KidsWorld* (Miami: Behrens Company).

38. Colorado Women's Hall of Fame, "Interview with Lena Archuleta" (video recording), www.youtube.com/watch?x-yt-ts = 1421914688&x-yt-cl = 84503534&v = N25BokvLcCI (accessed July 28, 2017); Latin American Research and Service Agency, "Our Story," www.larasa.org/ (accessed July 28, 2017); Jeanne Varnell, *Women of Consequence: The Colorado Women's Hall of Fame* (Boulder, CO: Johnson Books, 1999).

39. Archuleta, "Rodeo and Cattle Industry."

40. Archuleta, "Rodeo and Cattle Industry," 2. See also Alan Eladio Gómez, *The Revolutionary Imaginations of Greater Mexico: Chicana/o Radicalism, Solidarity Politics, and Latin American Social Movements* (Austin: University of Texas Press, 2016).

41. Archuleta, "Rodeo and Cattle Industry," 2.

42. Archuleta, "Rodeo and Cattle Industry," 4.

43. Archuleta, "Rodeo and Cattle Industry," 1.

44. Archuleta, "Rodeo and Cattle Industry," 6–9.

45. Archuleta, "Rodeo and Cattle Industry," 6; italics in original.

46. Archuleta, "Rodeo and Cattle Industry," 27–32.

47. Chungmei Lee, "Denver Public Schools: Resegregation, Latino Style," The Civil Rights Project (2006), 3, http://escholarship.org/uc/item/7mk9j9pf (accessed July 28, 2017).

48. Colorado Advisory Committee to the U.S. Commission on Civil Rights, *Hispanic Student Dropout Problem in Colorado* (Denver, 1987).

49. Lee, "Denver Public Schools."

50. David Márquez, "'The Chicano Wars': The Advent of the Chicano Movement in Pueblo, Colorado" (unpublished manuscript, 1983), David Márquez Papers, Archives and Special Collections, Colorado State University, Pueblo. See also Mary Therese Anstey, Chery Yost, and Adam Thomas, *In Pursuit of the American Dream: Pueblo in the Modern Age, 1940–1982* (Pueblo, CO: Historitecture, 2012), 108–14; Sandoval, *Spanish/Mexican Legacy,* 70–76.

51. Gómez, *Revolutionary Imaginations.*

52. Juan Espinosa, "A Time to Reflect," *Pueblo Chieftain,* September 21, 2003.

53. "Slamming the Door—No Mexicans or Dogs Allowed," *Pueblo Chieftain,* December 23, 2003.

54. "Slamming the Door."

55. Colorado State Fair Fiesta Committee, "General Information," https://sites.google.com/a/fiestacommittee.org/csf-fiesta-committee/ (accessed July 11, 2017).

56. James Mills, "Águilar Brings Mexican Pride to Festival, Rodeo," *Denver Post,* August 27, 1976, 27; see also "Mariachi Icon Antonio Águilar Dies at 88," *Billboard,* June 20, 2007.

57. Colorado State Fair Fiesta Committee, "General Information."

58. Espinosa, "A Time to Reflect."

59. "State Sen. Paul Sandoval, D-Denver, Hears about Mexican-Style Rodeo" (photo caption), *Denver Post,* January 13, 1979, via Getty Images; obituary for Florinda Romero Gallegos, www.findagrave.com/cgi-bin/fg.cgi?page = gr&GRid = 49382547 (accessed July 28, 2017).

60. Hero, "Hispanics in Urban Government."

61. Pueblo Sister Cities Commission, "Puebla, Mexico," www.pueblosistercities.org/puebla-mexico (accessed July 28, 2017).

62. Karen Vígil, "Bridging Borders," *Pueblo Chieftain,* December 9, 2003.

63. Juan Espinosa, "El Cinco de Mayo—Pueblo's Holiday," *Pueblo Chieftain,* May 2, 2010; Sandoval, *Spanish/Mexican Legacy,* 74.

64. Vígil, "Bridging Borders."

65. John Bodnar, *Remaking America: Public Memory, Commemoration, and Patriotism in the Twentieth Century* (Princeton: Princeton University Press, 1992), 234–37; David Ryan, "Re-Enacting Independence through Nostalgia: The 1976 U.S. Bicentennial after the Vietnam War," *Journal of the International Association of Inter-American Studies* 5, no. 3 (2012): n.p.; Malgorzata J. Rymsza-Pawlowska, *History Comes Alive: Between Past and Present in the Making of Postwar Histori-*

cal Consciousness (Chapel Hill: University of North Carolina Press, 2017); Tammy Stone-Gordon, *The Spirit of 1976: Commerce, Community, and the Politics of Commemoration* (Amherst: University of Massachusetts Press, 2013).

66. American Revolution Bicentennial Administration, "Questions and Answers about the Bicentennial" (Washington, DC: Government Printing Office, 1975).

67. "Multi-Ethnic Coalition Forms Plans to Aid in Bicentennial," *Afro-American,* July 13, 1974; Carol Bell, "U.S. Asked to 'Correct' History," *Denver Post,* September 12, 1975.

68. Matthew Frye Jacobson, *Roots Too: White Ethnic Revival in Post–Civil Rights America* (Cambridge: Harvard University Press, 2006).

69. Laura Barraclough, "The Western Spirit of '76: The Bicentennial of the American Revolution and the Making of Conservative Multiculturalism in the Mountain West," *Western Historical Quarterly* 47, no. 2 (2016): 161–81; Rymsza-Pawlowska, *History Comes Alive.*

70. Greater Pueblo Chamber of Commerce Centennial/Bicentennial Task Force, "1976 Charro Meet Set," *Centennial/Bicentennial Newsletter* 1, no. 1 (1976), 1, Julian Nava Papers, Box 19, Folder 12, California State University, Northridge, Urban Archives Center.

71. "Delegaciones de Agencias de Gobierno, Asociaciones Cívicas, y de la Ciudad de Pueblo," folder: "Colorado Correspondence, Oct–Dec 1974," Box 1, ARBA.

72. For example, early in the summer of 1974, a group of Mexican and U.S. officials convened in Pueblo to discuss organizational details. The meeting was attended by José Islas Salazar, president of the FMCH; Ignacio Arriola, the federation's special executive assistant to the United States; George Barrante, head of the Colorado Centennial-Bicentennial Committee (CCBC); Melvin Takaki, president of the Pueblo City Council and vice chairman of the CCBC; Mel Harmon, chairman of the Chamber of Commerce's Centennial-Bicentennial Committee; and Hispano members of the Pueblo Charro Association. Similarly diverse collectives would reconvene periodically throughout the planning stages. "Pueblo Bidding for Charreada Competition," *Colorado Springs Gazette Telegraph,* June 20, 1974, 18-D.

73. Members of the CCBC's Multi-Ethnic Committee included singer and activist John Denver; firefighter and veteran Lincoln Baca; Leonard Burch, tribal chairman of the Southern Utes; Native American historian Vine Deloria Jr.; African American librarian Juanita Gray; and Carlos Lucero, the first Hispanic president of the Colorado Bar Association, among others. "Hoffman at Bar Helm: Lucero President-Elect," *Denver Post,* October 3, 1976.

74. Multi-Ethnic Committee to Leopoldo Trujillo, August 27, 1974, in folder: "Colorado Correspondence, Jan–March 1976," Box 1, ARBA.

75. "Delegaciones de Agencias."

76. "Distinguished Guests Traveling to the XXIV Congress and National Charro Competition," October 22, 1974, in folder: "Colorado Correspondence, Oct–Dec 1974," Box 1, ARBA.

77. Pueblo City Council, "Proclamation: International Charro Week," October 13, 1974, in folder: "Colorado Correspondence, Oct–Dec 1974," Box 1, ARBA.

78. "Information Packet: Colorado's Centennial-Bicentennial International Charro Competition," enclosed with Ted Calantino to Joe Cerquone, February 9, 1976, in folder: "Colorado Correspondence, Oct–Dec 1974," Box 1, ARBA.

79. Pueblo Chamber of Commerce Centennial-Bicentennial Task Force, "1976 Charro Meet Set," *Focus '76* 1, no. 1 (January 1975), 1–2; Marcella F. Guerra, "La charrería," *La Luz,* May 2, 1975, 11.

80. "Minutes of the Colorado Centennial-Bicentennial Commission for March 22, 1975," in folder: "Colorado Correspondence, Jan–March 1975," Box 1, ARBA.

81. G. D. Barrante to Joe Albi, "Memorandum: Monthly Status Report," May 30, 1975, in folder: "Colorado Correspondence, April–June 1975," Box 1, ARBA; Joseph Albi to Joseph Dobal, "Request for Reimbursement, Two Fringed 3x5 Indoor Flags," April 30, 1975, in folder: "Flags," Box 7, ARBA.

82. "Lienzo Working Plans Near Completion," *Pueblo Charro Association Newsletter* 1, no. 1 (December 1975), 2.

83. Toby Madrid to Rae Hellen, December 22, 1975, in folder: "Colorado Correspondence, October–December 1975," Box 1, ARBA.

84. "Charros to Meet with Fair Commission," *Pueblo Charro Association Newsletter* 1, no. 1 (December 1975), 1.

85. "Charro Members Attend Seminar," *Pueblo Charro Association Newsletter* 1, no. 1 (December 1975), 2.

86. In the spring of 1975, the Pueblo charros held a dinner dance in observation of Mexican Independence Day at Pueblo's new Sangre de Cristo Arts Center. The event featured performances by Robert Griego, a popular Mexican American recording artist known for his corridos and other music honoring rural Hispano village life, as well as a ballet folklórico performance. Later that year, the charro association sponsored a New Year's Eve dance, again at the Sangre de Cristo Arts Center, where Francisco Lara gave a roping demonstration and local recording artist Juan Carlos performed his songs. They also hosted a children's party and sold tamales. The Pueblo Charro Ladies Auxiliary seems to have done most of the work in planning and hosting these events. "Griego Will Perform at Charro Show Here," *Pueblo Chieftain,* n.d., clipping in folder: "Colorado Correspondence, April–June 1976," Box 1, ARBA; "Charro New Years Eve Dance Draws Full House," *Pueblo Charro Association Newsletter* 2, no. 1 (January 1976), 2.

87. Pueblo Charro Association to John Warner, April 10, 1975, in folder: "Colorado Correspondence, April–June 1975," Box 1, ARBA.

88. Pueblo Charro Association to John Warner.

89. Kathleen Sands, *Charrería Mexicana: An Equestrian Folk Tradition* (Tucson: University of Arizona Press, 1993), 66–69.

90. Pueblo Charro Association to John Warner.

91. "Pueblo Charro Association Hires Staff," *Pueblo Charro Association Newsletter* 1, no. 1 (December 1975), 1.

92. "Charros to Perform in Western Stock Show," *Pueblo Charro Association Newsletter* 2, no. 1 (January 1976), 1.

93. For example, in May 1976 as part of ARBA-funded Cinco de Mayo celebrations, the Pueblo and Denver charro associations competed in the first-ever charreada to be held in the small town of Fountain, just south of Colorado Springs, which billed itself "the oldest town in the Pikes Peak region." Fountain Centennial-Bicentennial Committee, press release, April 15, 1976, in folder: "Colorado Correspondence, April–June 1976," Box 1, ARBA.

94. "Charreada Schedule Set by Pueblo Charros," *Pueblo Charro Association Newsletter* 2, no. 1 (January 1976), 1.

95. Ron Martínez, "International Charro Contests Begin This week," *Pueblo Chieftain,* August 22, 1976, 16B.

96. The queens who participated in the parade included Miss Rodeo Colorado, Bobbi Jo Etter of Grand Junction, Agnes Padilla of Colorado Springs, and Dawn Gonzáles and Rose May Sánchez, representing the Fiesta de Colores in Las Animas. Grand Junction and Colorado Springs are both cities associated with white settlement and resource exploitation, especially through mining, the military, and corporate ranching, while Las Animas is a small city in the heart of the Hispano homeland. Jim Harmon, "Fiesta Parade: Rich Mexican Culture Celebrated," *Pueblo Chieftain,* August 30, 1976, 5B.

97. Pueblo Charro Association, "First International Charro Competitions Tentative Schedule of Events," Folder: "Colorado Correspondence, Jan–March 1976," Box 1, ARBA.

98. Ron Martínez, "Phoenix Blanks Denver," *Pueblo Chieftain,* August 26, 1976, 6B.

99. Ron Martínez, "Phoenix Charros Unseat Del Rio Champs," *Pueblo Chieftain,* August 28, 1976, 8A.

100. Mike Spence, "'Respectable Showing': International Charro Contests Termed Learning Experience for Pueblo Team," *Pueblo Chieftain,* August 30, 1976, 1B.

101. Linda C. Delgado, "Baca Barragán, Polly," in *Latinas in the United States: A Historical Encyclopedia,* ed. Vicki Ruíz and Virginia Sánchez Korrol (Bloomington: Indiana University Press, 2006), 75–76; Gould, *Life and Times of Richard Castro;* Emma Lynch, "Richard Castro: And Justice for All," *La Voz Bilingüe,* October 13, 2010; Sandoval, *Spanish/Mexican Legacy,* 76.

102. "Charro Statue to Be Placed West of Capitol," *Rocky Mountain News,* September 29, 1981, 11.

103. Nancy Clegg, "Manuel Martínez," *Muse,* June/July 1985, 3; Carol Dickinson, "Power Period: Social Issues Find Expression through Artist's Creations," *Rocky Mountain News Sunday Magazine,* May 3, 1992, 12–14.

104. Irene Clubman, "Charro Statue for Capitol?" *Rocky Mountain News,* July 24, 1981, 6-C.

105. Geraldo Cadava, "Two Horsemen," in *Standing on Common Ground: The Making of a Sunbelt Borderland* (Cambridge: Harvard University Press, 2013): 212–44.

106. "Charro Statue Unveiled," *Rocky Mountain News,* September 15, 1981, 16.

107. Guy Kelly, "Artist Crafts Enduring Park Tribute to War Hero," *Rocky Mountain News,* March 14, 1987, 7, 13.

108. Porter, "Lassoing Memories."

109. Porter, "Lassoing Memories."

110. H. Lee Scamehorn, *Mill and Mine: The CF&I in the Twentieth Century* (Lincoln: University of Nebraska Press, 1992), 181–96.

111. Porter, "Lassoing Memories."

112. The contemporary web page for the Unión de Asociaciones de Charros de Colorado lists six associations, none of which are the same as the first charro associations established in Denver, Pueblo, and elsewhere in Colorado during the 1970s and '80s. http://charroscolorado.com/teams/ (accessed July 28, 2017).

CHAPTER FOUR. CLAIMING SUBURBAN PUBLIC SPACE AND TRANSFORMING L.A.'S RACIAL GEOGRAPHIES

1. During the 1968 "blowouts" in which twenty thousand mostly Chicano students walked out of East L.A. high schools, Esparza served as liaison to the media, setting the stage for a career representing social struggles to broad audiences. His first documentary, *Requiem 29* (1970), portrayed the Chicano Moratorium against the Vietnam War in August 1970, a march of one hundred thousand participants that resulted in the killing of Mexican journalist Ruben Salazar by sheriff's deputies under Peter Pitchess—the same figure who had expelled charros from the Sheriff's Posse a decade earlier. Esparza's later films, *The Ballad of Gregorio Cortez* (1982) and *The Milagro Beanfield War* (1988), among others, have become canonical for students and teachers of Chicano and ethnic studies. Victor Payán, "Interview with Moctesuma Esparza: From the L.A. High School Walkouts to 'Selena' and 'The Disappearance of García Lorca,'" *Motion Magazine,* May 21, 1998; UCLA Alumni Association, "Moctesuma Esparza," https://alumni.ucla.edu/awards/moctesuma-esparza-71-m-f-a-73/ (accessed August 11, 2015).

2. Moctesuma Esparza, *Cinco Vidas/Five Lives,* 1973 (KNBC-Los Angeles).

3. Though East L.A. became the largest and most well-known urban barrio, proto-suburban Mexican communities remained in the form of agricultural colonias (worker colonies). Located close to the fields and packinghouses and marked by dilapidated housing, insufficient infrastructure, and civic neglect, these suburban communities were barrios in their own right. Though small in population relative to the expanding urban barrios of the Southwest's largest cities, they marked a consistent ethnic Mexican suburban presence. For studies of colonias in Southern California, see José Alamillo, *Making Lemonade out of Lemons: Mexican American Labor and Leisure in a Small California Town, 1880–1960* (Urbana: University of Illinois Press, 2006); Laura Barraclough, *Making the San Fernando Valley: Rural Landscapes, Urban Development, and White Privilege* (Athens: University of Georgia Press, 2011), esp. chap. 2; Matt García, *A World of Its Own: Race, Labor, and Citrus*

in the Making of Greater Los Angeles, 1900–1970 (Chapel Hill: University of North Carolina Press, 2001); Gilbert González, *Labor and Community: Mexican Citrus Worker Villages in a Southern California County, 1900–1950* (Urbana: University of Illinois Press, 1998); Jerry González, *In Search of the Mexican Beverly Hills: Latino Suburbanization in Postwar Los Angeles* (New Brunswick: Rutgers University Press, 2017). For studies of colonias in other parts of the U.S. Southwest, see Chris Lukinbeal, Daniel Arreola, and D. Drew Lucio, "Mexican Urban Colonias in the Salt River Valley of Arizona," *Geographical Review* 100, no. 1 (2010): 12–34.

4. Phoebe Kropp, *California Vieja: Culture and Memory in a Modern American Place* (Berkeley: University of California Press, 2008); Dydia DeLyser, *Ramona Memories: Tourism and the Shaping of Southern California* (Minneapolis: University of Minnesota Press, 2005).

5. For example, Barraclough, *Making the San Fernando Valley;* Mike Davis, *City of Quartz: Excavating the Future in Los Angeles* (New York: Verso, 1990); M. García, *A World of Its Own;* J. González, *In Search of the Mexican Beverly Hills.*

6. William Frey and William O'Hare, "Vivan los suburbios!" *American Demographics* 15, no. 4 (1993): 30–37; William Siembieda, "Suburbanization of Ethnics of Color," *Annals of the American Academy of Political and Social Scientists* 422 (1975): 118–28; Jeffrey Timberlake, Aaron Howell, and Amanda Staight, "Trends in the Suburbanization of Racial/Ethnic Groups in U.S. Metropolitan Areas, 1970–2000," *Urban Affairs Review* 47, no. 2 (2011): 218–55.

7. Genevieve Carpio, *Collisions at the Crossroads: How Place and Mobility Make Race* (Berkeley: University of California Press, 2019); Wendy Cheng, *The Changs Next Door to the Díazes: Remapping Race in Suburban California* (Minneapolis: University of Minnesota Press, 2013); J. González, *In Search of the Mexican Beverly Hills;* Mary Pardo, *Mexican American Women Activists: Identity and Resistance in Two Los Angeles Communities* (Philadelphia: Temple University Press, 1998).

8. William Flores and Rina Benmayor, eds., *Latino Cultural Citizenship: Claiming Identity, Space, and Rights* (Boston: Beacon Press, 1998); see also Don Mitchell, *The Right to the City: Social Justice and the Fight for Public Space* (New York: Guilford Press, 2003).

9. Genevieve Carpio, Laura Pulido, and Clara Irazábal, "The Right to the Suburb: Rethinking Lefebvre and Immigrant Activism," *Journal of Urban Affairs* 33, no. 2 (2011): 185–208.

10. Barraclough, *Making the San Fernando Valley,* 54–58.

11. Ruben Salazar, "Serape Belt Occupies City's Heart," *Los Angeles Times,* February 26, 1963, A8.

12. Marcia Meeker, *San Fernando Valley Profile* (Los Angeles: San Fernando Valley Welfare Planning Council, 1964); Kevin Roderick, *The San Fernando Valley: America's Suburb* (Los Angeles: Los Angeles Times Books, 2001), 137–50.

13. George Garrigues, "'Comfort' Is an $8,000 Income," *Los Angeles Times,* November 13, 1963, G8.

14. "Valley Population Near Million: Growth Slows," *Los Angeles Times,* April 29, 1971, SF1.

15. Jean-Paul DeGuzman, "'And Make the San Fernando Valley My Home': Contested Spaces, Identities, and Activism on the Edge of Los Angeles" (PhD diss., University of California, Los Angeles, 2014); Roderick, *San Fernando Valley*, 147–50.

16. Barraclough, *Making the San Fernando Valley,* chap. 4.

17. "Frontier Days Fete to Mark 20th Year," *Los Angeles Times,* June 8, 1968, SF10.

18. "Ground Roundup," *Los Angeles Times,* May 17, 1973, SF10.

19. Ken Lubas, "Riders Cinch Saddles for Two Rodeos," *Los Angeles Times,* May 10, 1979, SF3.

20. Charros Emiliano Zapata, "Installation of Officers," 1973, p. 1, Julian Nava Papers, California State University, Northridge (CSUN), Special Collections, Box 19, Folder 11.

21. Martha Willman, "Charros!" *Los Angeles Times,* September 26, 1976, SF-A1.

22. Los Angeles Department of Animal Regulation, "Hearing re: Advisability and Legality of Charro Rodeos," January 29, 1976, pp. 19, 24, Julian Nava Papers, CSUN, Box 20.

23. Julian Nava, *My Mexican-American Journey* (Houston: Arte Público Press, 2002), 127.

24. Nava, *My Mexican-American Journey.*

25. Julian Nava to Tom Bradley, February 5, 1974; and Julian Nava to Martin Stone, February 5, 1974. Both pieces of correspondence are housed in the Julian Nava Papers, CSUN, Box 19, Folder 17.

26. Los Angeles Board of Recreation and Park Commissioners, "Report of General Manager No. 636: Hansen Dam Equestrian Center First Amendment to License Agreement," May 16, 1974; Los Angeles Board of Recreation and Park Commissioners, "Minutes of May 30, 1974." Both are located in the Los Angeles City Records and Archives. See also "Horse Show Ring Due at Hansen Dam Center," *Los Angeles Times,* June 23, 1974, SF_A7.

27. Nava, *My Mexican-American Journey,* 126.

28. Nava, *My Mexican-American Journey,* 126.

29. Harold Blackman to Julian Nava, September 24, 1974, Julian Nava Papers, CSUN, Box 19, Folder 17.

30. Julian Nava to Cleo Russell, December 27, 1974, Julian Nava Papers, CSUN, Box 19, Folder 17.

31. Nava, *My Mexican-American Journey,* 127.

32. Julian Nava Papers, 1970–2000 (Collection No. 400), Chicano Studies Research Center, University of California, Los Angeles.

33. Charros Emiliano Zapata, "Installation of Officers."

34. "An Agreement to Abide by a Code of Ethics to Protect the Emiliano Zapata Corporation," n.d., Julian Nava Papers, CSUN, Box 19, Folder 11.

35. "Una invitación especial," January 22, 1975, Julian Nava Papers, CSUN, Box 19, Folder 11.

36. "Asociación de Charros Emiliano Zapata Annual Event Schedule," 1975, Julian Nava Papers, CSUN, Box 19, Folder 11.

37. Charros Emiliano Zapata, "First Annual International Horsemanship Exhibition," 1975, Julian Nava Papers, CSUN, Box 5, Folder 1.

38. Tony Kiss, "History on Parade at Orcas Park," *Foothill Record-Ledger,* August 28, 1975, 12.

39. Los Angeles Department of Animal Regulation, Permit No. 18826 (1975), Julian Nava Papers, CSUN, Box 19, Folder 18.

40. Los Angeles City Attorney, "Opinion re Enforcement of Penal Code Section 597(b) and Los Angeles Municipal Code Sections 53.50 and 53.58 re. Rodeos, Opinion No. 75–113," February 20, 1975, pp. 8–9, Julian Nava Papers, CSUN, Box 20, Folder 10.

41. "Hearing re: Advisability," 19, 24.

42. "Hearing re: Advisability," 10.

43. "Hearing re: Advisability," 14.

44. Julian Nava Papers, CSUN, Box 20, Folder 13.

45. "Hearing re: Advisability," 37–40.

46. "Hearing re: Advisability," 93.

47. "Hearing re: Advisability," 136.

48. "Hearing re: Advisability," 153.

49. "Sample Score Sheets for Charriadas Held in Tucson, Fresno, Marysville, and Los Angeles between 1971–1975," Julian Nava Papers, CSUN, Box 20, Folder 18.

50. Jorge Delgadillo Guerrero to Ignacio Arreola, January 16, 1976, Julian Nava Papers, CSUN, Box 19, Folder 19.

51. "Hearing re: Advisability," 66.

52. "Hearing re: Advisability," 77–79.

53. "Hearing re: Advisability," 164.

54. "Hearing re: Advisability."

55. Julian Nava to American Humane Association, July 9, 1975; and Milton Searle to Julian Nava, July 24, 1975. Both are located in the Julian Nava Papers, CSUN, Box 19, Folder 18.

56. Robert Rush to Julian Nava, April 22, 1976; City of Los Angeles Department of Animal Regulation, "Rules and Regulations Governing the Events Colas (Tailing of the Steer) and Manganas (Roping the Front Legs of a Horse)—Draft," 1976. Both are located in the Julian Nava Papers, CSUN, Box 19, Folder 20.

57. Julian Nava, "Proposed Rules and Regulations for Conduct of Mexican Rodeos in Los Angeles," 1976, p. iii, Julian Nava Papers, CSUN, Box 20, Folder 17.

58. California Franchise Tax Board to Charros Emiliano Zapata, June 24, 1976, Julian Nava Papers, CSUN, Box 20, Folder 3.

59. "Charriada/Charrodeo Balance Sheets," dated January 16, 23, and 30, and February 13 and 20, 1977. All are located in Julian Nava Papers, CSUN, Box 20, Folder 3.

60. "Charros Perform for Scholarships," *El Tigre,* February 1, 1977, Julian Nava Papers, CSUN, Box 20, Folder 9; Untitled photograph with caption, *Spotlight, Newsletter of Los Angeles City Schools,* vol. 25 (March 11, 1977), p. 1, Julian Nava Papers, CSUN, Box 19, Folder 12.

61. Julian Nava, telephone interview by author, November 11, 2010.

62. Nava, *My Mexican-American Journey,* 127.

63. Nava, *My Mexican-American Journey,* 127.

64. Nava, *My Mexican-American Journey,* 127.

65. Alamillo, *Making Lemonade;* Carpio, *Collisions at the Crossroads;* M. García, *World of Its Own;* J. González, *In Search of the Mexican Beverly Hills.*

66. Victor Valle and Rodolfo Torres, *Latino Metropolis* (Minneapolis: University of Minnesota Press, 2000); see also J. González, *In Search of the Mexican Beverly Hills;* Pardo, *Mexican American Women Activists.*

67. J. González, *In Search of the Mexican Beverly Hills.*

68. Jerry González, "A Place in the Sun': Mexican American Identity, Race, and the Suburbanization of Los Angeles, 1940–1980" (PhD diss., University of Southern California, 2009), 83.

69. Shana Bernstein, "Interracial Activism in the Los Angeles Community Service Organization: Linking the World War II and Civil Rights Eras," *Pacific Historical Review* 80, no. 2 (2011): 231–67; Pico Rivera History and Heritage Society, *Pico Rivera* (Charleston, SC: Arcadia), 8.

70. J. González, "A Place in the Sun," 123.

71. "Charros in Pico Rivera" (photo caption), Shades of L.A.: Mexican American Community, Los Angeles Public Library photo collection.

72. Victor Valle and Rodolfo Torres, "Significant Space: Public Areas in the Greater Eastside," in *Latino Metropolis* (Minneapolis: University of Minnesota Press, 2000).

73. Keith Takahashi, "Pico Rivera Plans Attempt to Annex Site of Whittier Narrows Area Sports Arena," *Los Angeles Times,* April 23, 1978, SE-A2.

74. Keith Takahashi, "Cost of Pico Rivera Horse Arena Mounts," *Los Angeles Times,* April 21, 1977, SE1.

75. Keith Takahashi, "Horsemen's Park Project in Pico Rivera Snagged," *Los Angeles Times,* September 18, 1975, SE1, SE7.

76. Takahashi, "Horsemen's Park Project in Pico Rivera Snagged."

77. Keith Takahashi, "Pico Rivera Council Acts to Clear Park Project Snag," *Los Angeles Times,* September 25, 1975, SE1, SE6.

78. Keith Takahashi, "Charro Group Signs Pact to Use City Sports Arena," *Los Angeles Times,* April 23, 1978, SE-A1.

79. Keith Takahashi, "Consultants Will Evaluate Use of Pico Rivera Arena," *Los Angeles Times,* August 21, 1977, SE6.

80. Takahashi, "Consultants Will Evaluate"; Keith Takahashi, "Pico Rivera Hopes to not Get Saddled with Limited Use of $2 Million Arena," *Los Angeles Times,* October 23, 1977, SE2.

81. Keith Takahashi, "New Sports Arena's Opening Is Delayed," *Los Angeles Times,* March 23, 1978, SE-A1.

82. Keith Takahashi, "Pico Rivera Plans Attempt."

83. Bethania Palma Markus, "Pico Rivera Extends Concessionaire Contract at Sports Arena," *Pasadena Star-News,* December 10, 2009.

84. Keith Takahashi, "Charros, Gentlemen 'Born to the Saddle,' Lend Style to Opening of Sports Arena," *Los Angeles Times,* July 6, 1978, SE2.

85. Takahashi, "New Sports Arena's Opening Is Delayed"; Takahashi, "Charros, Gentlemen."

86. Valle and Torres, "Significant Space," 157.

87. M. Davis, *City of Quartz;* Stephanie Pincetl, "Nonprofits and Park Provision in Los Angeles: An Exploration of the Rise of Governance Approaches to the Provision of Local Services," *Social Science Quarterly* 84, no. 4 (2003): 979–1001; Jennifer Wolch, John P. Wilson, and Jed Fehrenbauch, *Parks and Park Funding in Los Angeles: An Equity Mapping Analysis* (Los Angeles: University of Southern California Sustainable Cities Program, 2002).

88. William Fulton, "Suburbs of Extraction," in *The Reluctant Metropolis: The Politics of Urban Growth in Los Angeles* (Baltimore: Johns Hopkins University Press, 1997).

89. Similar patterns have been observed among Latino paparazzi, who absorb the economic risks of providing celebrity photos to the mainstream media, from which they are otherwise largely excluded. Vanessa Díaz, "Latinos at the Margins of Celebrity Culture: Image Sales and the Politics of Paparazzi," in *Contemporary Latina/o Media: Production, Circulation, Politics,* ed. Arlene Dávila and Yeidy Rivero (New York: New York University Press, 2014).

90. Stephanie Chavez, "Bidders Invited to Upgrade Hansen Dam Horse Center," *Los Angeles Times,* September 19, 1985, 6; Stephanie Chavez, "L.A. Again Seeks Developer for Hansen Horse Center," *Los Angeles Times,* June 13, 1989, VY-A8; Stephanie Chavez, "Hoity Toity or Rough and Ready?" *Los Angeles Times,* December 3, 1990, 3; Dade Hayes, "Equestrian Center Operator Objects to City Lease," *Los Angeles Times,* June 10, 1997, 3.

91. Michael Connelly, "Officials Confront Drinking, Crowding at Orcas Park," *Los Angeles Times,* July 7, 1992, VY-B3; Julie Tamaki, "Popular Park Gets Improved Facilities," *Los Angeles Times,* August 1, 1992, VY-B2; John Schwada, "Parks Commission Seeks a Dusk-to-Dawn Curfew," *Los Angeles Times,* November 24, 1992, VY-B3; Julie Tamaki, "Changing Tunes: Orcas Park," *Los Angeles Times,* August 9, 1992, 3.

92. Tim May, "Orcas Park to Get Overhaul as Equestrian Facility," *Los Angeles Times,* November 29, 1995, 7; Michael Coit, "Gabrielino Dedication: New Equestrian Center Opens Its Gates," *Los Angeles Daily News,* October 28, 1999.

93. Bronco Entertainment, "About Us," www.elorcas.com/who-we-are.html (accessed March 6, 2017).

94. Experian Commercial Risk Database, "Bronco Entertainment, Inc." http://search.proquest.com/printviewfile?accountid = 15172 (accessed September 19, 2016).

95. Virginia Escalante, "New Era for Arena? Promoter Hopes Big-Name Entertainment Will Revive Pico Rivera Facility," *Los Angeles Times,* April 21, 1985.

96. Escalante, "New Era."

97. Agustín Gurza, "Obituary: Ralph Hauser III, 41: Promoter of Latin Music," *Los Angeles Times,* February 19, 2003.

98. James Gómez and Tina Daunt, "Pico Rivera Acts to Put Park under Private Management," *Los Angeles Times,* July 23, 1989.

99. "Unstable Situation," *San Gabriel Valley Tribune,* January 15, 2003; Ben Baeder, "Army Weighs Park Compromise," *San Gabriel Valley Tribune,* August 10, 2003; Debbie Pfeiffer Trunnell, "One Wild Ride," *San Gabriel Valley Tribune,* May 19, 2004; Jessica Garrison, "Equestrian Culture May Be Fading into the Sunset," *Los Angeles Times,* January 26, 2009.

100. "LEBA, Inc. (The Headquarters)," http://listings.findthecompany .com/l/9383664/Leba-Inc-in-Los-Angeles-CA (accessed March 9, 2017).

101. "Entrevista con Eduardo López," *Lienzo! Magazine,* July/August 2012, www.lienzomagazine.com/entrevista_con_eduardo_López (accessed September 21, 2016).

102. Markus, "Pico Rivera Extends."

103. City of Pico Rivera, "Pico Rivera Sports Arena," www.pico-rivera.org /thingstodo/sports.asp (accessed August 13, 2015).

CHAPTER FIVE. SHAPING ANIMAL WELFARE LAWS AND
BECOMING FORMAL POLITICAL SUBJECTS

1. David Bacon, *Illegal People: How Globalization Creates Migration and Criminalizes Migrants* (Boston: Beacon Press, 2008); Bill Ong Hing, *Ethical Borders: NAFTA, Globalization, and Mexican Migration* (Philadelphia: Temple University Press, 2010); Alicia Schmidt Camacho, *Migrant Imaginaries: Latino Cultural Politics in the U.S.-Mexico Borderlands* (New York: New York University Press, 2009).

2. Perla Guerrero, *Nuevo South: Latinas/os, Asians, and the Remaking of Place* (Austin: University of Texas Press, 2017); Gabriela Núñez, "The Latino Pastoral Narrative: Backstretch Workers in Kentucky," *Latino Studies* 10 (2012): 107–27; Sujey Vega, *Latino Heartland: Of Borders and Belonging in the Midwest* (New York: New York University Press, 2015); Julie Weise, *Corazón de Dixie: Mexicanos in the U.S. South since 1910* (Chapel Hill: University of North Carolina Press, 2015).

3. Mae Ngai, *Impossible Subjects: Illegal Aliens and the Making of Modern America* (Princeton: Princeton University Press, 2004); see also Douglas Massey and Karen Pren, "Origins of the New Latino Underclass," *Race and Social Problems* 4, no. 1 (2012): 5–17.

4. Kelly Lytle Hernández, *Migra! A History of the U.S. Border Patrol* (Berkeley: University of California Press, 2010); Ngai, *Impossible Subjects.*

5. Lisa Marie Cacho, "'The People of California Are Suffering': The Ideology of White Injury in Discourses of Immigration," *Cultural Values* 4, no. 4 (2000): 389–418; Leo Chávez, *The Latino Threat: Constructing Immigrants, Citizens, and the Nation* (Stanford: Stanford University Press, 2008); Nicholas De Genova, "Migrant 'Illegality' and Deportability in Everyday Life," *Annual Review of Anthropology* 31, no. 1 (2002): 419–47; Nicholas De Genova, *Working the Boundaries: Race, Space, and "Illegality" in Mexican Chicago* (Durham: Duke University Press, 2005); Jill

Harrison and Sarah Lloyd, "Illegality at Work: Deportability and the Productive New Era of Immigration Enforcement," *Antipode* 44, no. 2 (2012): 365–85; Joseph Nevins, *Operation Gatekeeper and Beyond: The War on "Illegals" and the Remaking of the U.S.–Mexico Boundary,* 2nd ed. (New York: Routledge, 2010); Ngai, *Impossible Subjects.*

6. Chávez, *Latino Threat,* 5–6.

7. Lisa Marie Cacho, *Social Death: Racialized Rightlessness and the Criminalization of the Unprotected* (New York: New York University Press, 2012).

8. De Genova, *Working the Boundaries;* Harrison and Lloyd, "Illegality at Work"; Monica Varsanyi, ed. *Taking Local Control: Immigration Policy Activism in U.S. Cities and States* (Stanford: Stanford University Press, 2008).

9. On banda and quebradita, see Sidney Hutchinson, *From Quebradita to Duranguense: Dance in Mexican American Youth Culture* (Tucson: University of Arizona Press, 2007); Helena Simonett, "Waving Hats and Stomping Boots: A Transborder Music and Dance Phenomenon in Los Angeles's Mexican American Communities," *Pacific Review of Ethnomusicology* 8, no. 1 (1996–97): 41–50; Helena Simonett, *Banda: Mexican Musical Life across Borders* (Middletown: Wesleyan University Press, 2001). On mariachi festivals, see Ana María Lasso, "Planning a Community Cultural Festival: The Power of Politics," MA thesis, Massachusetts Institute of Technology, 2001; Lauryn Camille Sálazar, "From Fiesta to Festival: Mariachi Music in California and the Southwestern United States," PhD diss., University of California, Los Angeles, 2011.

10. For example, Romeo Guzmán, "My Father's Charrería, My Rodeo: A Paisa Journey," *Boom! A Journal of California* 4, no. 1 (2014): 70–77.

11. On the recent history of the animal welfare movement in the United States and its legal accomplishments, see Diane Beers, *For the Prevention of Cruelty: The History and Legacy of Animal Rights Activism in the United States* (Athens: Swallow Press/Ohio University Press, 2006); Jordan Curnutt, *Animals and the Law: A Sourcebook* (Santa Barbara: ABC-CLIO, 2001); Lawrence Finsen and Susan Finsen, *The Animal Rights Movement in America: From Compassion to Respect* (New York: Twayne, 1994). On the complicated relationships between the animal welfare movement and immigrant animal practices, see Claire Jean Kim, "Multiculturalism Goes Imperial: Immigrants, Animals, and the Suppression of Moral Dialogue," *Du Bois Review: Social Science Research on Race* 4, no. 1 (2007): 233–49; Claire Jean Kim, *Dangerous Crossings: Race, Species, and Nature in a Multicultural Age* (New York: Cambridge University Press, 2015); Olga Nájera-Ramírez, "The Racialization of a Debate: The Charreada as Tradition or Torture," *American Anthropologist* 98, no. 3 (1996): 505–11.

12. Curnutt, *Animals and the Law,* 153.

13. For example, Richard Ballard, "'Slaughter in the Suburbs': Livestock Slaughter and Race in Post-Apartheid Cities," *Ethnic and Racial Studies* 33, no. 6 (2010): 1069–87; Laura Barraclough, "'Horse Tripping': Animal Welfare Laws and the Production of Immigrant Illegality," *Ethnic and Racial Studies* 37, no. 1 (2013): 2110–28; Glen Elder, Jennifer Wolch, and Jody Emel, "Le pratique savage: Race, Place, and

the Human-Animal Divide," in *Animal Geographies: Place, Politics, and Identity in the Nature-Culture Borderlands,* ed. Jennifer Wolch and Jody Emel (New York: Verso, 1998), 72–90; Marcie Griffith, Jennifer Wolch, and Unna Lassiter, " Animal Practices and the Racialization of Filipinas in Los Angeles," *Society and Animals* 10, no. 3 (2002): 221–48; Kim, "Multiculturalism Goes Imperial"; Michael Lundblad, "Archaeology of a Humane Society: Animality, Savagery, Blackness," in *Species Matters: Humane Advocacy and Cultural Theory,* ed. Marianne DeKoven and Michael Lundblad (New York: Columbia University Press, 2012), 75–102; Molly Mullin, "Mirrors and Windows: Sociocultural Studies of Human-Animal Relationships," *Annual Review of Anthropology* 28, no. 1 (1999): 201–24.

14. Lyanne Alfaro, "How an All-Woman Mariachi Band Is Owning the Genre," *NBC News* online, May 23, 2016, www.nbcnews.com/news/latino/how-all-woman-mariachi-band-owning-genre-n577731 (accessed February 14, 2017); Abel Salas, "L.A.'s Only All-Gay Mariachi Band," *L.A. Weekly,* December 8, 2014, www.laweekly.com/arts/las-only-all-gay-mariachi-band-5226910 (accessed February 14, 2017).

15. Adrián Pantoja, Ricardo Ramírez, and Gary Segura, "Citizens by Choice, Voters by Necessity: Patterns in Political Mobilization by Naturalized Latinos," *Political Research Quarterly* 54, no. 4 (2001): 729–50; Amy Pyle, Patrick McDonnel, and Héctor Tobar, "Latino Voter Participation Doubled since '94 Primary," *Los Angeles Times,* June 4, 1998, part A, 1–1.

16. Cacho, "The People of California"; Cacho, *Social Death.*

17. Kara Platoni, "Eric Mills and the Horse He Rode in on," *East Bay Express,* June 4, 2003.

18. Platoni, "Eric Mills."

19. Miguel Bustillo, "A Question of Culture or Cruelty?" *Los Angeles Times,* April 18, 1994.

20. Bustillo, "A Question of Culture."

21. Platoni, "Eric Mills."

22. Bustillo, "A Question of Culture."

23. California Penal Code 597g.

24. Nájera-Ramírez, "The Racialization of a Debate."

25. California State Legislature, House Assembly Committee on Public Safety, "Transcript of the Meeting of March 15, 1994," p. 2, http://leginfo.ca.gov/pub/93–94/bill/asm/ab_0001–0050/abx1_49_cfa_940331_200936_asm_comm (accessed August 16, 2018).

26. Bustillo, "A Question of Culture."

27. All three were quoted in Bustillo, "A Question of Culture."

28. California State Legislature, House Assembly Committee on Public Safety, "Transcript of the Meeting of March 15, 1994."

29. California State Legislature, House Assembly Committee on Public Safety, "Transcript."

30. California State Legislature, House Assembly Committee on Public Safety, "Transcript."

31. Bustillo, "A Question of Culture."

32. Platoni, "Eric Mills."

33. Platoni, "Eric Mills."

34. Platoni, "Eric Mills."

35. Rene Guzmán, "Preserving the Charro Tradition," *San Antonio Express-News,* September 26, 1999, 8H.

36. Toby de la Torre, personal communication, July 11, 2013.

37. "States Move to Outlaw Mexican Rodeo Event of Horse Tripping," *New York Times,* April 2, 1995; *OK* Statute §21–1700; Teresa Puente, "Ban Throws Mexican Horse Tradition," *Chicago Tribune,* June 24, 1996.

38. On recent Latino politics in San Antonio, see Rodolfo Rosales, *The Illusion of Inclusion: The Untold Political Story of San Antonio* (Austin: University of Texas Press, 2000). On the use of Mexican identity to promote contemporary tourism in San Antonio, see Miguel de Oliver, "Multicultural Consumerism and Racial Hierarchy: A Case Study of Market Culture and the Structural Harmonization of Contradictory Doctrines," *Antipode* 33, no. 2 (2001): 228–59.

39. On the "Charreada Blitzkrieg" strategy, see "VOICE Meeting Agenda, May 3, 1994," Fiesta San Antonio Commission Records (hereafter FSAC), Box 137, Folder 13, Institute of Texan Cultures. The letters to the Fiesta San Antonio Commission are in the same location.

40. Mr. and Mrs. Milton Knopoff to Marleen Pedroza, June 11, 1994, FSAC, Box 137, Folder 13.

41. Mr. and Mrs. Edgar Brown to Marleen Pedroza, June 15, 1994, FSAC, Box 137, Folder 13.

42. Sandra James, unpublished letter to the editor of the *San Antonio Express/News,* April 11, 1994, FSAC, Box 137, Folder 13.

43. George and Louise Taylor to Marleen Pedroza, May 10, 1994, FSAC, Box 137, Folder 13.

44. Greta Bunting to Marleen Pedroza, June 20, 1994, FSAC, Box 137, Folder 13.

45. Nanette Bradley, "Application for Participating Member Organization Status: Bobbit's B'ris Booth," May 23, 1994, FSAC, Box 137, Folder 13.

46. Marleen Pedroza to Nanette Bradley, November 7, 1994, FSAC, Box 137, Folder 13.

47. Dan Morales to John Whitmire, Chair of the Criminal Justice Committee, Texas State Senate, December 21, 1994, FSAC.

48. Texas Penal Code, Title 9, Chapter 42—§ 42.09, "Disorderly Conduct and Related Offenses," (a)(8); (c)(6); and (f).

49. Quoted in Jasmina Wellinghoff, "Horse Power," *San Antonio Express-News,* April 28, 1996, 5.

50. Quoted in Rene Guzmán, "Preserving."

51. Gabriel C. Pérez, "Unidos por charrería," www.gabrielcperez.com/Charrería (accessed November 8, 2017); Federación Mexicana de Charrería A.C., U.S.A. Chapter, website, www.fmchusa.com/?lang = en (accessed November 10, 2017).

52. *Art of the Charrería: A Mexican Tradition,* exhibit and accompanying book published by the Autry National Center, 2002; for the Smithsonian exhibit, see *Tales of Lienzos* (online exhibit), Smithsonian Latino Initiative, www.latino.si.edu /virtualgallery/TalesofLienzos (accessed November 8, 2017).

53. Toby de la Torre, personal communication, July 18, 2013.

54. Kindra Gordon, "Taking the Reins: Nevada and Idaho have taken a Proactive Stance on Selling Ranch Stewardship to the Public," *Rangelands* 28, no. 4 (2006): 33–34; Jerry Hawkes, Jay Lillywhite, and James Libbin, "A Sporting Alternative: Sport Cattle May Help Cattle Growers Round up Their Profits," *Rangelands* 28, no. 6 (2006): 15–17; Thomas Sheridan, "Embattled Ranchers, Endangered Species, and Urban Sprawl: The Political Ecology of the New American West," *Annual Review of Anthropology* 36 (2007): 121–38.

55. Smithsonian, *Tales of Lienzos.*

56. Platoni, "Eric Mills."

57. Jonathan Paton, "Floor Amendment to Senate Bill 1115," Arizona Forty-Ninth Legislature (2009), First Regular Session.

58. Marvin Miranda, *A History of Hispanics in Southern Nevada* (Reno: University of Nevada Press, 1997); JoAnne Skelly, Loretta Singletary, Jessica Angle, and Emma Sepúlveda-Pulvirenti, *Addressing the Needs of Nevada's Growing Latino Population: Results of a Statewide Needs Assessment* (Reno: University of Nevada Cooperative Extension/Latino Research Center, 2010); John Tuman, David Damore, and María José Flor Ágreda, "Immigration and the Contours of Nevada's Latino Population," *Brookings Mountain West* (Washington, DC: Brookings Institute, 2013).

59. Steve Sebilius, "Mayor to Introduce Bill to Ban Horse Tripping," *Las Vegas Sun,* September 30, 1996.

60. Suburban Stats, "Population Demographics for Winnemucca, Nevada in 2016 and 2015," https://suburbanstats.org/population/nevada/how-many-people-live-in-winnemucca (accessed July 27, 2017).

61. Nevada Senate Committee on Natural Resources, "Minutes of Hearing Held April 6, 2011," Carson City, Nevada.

62. Nevada Senate Committee on Natural Resources, "Minutes of Hearing Held April 6, 2011."

63. Nevada Senate Committee on Natural Resources, "Minutes of Hearing Held April 6, 2011"; on the Colorado law, see Kyle Glazier, "Bill Banning Mexican Rodeo Events Horse-Tripping and Steer-Tailing Dies," *Denver Post,* January 24, 2011.

64. Nevada Senate Committee on Natural Resources, "Minutes of Hearing held April 6, 2011."

65. Nevada Senate Committee on Natural Resources, "Minutes of Hearing held April 6, 2011."

66. Nevada Senate Committee on Natural Resources, "Minutes of Hearing Held April 15, 2011," Carson City, Nevada.

67. Animal Law Coalition 2013, "NV Horse Tripping Bill Signed into Law, June 4, 2013," https://animallawcoalition.com/nv-horse-tripping-bill-closerto-becoming-law (accessed July 27, 2017).

68. Ben Botkin, "Mexican Rodeo Canceled at South Point Arena," *Las Vegas Review Journal,* August 23, 2013, www.reviewjournal.com/news/las-vegas/mexican-rodeo-canceled-south-point-arena (accessed July 27, 2017).

69. Botkin, "Mexican Rodeo Canceled."

70. Roger Davis, "Latinos along the Platte: The Hispanic Experience in Central Nebraska," *Great Plains Research* 12, no. 1 (2002): 27–50.

71. Karen Sloan and Andrew Nelson, "Omaha May Ban Steer Tailing, Horse Tripping," *Omaha World Herald,* December 16, 2007.

72. Sloan and Nelson, "Omaha."

73. Sloan and Nelson, "Omaha."

74. Sloan and Nelson, "Omaha."

75. Toby de la Torre email to author, June 22, 2013.

76. Nebraska Legislative Bill 865 (2010); Nebraska Revised Statute 54–911.

77. Pat Raia, "Horse Tripping Ban a Tough Sell in Some States," *Horse,* July 29, 2008; "Horse Tripping Banned in Nine States," *Equus,* September 3, 2009.

78. Thomas G. Alexander, "The Rise of Utah's Latino Population," Utah History-to-Go, not dated, https://historytogo.utah.gov/utah_chapters/utah_today/theriseofutahslatinopopulation.html (accessed August 13, 2018); Dennis Nodín Valdés, "Betabeleros: The Formation of an Agricultural Proletariat in the Midwest, 1897–1930," *Labor History* 30, no. 4 (1989): 536–62.

79. Lee Davidson, "Census: Utah's Latino Population Grows to More than 400,000," *Salt Lake Tribune,* June 23, 2016, http://archive.sltrib.com/article.php?id = 4035282&itype = CMSID (accessed August 13, 2018); Utah State University, *Latino Voices* (digital exhibit), http://exhibits.usu.edu/exhibits/show/latinovoices (accessed August 13, 2018).

80. Amy Joi O'Donoghue, "Lawmakers Back off Horse-Tripping Ban," KSL-FM Radio online, February 25, 2015, www.ksl.com/?nid = 148&sid = 33592112.

81. Utah Department of Agriculture and Food, "Horse Tripping Information" (online webform), www.ag.utah.gov/animal.html?id = 542 (accessed August 13, 2018); "What You Need to Know about Horse Tripping Events" (brochure), 2015, www.ag.utah.gov/documents/Horse%20Tripping%20brochure-2015—final.pdf (accessed August 13, 2018); LuAnn Adams, "Letter regarding Horse Tripping Reporting Requirements," Utah Department of Agriculture and Food, May 29, 2015, www.ag.utah.gov/documents/HorseTrippingFinalLetter.pdf (accessed August 13, 2018).

82. Toby de la Torre email to author, July 28, 2013.

83. Wikipedia, "Charreada," https://en.wikipedia.org/wiki/Charreada (accessed November 8, 2017).

84. San Antonio Charro Association, "Mangana and Piales (Horse Tripping) Are Safe! Peta and the HSUS Are Wrong," not dated, with embedded videos, www.sacharro.com/page13 (accessed September 22, 2017).

85. Melissa Howell, "Charrería Exhibit Corrals Traditions," *Oklahoman,* November 24, 2009.

86. Chip Chandler, "AQHA to Pay Tribute to Mexican Horse-Handling in New Museum Exhibition," *Panhandle PBS,* January 23, 2017, www.panhandlepbs

.org/blogs/play-here/aqha-to-pay-tribute-to-mexican-horse-handling-in-new-museum-exhibition/ (accessed November 8, 2017).

87. FMCH-USA, "FMCH-USA participates in Agriculture Day in Sacramento, CA," March 21, 2015, www.fmchusa.com/2015/03/216/?lang = en (accessed November 10, 2017).

88. Hispanic Western Heritage PAC website, www.hwhpacblog.com/hwhpac/ (accessed November 10, 2017).

89. Hispanic Western Heritage, "Charrería against Cancer," https://gogetfunding.com/charrería-against-cancer/ (accessed November 10, 2017); Hispanic Western Heritage PAC, "Rafael Rivera Trail Ride," January 18, 2016, www.hwhpacblog.com/2016/01/rafael-rivera-trail-ride/ (accessed September 25, 2017).

90. FMCH-USA, "FMCH-USA Surprises First Recipient with Scholarship at Charro Dance," www.fmchusa.com/2015/04/fmch-usa-surprises-first-recipient-with-scholarship-at-charro-dance/?lang = en (accessed September 25, 2017).

CONCLUSION

1. Melissa Repko, "A Deadly Ride," *Dallas Morning News,* March 3, 2016, http://interactives.dallasnews.com/2016/unregulated-rodeos/ (accessed January 3, 2018).

2. Rodeo Tierra Caliente web page, www.rodeotierracaliente.com/.

3. Sarah Lynn Lopez, "El Jaripeo: The Gendered Spectacle of Remittance," in *The Remittance Landscape: Spaces of Migration in Rural Mexico and Urban U.S.A.* (Chicago: University of Chicago Press, 2015).

BIBLIOGRAPHY

Abbott, Carl. "Suburb and City: Changing Patterns of Socioeconomic Status in Metropolitan Denver since 1940." *Social Science History* 2, no. 1 (1977): 53–71.

———. "Plural Society in Colorado: Ethnic Relations in the Twentieth Century." *Phylon* 39, no. 3 (1978): 250–60.

Agnew, Jeremy. *The Creation of the Cowboy Hero: Fiction, Film, and Fact.* Jefferson, NC: McFarland, 2015.

Agrasánchez, Rogelio. *Mexican Movies in the United States: A History of the Films, Theaters, and Audiences, 1920–1960.* Jefferson, NC: McFarland, 2006.

Alamillo, José. *Making Lemonade out of Lemons: Mexican American Labor and Leisure in a Small California Town, 1880–1960.* Urbana: University of Illinois Press, 2006.

Albro, Ward. *Always a Rebel: Ricardo Flores Magón and the Mexican Revolution.* Fort Worth: Texas Christian University Press, 1992.

Almaguer, Tomás. *Racial Fault Lines: The Historical Origins of White Supremacy in California.* Berkeley: University of California Press, 1994.

Álvarez, Luis. *The Power of the Zoot: Youth Culture and Resistance during World War II.* Berkeley: University of California Press, 2009.

Álvarez del Villar, José. *Orígenes del charro mexicano.* Mexico City: Librería A. Pola, 1968.

Anstey, Mary Therese, Chery Yost, and Adam Thomas. *In Pursuit of the American Dream: Pueblo in the Modern Age, 1940–1982.* Pueblo, CO: Historitecture, 2012.

Archuleta, Lena. "The Rodeo and Cattle Industry: Its Rich Spanish-Mexican Heritage." Denver Public Schools, 1973.

Arciniega, Guillermo Miguel, Thomas Anderson, Zoila Tovar-Blank, and Terence Tracey. "Toward a Fuller Conception of Machismo: Development of a Traditional Machismo and Caballerismo Scale." *Journal of Counseling Psychology* 55, no. 1 (2008): 19–33.

Arreola, Daniel. "Urban Ethnic Landscape Identity." *Geographical Review* 85, no. 4 (1995): 518–34.

Bacon, David. *Illegal People: How Globalization Creates Migration and Criminalizes Migrants.* Boston: Beacon Press, 2008.

Ballard, Richard. "'Slaughter in the Suburbs': Livestock Slaughter and Race in Post-Apartheid Cities." *Ethnic and Racial Studies* 33, no. 6 (2010): 1069–87.

Ballesteros, José Ramón. *Origen y evolución del charro mexicano.* Mexico City: Manuel Porrúa, 1972.

Barraclough, Laura. "Rural Urbanism: Producing Western Heritage and the Racial Geography of Postwar Los Angeles." *Western Historical Quarterly* 39, no. 2 (2008): 177–202.

———. *Making the San Fernando Valley: Rural Landscapes, Urban Development, and White Privilege.* Athens: University of Georgia Press, 2011.

———. "'Horse Tripping': Animal Welfare Laws and the Production of Immigrant Illegality." *Ethnic and Racial Studies* 37, no. 1 (2013): 2110–28.

———. "The Western Spirit of '76: The American Bicentennial and the Making of Conservative Multiculturalism in the Mountain West." *Western Historical Quarterly* 47, no. 2 (2016): 161–81.

Barragán López, Esteban. *Con un pie en el estribo: Formación y deslizamientos de las sociedades rancheras en la construcción del México moderno.* Zamora, Michoacán: El Colegio de Michoacán, 1997.

Basch, Linda, Nina Glick Schiller, and Cristina Szanton Blanc. *Nations Unbound: Transnational Projects, Postcolonial Predicaments and Deterritorialized Nation-States.* New York: Routledge, 1993.

Beachley Brear, Holly. *Inherit the Alamo: Myth and Ritual at an American Shrine.* Austin: University of Texas Press, 1995.

Beasley, Betsy. "Exporting Service: Houston and the Globalization of Oil Expertise, 1945–2008." PhD diss., Yale University, 2016.

Beers, Diane. *For the Prevention of Cruelty: The History and Legacy of Animal Rights Activism in the United States.* Athens: Swallow Press/Ohio University Press, 2006.

Bender, Steven. *Tierra y Libertad: Land, Liberty, and Latino Housing.* New York: New York University Press, 2010.

Bennett, Marilyn. *It Happened in San Antonio.* Guilford, CT: Globe Pequot Press, 2006.

Bernstein, Shana. "Interracial Activism in the Los Angeles Community Service Organization: Linking the World War II and Civil Rights Eras." *Pacific Historical Review* 80, no. 2 (2011): 231–67.

Bingmann, Melissa. *Prep School Cowboys: Ranch Schools in the American West.* Albuquerque: University of New Mexico Press, 2015.

Blanton, Carlos. "George I. Sánchez, Ideology, and Whiteness in the Making of the Mexican American Civil Rights Movement, 1930–1960." *Journal of Southern History* 72, no. 3 (2006): 569–604.

Bodnar, John. *Remaking America: Public Memory, Commemoration, and Patriotism in the Twentieth Century.* Princeton: Princeton University Press, 1992.

Boehmer, Elleke. *Stories of Women: Gender and Narrative in the Postcolonial Nation.* Manchester, U.K.: Manchester University Press, 2005.

Bokovoy, Matthew. *The San Diego World's Fairs and Southwestern Memory, 1880–1940*. Albuquerque: University of New Mexico Press, 2005.

Bowman, Timothy. *Blood Oranges: Colonialism and Agriculture in the South Texas Borderlands*. College Station: Texas A&M University Press, 2016.

Burt, Kenneth. *The Search for a Civic Voice: California Latino Politics*. Claremont, CA: Regina Books, 2007.

Bynum, Lindley, and Idwal Jones. *Biscailuz: Sheriff of the New West*. New York: William Morrow, 1950.

Cacho, Lisa Marie. "'The People of California are Suffering': The Ideology of White Injury in Discourses of Immigration." *Cultural Values* 4, no. 4 (2000): 389–418.

———. *Social Death: Racialized Rightlessness and the Criminalization of the Unprotected*. New York: New York University Press, 2012.

Cadava, Geraldo. *Standing on Common Ground: The Making of a Sunbelt Borderland*. Cambridge: Harvard University Press, 2013.

Calavita, Kitty. *Inside the State: The Bracero Program, Immigration, and the I.N.S.* New York: Routledge, 1992.

Camarillo, Albert. *Chicanos in a Changing Society: From Mexican Pueblos to American Barrios in Santa Barbara and Southern California, 1848–1930*. Cambridge: Harvard University Press, 1979.

Carpio, Genevieve. "Multiracial Suburbs and Unrest in the California Inland Empire." Paper presented at the American Association of Geographers annual meeting, San Francisco. April 2, 2016.

———. *Collisions at the Crossroads: How Place and Mobility Make Race*. Berkeley: University of California Press, 2019.

Carpio, Genevieve, Laura Pulido, and Clara Irazábal. "The Right to the Suburb: Rethinking Lefebvre and Immigrant Activism." *Journal of Urban Affairs* 33, no. 2 (2011): 185–208.

Carreño King, Tania. *El charro: La construcción de un estereotipo nacional, 1920–1940*. Mexico City: Instituto Nacional de Estudios Históricos de la Revolución Mexicana, 2000.

Chang, Beth Helen Bruinsma. "Complicated Lives: Engendering Self-Sufficiency after Welfare Reform in San Antonio, TX." PhD diss, University of Texas at Austin, 2007.

Chávez, Leo. *The Latino Threat: Constructing Immigrants, Citizens, and the Nation*. Stanford: Stanford University Press, 2008.

Chávez-García, Miroslava. *Negotiating Conquest: Gender and Power in California, 1770s to 1880s*. Tucson: University of Arizona Press, 2004.

Cheng, Wendy. *The Changs Next Door to the Díazes: Remapping Race in Suburban California*. Minneapolis: University of Minnesota Press, 2013.

Clark, David Anthony Tyeeme, and Joanne Nagel. "White Men, Red Masks: Appropriations of 'Indian' Manhood in Imagined Wests." In *Across the Great Divide: Cultures of Manhood in the American West*, edited by Matthew Basso, Laura McCall, and Dee Garceau, 109–30. New York: Routledge, 2001.

Connolly, Nathan D. B. *A World More Concrete: Real Estate and the Making of Jim Crow South Florida.* Chicago: University of Chicago Press, 2014.

Contreras, A. Reynaldo. "Impact of *Brown* on Multicultural Education of Hispanic Americans." *Journal of Negro Education* 73, no. 3 (2004): 314–27.

Corkin, Stanley. *Cowboys as Cold Warriors: The Western and U.S. History.* Philadelphia: Temple University Press, 2004.

Correia, David. *Properties of Violence: Law and Land Grant Struggle in Northern New Mexico.* Athens: University of Georgia Press, 2013.

Cosgrove, Stuart. "The Zoot-Suit and Style Warfare." *History Workshop Journal* 18, no. 1 (1984): 77–91.

Cummings, Alex Sayf. "'Brain Magnet': Research Triangle Park and the Origins of the Creative City, 1953–1965." *Journal of Urban History* 43, no. 3 (2017): 470–92.

Curnutt, Jordan. *Animals and the Law: A Sourcebook.* Santa Barbara: ABC-CLIO.

Davis, Mike. *City of Quartz: Excavating the Future in Los Angeles.* New York: Verso, 1990.

———. "Sunshine and the Open Shop." In *Metropolis in the Making: Los Angeles in the 1920s,* edited by Tom Sitton and William Deverell, 96–122. Berkeley: University of California Press, 2001.

Davis, Roger. "Latinos along the Platte: The Hispanic Experience in Central Nebraska." *Great Plains Research* 12, no. 1 (2002): 27–50.

De Baca, Vincent, ed. *La Gente: Hispano History and Life in Colorado.* Denver: Colorado Historical Society, 1998.

De Genova, Nicholas. "Migrant 'Illegality' and Deportability in Everyday Life." *Annual Review of Anthropology* 31, no. 1 (2002): 419–47.

———. *Working the Boundaries: Race, Space, and "Illegality" in Mexican Chicago.* Durham: Duke University Press, 2005.

DeGuzman, Jean-Paul. "'And Make the San Fernando Valley My Home': Contested Spaces, Identities, and Activism on the Edge of Los Angeles." PhD diss., University of California, Los Angeles, 2014.

De León, Arnoldo. *They Called Them Greasers: Anglo Attitudes toward Mexicans in Texas, 1821–1900.* Austin: University of Texas Press, 1983.

DeLyser, Dydia. *Ramona Memories: Tourism and the Shaping of Southern California.* Minneapolis: University of Minnesota Press, 2005.

Denver Area Welfare Council. *The Spanish-American Population of Denver: An Exploratory Survey.* Denver: Denver Area Welfare Council, 1950.

Denver Unity Council. *The Spanish-Speaking Population of Denver: Housing, Employment, Health, Recreation, Employment.* Denver: Denver Unity Council, 1946.

De Oliver, Miguel. "Multicultural Consumerism and Racial Hierarchy: A Case Study of Market Culture and the Structural Harmonization of Contradictory Doctrines." *Antipode* 33, no. 2 (2001): 228–59.

De Onís, José, ed. *The Hispanic Contribution to the State of Colorado.* Boulder: Westview Press, 1976.

Deutsch, Sarah. *No Separate Refuge: Culture, Class, and Gender on an Anglo-Hispanic Frontier in the American Southwest, 1880–1940.* New York: Oxford University Press, 1987.

Deverell, William. *Whitewashed Adobe: The Rise of Los Angeles and the Remaking of Its Mexican Past.* Berkeley: University of California Press, 2004.

Díaz, Vanessa. "Latinos at the Margins of Celebrity Culture: Image Sales and the Politics of Paparazzi." In *Contemporary Latina/o Media: Production, Circulation, Politics,* edited by Arlene Dávila and Yeidy Rivero, 125–45. New York: New York University Press, 2014.

Donato, Rubén. *Mexicans and Hispanos in Colorado Schools and Communities.* Albany: State University of New York Press, 2007.

Dunham, Harold. "Spanish and Mexican Land Grants in the Southwest." In *The Hispanic Contribution to the State of Colorado,* edited by José de Onís, 43–63. Boulder: Westview Press, 1976.

Elder, Glen, Jennifer Wolch, and Jody Emel. "Le pratique savage: Race, Place, and the Human-Animal Divide." In *Animal Geographies: Place, Politics, and Identity in the Nature-Culture Borderlands,* edited by Jennifer Wolch and Jody Emel, 72–90. New York: Verso, 1998.

Escobar, Edward. *Race, Police, and the Making of a Political Identity: Mexican Americans and the Los Angeles Police Department, 1900–1945.* Berkeley: University of California Press, 1999.

Escobedo, Elizabeth. *From Coveralls to Zoot Suits: The Lives of Mexican American Women on the World War II Home Front.* Chapel Hill: University of North Carolina Press, 2013.

Estrada, William. "Los Angeles' Old Plaza and Olvera Street: Imagined and Contested Space." *Western Folklore* 58, no. 2 (1999): 107–29.

Fairbanks, Robert. *The War on Slums in the Southwest: Public Housing and Slum Clearance in Texas, Arizona, and New Mexico, 1935–1965.* Philadelphia: Temple University Press, 2014.

Faragher, John Mack. *Eternity Street: Violence and Justice in Frontier Los Angeles.* New York: W. W. Norton, 2015.

Finsen, Lawrence, and Susan Finsen. *The Animal Rights Movement in America: From Compassion to Respect.* New York: Twayne, 1994.

Fisher, Lewis. "Preservation of San Antonio's Built Environment." In *On the Border: An Environmental History of San Antonio,* edited by Char Miller, 199–221. Pittsburgh: University of Pittsburgh Press, 2007.

Flores, Lori. "Mexican American Civil Rights Organizations' Queen Contests and the Pageantry of Respectability." Paper presented at the Newberry Library, Borderlands and Latino History Seminar, Chicago, May 12, 2017.

Flores, Miguel. *El Charro en U.S.A.* Glendora, CA: Associated Publications, 1998.

Flores, Richard. *Remembering the Alamo: Memory, Modernity, and the Master Symbol.* Austin: University of Texas Press, 2002.

Flores, William, and Rina Benmayor, eds. *Latino Cultural Citizenship: Claiming Identity, Space, and Rights.* Boston: Beacon Press, 1998.

Fogelson, Robert. *Fragmented Metropolis: Los Angeles, 1850–1930.* Berkeley: University of California Press, 1993.

Foley, Neil. *The White Scourge: Mexicans, Blacks, and Poor Whites in Texas Cotton Culture.* Berkeley: University of California Press, 1997.

———. "Becoming Hispanic: Mexican Americans and the Faustian Pact with Whiteness." In *Reflexiones: New Directions in Mexican American Studies,* edited by Neil Foley, 53–70. Austin: University of Texas Press, 1998.

Fregoso, Rosa Linda. *MeXicana Encounters: The Making of Social Identities on the Borderlands.* Berkeley: University of California Press, 2003.

Frey, William, and William O'Hare. "Vivan Los Suburbios!" *American Demographics* 15, no. 4 (1993): 30–37.

Fulton, William. *The Reluctant Metropolis: The Politics of Urban Growth in Los Angeles.* Baltimore: Johns Hopkins University Press, 1997.

Gallardo, Carlos Rincón. *El charro mexicano.* Mexico City: Miguel Ángel Porrúa, 1939.

García, Desirée. *The Migration of Musical Film: From Ethnic Margins to American Mainstream.* New Brunswick: Rutgers University Press, 2014.

García, Mario. *Mexican Americans: Leadership, Ideology, and Identity, 1930–1960.* New Haven: Yale University Press, 1989.

García, Matt. *A World of Its Own: Race, Labor, and Citrus in the Making of Greater Los Angeles, 1900–1970.* Chapel Hill: University of North Carolina Press, 2001.

García, Richard. *Rise of the Mexican American Middle Class: San Antonio, 1929–1941.* College Station: Texas A&M University Press, 1991.

Goldberg, Robert. "Racial Change on the Southern Periphery: The Case of San Antonio, Texas, 1960–1965." *Journal of Southern History* 49, no. 3 (1983): 349–74.

Gómez, Alan Eladio. *The Revolutionary Imaginations of Greater Mexico: Chicana/o Radicalism, Solidarity Politics, and Latin American Social Movements.* Austin: University of Texas Press, 2016.

Gonzales, Manuel. *The Hispanic Elite of the Southwest.* El Paso: Texas Western Press/University of Texas at El Paso, 1989.

Gonzales, Nicki M. "'Sin Tierra, No Hay Libertad': The Land Rights Council and the Battle for La Sierra, San Luis, Colorado, 1863–2002." PhD diss., University of Colorado at Boulder, 2007.

González, Gilbert. *Labor and Community: Mexican Citrus Worker Villages in a Southern California County, 1900–1950.* Urbana: University of Illinois Press, 1998.

González, Jerry. "'A Place in the Sun': Mexican American Identity, Race, and the Suburbanization of Los Angeles, 1940–1980." PhD diss., University of Southern California, 2009.

———. *In Search of the Mexican Beverly Hills: Latino Suburbanization in Postwar Los Angeles.* New Brunswick: Rutgers University Press, 2017.

Gonzales-Day, Ken. *Lynching in the West: 1850–1935.* Durham: Duke University Press, 2006.

Gordon, Kindra. "Taking the Reins: Nevada and Idaho Have Taken a Proactive Stance on Selling Ranch Stewardship to the Public." *Rangelands* 28, no. 4 (2006): 33–34.

Gould, Richard. *The Life and Times of Richard Castro*. Denver: Colorado Historical Society, 2007.

Griffith, Marcie, Jennifer Wolch, and Unna Lassiter. "Animal Practices and the Racialization of Filipinas in Los Angeles." *Society and Animals* 10, no. 3 (2002): 221–48.

Gross, Ariela. "'The Caucasian Cloak': Mexican Americans and the Politics of Whiteness in the Twentieth-Century Southwest." *Georgetown Law Journal* 95, no. 2 (2007): 337–92.

Guerrero, Perla. *Nuevo South: Latinas/os, Asians, and the Remaking of Place*. Austin: University of Texas Press, 2017.

Guidotti-Hernández, Nicole. *Unspeakable Violence: Remapping U.S. and Mexican National Imaginaries*. Durham: Duke University Press, 2011.

Gunckel, Colin. *Mexico on Main Street: Transnational Film Culture in Los Angeles before World War II*. New Brunswick: Rutgers University Press, 2015.

Gutmann, Matthew. *The Meanings of Macho: Being a Man in Mexico City*. Berkeley: University of California Press, 2006.

Guzmán, Romeo. "My Father's *Charrería,* My Rodeo: A *Paisa* Journey." *Boom! A Journal of California* 4, no. 1 (2014): 70–77.

Haas, Lisbeth. *Conquests and Historical Identities in California, 1769–1936*. Berkeley: University of California Press, 1995.

Hackel, Steven. *Children of Coyote, Missionaries of Saint Francis: Indian-Spanish Relations in Colonial California, 1769–1850*. Chapel Hill: University of North Carolina Press, 2005.

Hafertepe, Kenneth. "Restoration, Reconstruction or Romance? The Case of the Spanish Governor's Palace in Hispanic-Era San Antonio Texas." *Journal of the Society of Architectural Historians* 67, no. 3 (2008): 412–33.

Harrison, Jill, and Sarah Lloyd. "Illegality at Work: Deportability and the Productive New Era of Immigration Enforcement." *Antipode* 44, no. 2 (2012): 365–85.

Hawkes, Jerry, Jay Lillywhite, and James Libbin. "A Sporting Alternative: Sport Cattle May Help Cattle Growers Round Up Their Profits." *Rangelands* 28, no. 6 (2006): 15–17.

Henriques, Donald. "Performing Nationalism: Mariachi, Media, and the Transformation of a Tradition (1920–1942)." PhD diss., University of Texas at Austin, 2006.

Herbert, Steve. *Policing Space: Territoriality and the Los Angeles Police Department*. Minneapolis: University of Minnesota Press, 1997.

Hernández, Kelly Lytle. *Migra! A History of the U.S. Border Patrol*. Berkeley: University of California Press, 2010.

———. *City of Inmates: Conquest, Rebellion, and the Rise of Human Caging in Los Angeles, 1771–1965*. Chapel Hill: University of North Carolina Press, 2017.

Hernández-Ehrisman, Laura. *Inventing the Fiesta City: Heritage and Carnival in San Antonio*. Albuquerque: University of New Mexico Press, 2008.

Hero, Rodney. "Hispanics in Urban Government and Politics: Some Findings, Comparisons and Implications." *Western Political Quarterly* 43, no. 2 (1990): 403–14.

Highsmith, Andrew. *Demolition Means Progress: Flint, Michigan, and the Fate of the American Metropolis.* Chicago: University of Chicago Press, 2015.

Hing, Bill Ong. *Ethical Borders: NAFTA, Globalization, and Mexican Migration.* Philadelphia: Temple University Press, 2010.

Hunt, Darnell. *Screening the Los Angeles "Riots": Race, Seeing, and Resistance.* Cambridge, U.K.: Cambridge University Press, 1997.

Hurtado, Aída, and Mrinal Sinha. "More than Men: Latino Feminist Masculinities and Intersectionality." *Sex Roles* 59, no. 5–6 (2008): 337–49.

Hurtado, Albert. *Intimate Frontiers: Sex, Gender, and Culture in Old California.* Albuquerque: University of New Mexico Press, 1999.

Hutchinson, Sidney. *From Quebradita to Duranguense: Dance in Mexican American Youth Culture.* Tucson: University of Arizona Press, 2007.

Hutton, John. "Landscape, Architecture, and the Social Matrix." In *On the Border: An Environmental History of San Antonio,* edited by Char Miller, 222–37. Pittsburgh: University of Pittsburgh Press, 2007.

Iber, Jorge, and Samuel Regalado, eds. *Mexican Americans and Sport.* College Station: Texas A&M University Press, 2007.

Iber, Jorge, Samuel Regalado, and José Alamillo. *Latinos in U.S Sport: A History of Isolation, Cultural Identity, and Acceptance.* Champaign: Human Kinetics, 2011.

Isenberg, Andrew. "Between Mexico and the United States: From *Indios* to Vaqueros in the Pastoral Borderlands." In *Mexico and Mexicans in the Making of the United States,* edited by John Tutino, 83–109. Austin: University of Texas Press, 2012.

Iverson, Peter. *When Indians Became Cowboys: Native Peoples and Cattle Ranching in the American West.* Norman: University of Oklahoma Press, 1994.

Jacobson, Matthew Frye. *Roots Too: White Ethnic Revival in Post-Civil Rights America.* Cambridge: Harvard University Press, 2006.

Jones, Richard C. "San Antonio's Spatial Economic Structure, 1955–1980." In *The Politics of San Antonio: Community, Progress, and Power,* edited by David Johnson, John Booth, and Richard Harris, 28–52. Lincoln: University of Nebraska Press, 1983.

Jordan, Terry. *Trails to Texas: The Southern Roots of Western Cattle Ranching.* Lincoln: University of Nebraska Press, 1981.

Kelley, Robin D. G. "Notes on Deconstructing 'The Folk.'" *American Historical Review* 97, no. 5 (1992): 1400–1408.

Kim, Claire Jean. "Multiculturalism Goes Imperial: Immigrants, Animals, and the Suppression of Moral Dialogue." *Du Bois Review: Social Science Research on Race* 4, no. 1 (2007): 233–49.

———. *Dangerous Crossings: Race, Species, and Nature in a Multicultural Age.* New York: Cambridge University Press, 2015.

Knopp, Anthony, Manuel Medrano, Priscilla Rodríguez, and the Brownsville Historical Association. *Charro Days in Brownsville.* Charleston, SC: Arcadia, 2009.

Kriken, John. "The Arts and City Livability." *Ekistics* 48, no. 288 (1981): 181–91.

Kropp, Phoebe. *California Vieja: Culture and Memory in a Modern American Place.* Berkeley: University of California Press, 2006.

Kruse, Kevin. *White Flight: Atlanta and the Making of Modern Conservatism.* Princeton: Princeton University Press, 2005.

La Chapelle, Peter. *Proud to Be an Okie: Cultural Politics, Country Music, and Migration to Southern California.* Berkeley: University of California Press, 2007.

Laguna, Albert Sergio. *Diversión: Play and Popular Culture in Cuban America.* New York: New York University Press, 2017.

Lane, John Hart. *Voluntary Associations among Mexican Americans in San Antonio, Texas: Organizational and Leadership Characteristics.* New York: Arno Press, 1976.

Larralde, Carlos. "Josefina Fierro and the Sleepy Lagoon Crusade, 1942–1945." *Southern California Quarterly* 92, no. 2 (2010): 117–60.

Lasso, Ana María. "Planning a Community Cultural Festival: The Power of Politics." MA thesis, Massachusetts Institute of Technology, 2001.

LeCompte, Mary Lou. "The Hispanic Influence on the History of Rodeo, 1823–1922." *Journal of Sport History* 12, no. 1 (1985): 21–38.

Lee, Chungmei. "Denver Public Schools: Resegregation, Latino Style." The Civil Rights Project. University of California, Los Angeles, 2006.

Licón, Gerardo. "Pachucas, Pachucos, and Their Culture: Mexican American Youth Culture of the Southwest, 1910–1955." PhD diss., University of Southern California, 2009.

Lloyd, David, and Laura Pulido. "In the Long Shadow of the Settler: On Israeli and U.S. Colonialisms." *American Quarterly* 62, no. 4 (2010): 795–809.

Lopez, Sarah Lynn. *The Remittance Landscape: Spaces of Migration in Rural Mexico and Urban U.S.A.* Chicago: University of Chicago Press, 2015.

Lovrich, Nicholas Jr., and Otwin Marenin. "A Comparison of Black and Mexican American Voters in Denver: Assertive versus Acquiescent Political Orientations and Voting Behavior in an Urban Electorate." *Western Political Quarterly* 29, no. 2 (1976): 284–94.

Luis-Brown, David. *Waves of Decolonization: Discourses of Race and Hemispheric Citizenship in Cuba, Mexico, and the United States.* Durham: Duke University Press, 2008.

Lukinbeal, Chris, Daniel Arreola, and D. Drew Lucio. "Mexican Urban Colonias in the Salt River Valley of Arizona." *Geographical Review* 100, no. 1 (2010): 12–34.

Lundblad, Michael. "Archaeology of a Humane Society: Animality, Savagery, Blackness." In *Species Matters: Humane Advocacy and Cultural Theory,* edited by Marianne DeKoven and Michael Lundblad, 75–102. New York: Columbia University Press, 2012.

Macías, Anthony. *Mexican American Mojo: Popular Music, Dance, and Urban Culture in Los Angeles, 1935–1968.* Durham: Duke University Press, 2008.

MacLean, Nancy. "The Civil Rights Act and the Transformation of Mexican American Identity and Politics." *Berkeley La Raza Law Journal* 18, no. 10 (2007): 123–33.

Magliari, Michael. "Free Soil, Unfree Labor: Cave Johnson Couts and the Binding of Indian Workers in California, 1850–1867." *Pacific Historical Review* 73, no. 3 (2004): 349–90.

Marín, Christine. *A Spokesman of the Mexican American Movement: Rodolfo "Corky" Gonzales and the Fight for Chicano Liberation, 1966–1972.* San Francisco: R and E Research Associates, 1977.

Martínez, John. "Leadership and Politics." In *La Raza: Forgotten Americans,* edited by Julian Samora, 47–62. Notre Dame: University of Notre Dame Press, 1962.

Massey, Douglas, and Karen Pren. "Origins of the New Latino Underclass." *Race and Social Problems* 4, no. 1 (2012): 5–17.

Mayer, Vicki. "From Segmented to Fragmented: Latino Media in San Antonio, Texas." *Journalism and Mass Communication Quarterly* 78, no. 2 (2001): 291–306.

McIlwaine, Cathy. "Migrant Machismos: Exploring Gender Ideologies and Practices among Latin American Migrants in London from a Multi-Scalar Perspective." *Gender, Place, and Culture: A Journal of Feminist Geography* 17, no. 3 (2010): 281–300.

McWilliams, Carey. *North from Mexico: The Spanish-Speaking People of the United States.* Philadelphia: J. B. Lippincott, 1949.

Meeker, Marcia. *San Fernando Valley Profile.* Los Angeles: San Fernando Valley Welfare Planning Council, 1964.

Meinig, Donald W. *Southwest: Three Peoples in Geographic Change, 1600–1970.* New York: Oxford University Press, 1971.

Messner, Michael. *Taking the Field: Women, Men, and Sports.* Minneapolis: University of Minnesota Press, 2002.

Millán, Amalia, and Beatrice Krone. *Cantos de México (Folk songs of Mexico): A Supplementary Book of Songs in Spanish for Beginning Classes.* Park Ridge, IL: Neil A. Kjos Music Co., c1968.

Miller, Char. "Where the Buffalo Roamed: Ranching, Agriculture, and the Urban Marketplace." In *On the Border: An Environmental History of San Antonio,* edited by Char Miller, 56–80. Pittsburgh: University of Pittsburgh Press, 2007.

Miranda, Marvin. *A History of Hispanics in Southern Nevada.* Reno: University of Nevada Press, 1997.

Mirandé, Alfredo. *Hombres y Machos: Masculinity and Latino Culture.* Boulder: Westview Press, 1997.

Mitchell, Don. *The Right to the City: Social Justice and the Fight for Public Space.* New York: Guilford Press, 2003.

Monroy, Douglas. *Rebirth: Mexican Los Angeles from the Great Migration to the Great Depression.* Berkeley: University of California Press, 1999.

Montejano, David. *Anglos and Mexicans in the Making of Texas, 1836–1986.* Austin: University of Texas Press, 1987.

———. *Quixote's Soldiers: A Local History of the Chicano Movement.* Austin: University of Texas Press, 2010.

Montgomery, Charles. *The Spanish Redemption: Heritage, Power, and Loss on New Mexico's Upper Rio Grande.* Berkeley: University of California Press, 2002.

Montoya, Fawn-Amber. "From Mexicans to Citizens: Colorado Fuel and Iron's Representation of Nuevo Mexicans, 1901–1919." *Journal of the West* 45, no. 4 (2006): 29–35.

Montoya, María. *Translating Property: The Maxwell Land Grant and the Conflict over Land in the American West, 1840–1900.* Berkeley: University of California Press, 2002.

Moore, Jacqueline. *Cow Boys and Cattle Men: Class and Masculinities on the Texas Frontier, 1865–1900.* New York: New York University Press, 2009.

Moreno, Gary. "Charro: The Transnational History of a Cultural Icon." PhD diss., University of Oklahoma, 2014.

Mullin, Molly. "Mirrors and Windows: Sociocultural Studies of Human-Animal Relationships." *Annual Review of Anthropology* 28, no. 1 (1999): 201–24.

Murià, José. "En defensa de la originalidad." In *Orígenes de la charrería y de su nombre,* 87–96. Mexico City: Miguel Ángel Porrúa, 2010.

Nájera-Ramírez, Olga. "Engendering Nationalism: Identity, Discourse, and the Mexican Charro." *Anthropological Quarterly* 67, no. 1 (1994): 1–14.

———. "The Racialization of a Debate: The Charreada as Tradition or Torture." *American Anthropologist* 98, no. 3 (1996): 505–11.

———. "Mounting Traditions: The Origin and Evolution of La Escaramuza Charra." In *Chicana Traditions: Continuity and Change,* edited by Norma Cantú and Olga Nájera-Ramírez, 207–23. Urbana: University of Illinois Press, 2002.

———. "Unruly Passions: Poetics, Performance, and Gender in the Ranchera Song." In *Chicana Feminisms: A Critical Reader,* edited by Gabriela Arredondo and Aída Hurtado, 184–210. Durham: Duke University Press, 2003.

Nava, Julian. *My Mexican-American Journey.* Houston: Arte Público Press, 2002.

Nevins, Joseph. *Operation Gatekeeper and Beyond: The War on "Illegals" and the Remaking of the US–Mexico Boundary,* 2nd ed. New York: Routledge, 2010.

Ngai, Mae. *Impossible Subjects: Illegal Aliens and the Making of Modern America.* Princeton: Princeton University Press, 2004.

Nichols, John. *St. Francis Dam Disaster.* Charleston, SC: Arcadia, 2002.

Nicolaides, Becky. *My Blue Heaven: Life and Politics in the Working-Class Suburbs of Los Angeles, 1920–1965.* Chicago: University of Chicago Press, 2002.

Norman, James. *Charro: Mexican Horseman.* New York: Putnam, 1969.

Nostrand, Richard. *The Hispano Homeland.* Norman: University of Oklahoma Press, 1992.

Núñez, Gabriela. "The Latino Pastoral Narrative: Backstretch Workers in Kentucky." *Latino Studies* 10, no. 1–2 (2012): 107–27.

Olden, Danielle. "Becoming Minority: Mexican Americans, Race, and the Legal Struggle for Educational Equity in Denver, Colorado." *Western Historical Quarterly* 48, no. 1 (2017): 43–66.

Pagán, Eduardo Obregón. *Murder at the Sleepy Lagoon: Zoot Suits, Race, and Riot in Wartime L.A.* Chapel Hill: University of North Carolina Press, 2006.

Palomar, Cristina. "El papel de la charrería como fenómeno cultural en la construcción del Occidente de México." *Revista Europea de Estudios Latinoamericanos y del Caribe* 76 (2004): 83–98.

Pantoja, Adrian, Ricardo Ramírez, and Gary Segura. "Citizens by Choice, Voters by Necessity: Patterns in Political Mobilization by Naturalized Latinos." *Political Research Quarterly* 54, no. 4 (2001): 729–50.

Pardo, Mary. *Mexican American Women Activists: Identity and Resistance in Two Los Angeles Communities.* Philadelphia: Temple University Press, 1998.

Paredes, Américo. "The Problem of Identity in a Changing Culture: Popular Expressions of Culture Conflict along the Lower Rio Grande Border." In *Views across the Border: The United States and Mexico,* edited by Stanley Ross, 68–94. Albuquerque: University of New Mexico Press, 1978.

Pérez, Vincent. *Remembering the Hacienda: History and Memory in the Mexican American Southwest.* College Station: Texas A&M University Press, 2006.

Pescador, Juan Javier. "*Los Heroes del Domingo:* Soccer, Borders, and Social Spaces in Great Lakes Mexican Communities, 1940–1970." In *Mexican Americans and Sport,* edited by Jorge Iber and Samuel Regalado, 73–88. College Station: Texas A&M University Press, 2007.

Pico Rivera History and Heritage Society. *Pico Rivera.* Charleston, SC: Arcadia, 2008.

Pincetl, Stephanie. "Nonprofits and Park Provision in Los Angeles: An Exploration of the Rise of Governance Approaches to the Provision of Local Services." *Social Science Quarterly* 84, no. 4 (2003): 979–1001.

Pitt, Leonard. *Decline of the Californios: A Social History of the Spanish-Speaking Californians, 1846–1890.* Berkeley: University of California Press, 1999.

Pulido, Laura. "Geographies of Race and Ethnicity III: Settler Colonialism and Nonnative People of Color." *Progress in Human Geography* 42, no. 2 (2018): 309–18.

Pycior, Julie. *Democratic Renewal and the Mutual Aid Legacy of U.S. Mexicans.* College Station: Texas A&M University Press, 2014.

Ramírez, Ana C. "Escaramuzas Charras: Paradoxes of Performance in a Mexican Women's Equestrian Sport." In *The Meaning of Horses: Biosocial Encounters,* edited by Dona Lee Davis and Anita Maurstad, 164–76. New York: Routledge, 2016.

Ramírez, Catherine. *The Woman in the Zoot Suit: Gender, Nationalism, and the Cultural Politics of Memory.* Durham: Duke University Press, 2009.

Ramírez, Dixa. *Colonial Phantoms: Belonging and Refusal in the Dominican Americas, from the 19th Century to the Present.* New York: New York University Press, 2018.

Rendón, Al. *Charreada: Mexican Rodeo in Texas.* Denton: University of North Texas Press, 2002.

Rico, Monica. *Nature's Noblemen: Transatlantic Masculinities and the Nineteenth-Century American West.* New Haven: Yale University Press, 2013.

Rivas-Rodríguez, Maggie. "Ignacio E. Lozano: The Mexican Exile Publisher Who Conquered San Antonio and Los Angeles." *American Journalism* 21, no. 1 (2004): 75–89.

Roderick, Kevin. *The San Fernando Valley: America's Suburb.* Los Angeles: Los Angeles Times Books, 2001.

Romero, Tom, II. "Our Selma Is Here: The Political and Legal Struggle for Educational Equality in Denver, Colorado, and Multiracial Conundrums in American Jurisprudence." *Seattle Journal for Social Justice* 3, no. 1 (2004): 72–142.

Romero, Tom, II, and Nicki M. Gonzalez. "Colorado." In *Latino America: A State-by-State Encyclopedia*. Vol. 1, edited by Stephen Pitti, 105–24. Westport, CT: Greenview Press, 2008.

Romo, Ricardo. *East Los Angeles: History of a Barrio*. Austin: University of Texas Press, 1983.

Rosales, Rodolfo. *The Illusion of Inclusion: The Untold Political Story of San Antonio*. Austin: University of Texas Press, 2000.

Ruíz, Vicki, and Virginia Sánchez Korrol, eds. *Latinas in the United States: A Historical Encyclopedia*. Bloomington: Indiana University Press, 2006.

Ryan, David. "Re-Enacting Independence through Nostalgia: The 1976 US Bicentennial after the Vietnam War." *Journal of the International Association of Inter-American Studies* 5, no. 3 (2012): n.p.

Rymsza-Pawlowska, Malgorzata. *History Comes Alive: Between Past and Present in the Making of Postwar Historical Consciousness*. Chapel Hill: University of North Carolina Press, 2017.

Sackman, Douglas. *Orange Empire: California and the Fruits of Eden*. Berkeley: University of California Press, 2005.

Saez, Pedro, Adonaid Casao, and Jay Wade. "Factors Influencing Masculinity Ideology among Latino Men." *Journal of Men's Studies* 17, no. 2 (2009): 116–28.

Salazar, Lauryn Camille. "From Fiesta to Festival: Mariachi Music in California and the Southwestern United States." PhD diss., University of California, Los Angeles, 2011.

Sánchez, George. *Becoming Mexican American: Ethnicity, Culture, and Identity in Chicano Los Angeles, 1900–1945*. New York: Oxford University Press, 1995.

Sánchez, Rosaura, and Beatrice Pita. "Rethinking Settler Colonialism." *American Quarterly* 66, no. 4 (2014): 1039–55.

Sandoval, David. *Spanish/Mexican Legacy of Latinos in Pueblo County*. Pueblo, CO: Pueblo City-County Library District, 2012.

Sands, Kathleen. *Charrería Mexicana: An Equestrian Folk Tradition*. Tucson: University of Arizona Press, 1993.

San Miguel, Guadalupe. *Chicana/o Struggles for Education: Activism in the Community*. College Station: Texas A&M University Press, 2013.

Scamehorn, H. Lee. *Mill and Mine: The CF&I in the Twentieth Century*. Lincoln: University of Nebraska Press, 1992.

Schmidt Camacho, Alicia. *Migrant Imaginaries: Latino Cultural Politics in the U.S.-Mexico Borderlands*. New York: New York University Press, 2009.

Scruggs, Otey. "Texas and the Bracero Program, 1942–47." *Pacific Historical Review* 32, no. 3 (1963): 251–64.

Sheridan, Thomas. "Embattled Ranchers, Endangered Species, and Urban Sprawl: The Political Ecology of the New American West." *Annual Review of Anthropology* 36 (2007): 121–38.

Siembieda, William. "Suburbanization of Ethnics of Color." *Annals of the American Academy of Political and Social Scientists* 422 (1975): 118–28.

Simonett, Helena. "Waving Hats and Stomping Boots: A Transborder Music and Dance Phenomenon in Los Angeles's Mexican American Communities." *Pacific Review of Ethnomusicology* 8, no. 1 (1996–97): 41–50.

———. *Banda: Mexican Musical Life across Borders.* Middletown: Wesleyan University Press, 2001.

Sitton, Tom, and William Deverell, eds. *Metropolis in the Making: Los Angeles in the 1920s.* Berkeley: University of California Press, 2001.

Skelly, JoAnne, Loretta Singletary, Jessica Angle, and Emma Sepúlveda-Pulvirenti. *Addressing the Needs of Nevada's Growing Latino Population: Results of a Statewide Needs Assessment.* Reno: University of Nevada Cooperative Extension /Latino Research Center, 2010.

Smith, Jeffrey. "Rural Place Attachment in Hispano Urban Centers." *Geographical Review* 92, no. 3 (2002): 432–51.

Stone-Gordon, Tammy. *The Spirit of 1976: Commerce, Community, and the Politics of Commemoration.* Amherst: University of Massachusetts Press, 2013.

Tijerina, Reies López. *They Called Me "King Tiger": My Struggle for the Land and Our Rights.* Translated and edited by José Ángel Gutiérrez. Houston: Arte Público Press, 2000.

Timberlake, Jeffrey, Aaron Howell, and Amanda Staight. "Trends in the Suburbanization of Racial/Ethnic Groups in U.S. Metropolitan Areas, 1970–2000." *Urban Affairs Review* 47, no. 2 (2011): 218–55.

Torres-Rouff, David. *Before L.A.: Race, Space, and Municipal Power in Los Angeles, 1781–1894.* New Haven: Yale University Press, 2013.

Tuman, John, David Damore, and María José Flor Ágreda, "Immigration and the Contours of Nevada's Latino Population." *Brookings Mountain West.* Washington, DC: Brookings Institute, 2013.

Valdés, Dennis Nodín. "Betabeleros: The Formation of an Agricultural Proletariat in the Midwest, 1897–1930." *Labor History* 30, no. 4 (1989): 536–62.

Valle, Victor, and Rodolfo Torres. *Latino Metropolis.* Minneapolis: University of Minnesota Press, 2000.

Vargas, Deborah. "Rita's Pants: The *Charro Traje* and Trans-Sensuality." *Women and Performance: A Journal of Feminist Theory* 20, no. 1 (2010): 3–14.

Varnell, Jeanne. *Women of Consequence: The Colorado Women's Hall of Fame.* Boulder, CO: Johnson Books, 1999.

Varsanyi, Monica, ed. *Taking Local Control: Immigration Policy Activism in US Cities and States.* Stanford: Stanford University Press, 2008.

Vega, Sujey. *Latino Heartland: Of Borders and Belonging in the Midwest.* New York: New York University Press, 2015.

Vigil, Charles. "Mexican Land Grants in Colorado." In *The Hispanic Contribution to the State of Colorado,* edited by José de Onís, 65–77. Boulder, CO: Westview Press, 1976.

Weber, David. *The Mexican Frontier, 1821–1846*. Albuquerque: University of New Mexico Press, 1982.

Weber, John. *From South Texas to the Nation: The Exploitation of Mexican Labor in the Twentieth Century*. Chapel Hill: University of North Carolina Press, 2015.

Weise, Julie. *Corazón de Dixie: Mexicanos in the U.S. South since 1910*. Chapel Hill: University of North Carolina Press, 2015.

Wild, Mark. *Street Meeting: Multiethnic Neighborhoods in Early Twentieth-Century Los Angeles*. Berkeley: University of California Press, 2005.

Wilson, Chris. *The Myth of Santa Fe: Creating a Modern Regional Tradition*. Albuquerque: University of New Mexico Press, 1997.

Wolch, Jennifer, John P. Wilson, and Jed Fehrenbauch. *Parks and Park Funding in Los Angeles: An Equity Mapping Analysis*. Los Angeles: University of Southern California Sustainable Cities Program, 2002.

Wolford, Wendy. *This Land Is Ours Now: Social Mobilization and the Meanings of Land in Brazil*. Durham: Duke University Press, 2010.

Woods, Frances. *Mexican Ethnic Leadership in San Antonio, Texas*. Washington, DC: Catholic University of America Press, 1949.

INDEX

Page numbers in italics indicate illustrations.

charreada (Mexican rodeo) *(continued)*
  international, 87–88, 123
  in Los Angeles, 66, 142
  make-believe, 112
  in Mexico, 86, 122, 155
  opposition to, 21, 26, 175, 177, 178–179,
    188
  regulations, 145
  rodeo compared to, 15–16
  in San Antonio, 79, 80, 92, 93, 95
  spaces and rituals of, 6
  in Winnemucca, 125–126, 185, 186
charrería
  Anglo interest in, 92
  as response to anti-immigrant onslaught,
    165–166
  benefits of participation in, 24, 196–197
  colonial and nationalist imaginaries
    invoked by, 23
  crime, alleged link to, 178
  decline of, in Colorado, 131
  defense of, 171, 179
  domination at core of, 166–167
  ethics of, 21
  hierarchies and tensions, 197–198
  income requirements for participation
    in, 22
  institutionalization of, in Mexico, 14
  learning, 102–103, 127
  in Los Angeles, 61
  maps, 7
  "official" histories of, 14
  overview of, 1
  public space claimed through, 163
  regional differences, 9–10
  regulation of, 150, 168, 179
  student knowledge of, 113
  in suburbs, 133–134, 135, 141, 151
"charriadas," 144
charro and cowboy styles, blending, 53,
  56–57
Charro Association of Northern Nevada,
  185
charro associations
  administrative support to, 180
  as cultural and economic organizations,
    89
  establishment of, 14, 18–19, 97, 165

historic overview of, 3–4
institutional power of, 22
lienzo space leased or purchased by, 196
partnerships formed by members of, 5
Pico Rivera Sports Arena used by, 163
press coverage of, 90
suburban presence of, 133–134, 135, 136,
  141, 151
veterinarians sought by, 194
charro associations (Colorado)
  overview of, 101–114
  struggles of, 131
  suburban presence of, 136
  western and Mexican events, appearance
    at, 125
charro associations (Los Angeles)
  establishment of, 66, 134–135
  profiles of, 56–57, 133, 136
  transnationally accredited, 43
charro associations (San Antonio)
  Anglo-American members, 81–82
  awards and honors, 89–90
  clothing and dress, *76*
  education level within, 77, 218n24
  establishment of, 71
  gains by, 89
  overview of, 75–81
  post–World War II, 20
  transnationally accredited, 43
charro-businessmen, 73–74, 85, 137
"Charro Days" celebration, San Antonio,
  73
"charrodeos," 144
Charro en U.S.A., El (Flores), 39, 141
Charro Riding Club, San Antonio, 75, 79,
  85
charros
  American cowboy compared to, 14–16
  American history and culture, centrality
    to, 182
  as American subjects, 183
  Anglo-American growth machine,
    relationships with, 81–86
  animals, attitudes toward, 177, 179
  awareness campaign by, 193
  clothing and dress, 17–18, 57, 76 (*see also*
    traje de charro)
  composition of, 9

colonias, agricultural
  as barrios, 135, 231n3
  departure from, 136
  Mexicans confined to, 11
  in San Fernando Valley, 138
  in San Gabriel Valley, 152
colonialism, 4, 23
Colorado
  Anglo-American settlers in, 115
  groups urbanized in, 100
  Mexican cultural nationalism in, 99–100
  Mexican migration to, 100, 131
  Mexico, ties to, 98, 124
  as sister state, 121
Colorado Centennial-Bicentennial Committee (CCBC), 120, 121, 122
Colorado Fuel and Iron (CF&I), 102, 131
Colorado Latin American Conference, 108, 225n28
Colorado Multi-Ethnic Committee, 120–121
Colorado State Fair
  Fiesta Days, 115–116, 118, 123, 126
  integration of, 20, 100
Colorado State Fair Commission, 123
Colorado State University, Pueblo, 117
comedia ranchera, 13–14, 18, 39, 206n48
Committee to Save Horsemen's Park, 155, 156
community, patriarchal control of, 4
Community Service Organization, 50–51, 62
competition, personal opportunities for, 4
conquest, histories of, 26
conquest, resistance to, 16
Contreras, George, 50
Copening, Allison, 184, 186
Corman, James, 145
Cornett, Abbie, 190
Corro Ferrer, Jesús, 118
Cortinas, Elisa, 125
country western music industry, 13, 140
Covarrubias, José, 194
cowboys
  American corporate method impact on, 11
  construction of, 6
  disparities in workforce, 11

as masculine symbol, 12
meanings of, 2
mestizo and indigenous vaquero influence on, 10
Mexican charro compared to, 14–16
transnational history of, 195
whitewashed history of, 3, 13, 27, 83–84, 111, 125, 139, 140, 146
cowboys and Indians, playing, 12–13, 52
Crusade for Justice, 109, 113, 129
Cruz, Roberto, 79
Cruz, Tom, 133, 153
Cueva, Beto, 140–141
CUIDA program, 180
cultural hybridity, 10, 53

"Day of the Charro" (Mexican holiday), 14
death leap, *36*
debt peonage, 17, 204–205n41
Deferred Action for Childhood Arrivals (DACA) program, 165
deindustrialization, 137, 159, 173
de la Cruz, Sebastien, 1, 2
de la Madrid, Roberto, 59, 60–61
de la Mora, Gloria, 85, 220n53
de la Torre, Toby, 190
de los Santos, Fortunato, 77–78
de los Santos, José, 160
democracy, struggles for, 125
democratic institutions, American, 59
Democratic Party, 71, 83, 216n8, 219n46
Denver, Colorado
  charro influence in, 128
  Hispanos in, 100
  inequality and segregation in, 132
  maps, *106*
  Mexican migrants in, 100, 223n5
Denver, John, 120, 228n73
Denver Charro Association, 103–107, *105*, *106*, 112, 113, 114
Denver Commission on Cultural Affairs, 130
Denver Parks and Recreation Department, 130
Denver Public School District, 110
Department of Homeland Security, 165
deputies, U.S. citizenship required for, 64
desegregation, 97, 113–114, 139

middle class Mexican Americans *(continued)*
  growing scholarship on, 22
  in local power structure, 72
middle class Mexicans, ethnic
  Anglo relations with, 82
  businessmen, 20, 69
  class formation among, 21–22
  film depiction of, 60
  gains made by, 96
  perspectives and goals of, 198
  significance of, 21
  state power claims limited for, 67–68
  suburbs, 155
middle-class respectability, 91
middle class social life, 22
middle-class status, accessing, 4
migrant children separation from parents,
  165
migration, mitigating effects of, 18, 206n48
Milagro Beanfield War, The (film), 133,
  231n1
Milligan, Eddie, 160
Mills, Eric, 169, 172, 173, 181, 183, 184–185, 192
Minuteman Project, 168
missing persons, searches for, 47–48
Mission Area Plan, San Antonio, 92
Mission Revival architectural style, 9, 18,
  135
Mix, Tom, 47
modernity, 21, 198
Montebello, California, 157–158
Morales, Dan, 178
Morin, Shirley, 85
mounted posse program, Los Angeles,
  52–57
multiculturalism, 113–114, 147
música ranchera, 13–14

National Cowboy and Western Heritage
  Museum, 193
National Hispanic Heritage Week, 109
National Western Stock Show, 125
nationhood, 12
nation-state, modern, 6
"native sons," 45, 46, 67
Native Sons parades, 46–47
nativist groups, 168
Nava, Henry, 62, 141

Nava, Julian, 62, 140, 141, 142, 143, 146–
  147, 148, 150, 151, 160
Nebraska, charrería and politics in,
  188–190
Nebraska Humane Society, 189, 190
neoliberalism, 137, 158, 159
neoliberal trade arrangements, 5, 164
Nevada, charrería and politics in, 183–188
New Mexico
  as Hispano homeland, 98–99
  Spanish colonial legacy in, 99, 222n3
norteño music, 134–135
North American Free Trade Agreement
  (NAFTA), 4, 164
Northglenn, Colorado, 106
Northridge, California, 61, 62
Núñez, José R., 77, *78*, 78–79, 87

Obama, Barack, 2
open range, end of, 10–11
Operation Wetback, 74
Orcas Park, Los Angeles, *134*, 139–140, 159,
  160, 163
Order of the Alamo, 84, 220n51
"original cowboys"
  charros as, 1, 2, 16, 27, 83, 126, 146, 167,
    182, 183, 195
  language of, 20
  Mexican ranchers and vaqueros as,
    199–200
  school curricula covering, 111
Oropeza, Vicente, 147
Orozco Romero, Alberto, 122

Pacheco, Elmer, 185
pachucos, 3, 41–42
Pacoima, 138, 140S
Padilla, Agnes, 126, 230n96
Palencia, José, 48
Pan American Friendship Week, 85–86
Pan American Progressive Association
  (PAPA), 71, 77, 90
paparazzi, Latino, 159, 236n89
Parker, Ivan, 46–47
Parker, William, 64, 213n70
paso de la muerte (charreada event), *36*
Patino, Douglas, 120, 122
Pedroza, Marleen, 177

VOICE for Animals, 175–177
voting, federal protections on, 97

Walker, Carol, 82
Warner, John, 119, 120, 124
War on Poverty, 97
West, Old, charro role in, 73
western-central Mexico, 9, 14–15, 23
Western film industry, cowboy depiction by, 13
western-themed dime novels, collectors of, 55–56
Westside Coalition (Denver, Colo.), 109, 226n30
westward expansion, U.S., 16, 47, 70, 119, 139–140, 215n5
"wetbacks," 74
White, Jack, 85, 87
white American settler experience, celebrating, 119
white American settler power, 11, 60
white imperialist nostalgia, 69, 135
whiteness
    aspirations to, 4, 98, 198
    central-western Mexico associated with, 23
    ethnic Mexican relationship to, 21, 98
    law enforcement committed to norms and practices of, 64–65
    Mexican manhood framed around, 14–15
    tensions related to, 23
whitening, charrería role in, 23
white settlement, Colorado cities associated with, 126, 230n96
white settler West, memories and reenactments of, 140
white supremacy, 119, 128
Whitmore, John, 178
Whittier Narrows Dam and Recreation Area, 154, 157–158
Wild West shows, 13, 51, 147

Williams, Thelda, 183
Wilson, Pete, 172
women
    charreada events for, 37
    charrería, participation in, 24, 198
    charro used by, 4
    colonial Mexico, status in, 8
    domestic labor of, 6
    hacendados dependent on labor of, 9
    in law enforcement, 51
    paternalistic control of, 11
workers, paternalistic control of, 11
working-class Mexicans
    charro- and ranch-themed culture, immersion in, 17, 198, 199
    as charros, 140–141
    class-based exclusion of, 55
    displacement of, 94–95
    law enforcement, relations with, 41–42, 48–51, 55
    state power claims limited for, 67–68
    violence against, 52, 60
working-class ranch culture, 10
workplace raids, 74, 88
Works Progress Administration, 70
World Series of Charrería, 187, 187–188
World War II
    charros after, 18–19, 51–52
    economic conditions after, 71
    law enforcement-working-class Mexican relations during, 49
    Mexican American Generation participation in, 71, 130, 216n8
"wrangling" (term), 182, 185

The Young Land (film), 20, 43, 57–62, 67, 141

Zapata, Emiliano, 101, 129
Zisman, S. B., 93
zoot suiters, 41–42, 49, 54
Zoot Suit Riots, 1943, 49, 50–51, 57